Southern California

A DAY HIKER'S GUIDE

For more of John McKinney's

hiking tips and trails, take a hike to www.thetrailmaster.com

Southern California

A DAY HIKER'S GUIDE

by

JOHN McKINNEY

THE TRAILMASTER

Southern California: A Day Hiker's Guide

Portions of this book appeared in the author's hiking column in the Los Angeles Times, Westways and Sunset Magazines.

Cover illustration: *Santa Ynez Mountains* by Nadya Penoff
The Trailmaster Series Editor: Cheri Rae
Maps designed by Hélène Webb
Book Design and typography by Jim Cook

Published by: The Trailmaster Inc
www.TheTrailmaster.com
(805) 965-7200
Visit www.thetrailmaster.com for a complete listing of all
Trailmaster publications, products and services.

ACKNOWLEDGEMENTS

For their cooperation, field- and fact-checking, the author wishes to thank the rangers and administrators of the Cleveland, San Bernardino, Angeles and Los Padres national forests, Los Angeles County Department of Parks and Recreation, Orange County Harbors, Beaches and Parks, California Department of Parks & Recreation, National Park Service and the Santa Monica Mountains Conservancy. Re-hiking many of the hikes in this book was a particular pleasure with friends, family members (particularly my son, Daniel) and the enthusiastic members of the KPCC Hiking Club.

PHOTO CREDITS

Angeles National Forest, p. 109; Big Santa Anita Historical Society, p. 117; Richard Clinton, p. 111; Bob Howells, pp. 16, 304; Joshua Tree National Park, p. 311; Roy Murphy, p. 132; Palm Springs Aerial Tramway, p. 225; Pasadena Historical Society, p. 114; Trabuco Ranger District, United States Forest Service, pp. 170, 178, 180; David M. Werk, p. 208; all other photos by author.

SOUTHERN CALIFORNIA
A Day Hiker's Guide

A Word from The Trailmaster

I've climbed many a mountain above the SoCal metropolis and contemplated the Southland. Sometimes it's the summit view that inspires, sometimes it's the hike itself or one of the region's lovely parklands I've experienced along the way, but always I return home with a slightly different perspective on Southern California.

Today in our frenzied modern world, often so separated from the natural world, this "hiker's perspective" is more important than ever. I know, hikers know, the benefits of climbing the aerie heights, the freedom of the footpath, the joys of experiencing nature. Hiking helps restore the sense of peace and tranquility that our souls require and our hearts desire.

So hike. Contemplate what makes you happy and what would make you happier still. Hike. Enjoy the company of friends and family or the pleasure of your own company. Hike. Delight in the beauty of this world. Hike. Get fit and lift your spirits. Hike. Think about what you can do to expand your life and what you can do to simplify it. Hike.

See you on the trail,
John McKinney
The Trailmaster

On Hiking
Southern California

No guidebook has had such enthusiastic field-testers! By field-testers, I mean the many readers of my Los Angeles Times hiking column and visitors to The Trailmaster website, who took my words to the woods, deserts and coast, then wrote to me about their experiences on the trail.

By enthusiastic I mean the high you've felt high atop a mountain, that great aerobic workout you enjoyed, the fascination in the eyes of your children when you introduced them to nature's marvels.

I like to think I'm a rather enthusiastic field-tester myself. My job, as The Trailmaster, is to take a hike and write about it. I wander the world's trails looking for lonely beaches, desert dunes, dramatic summits, hills ablaze with wildflowers. (Yes, it's a dirty job, but somebody's got to do it.)

My enthusiasm increases every time I hear parents tell me how, with the help of one of my website tips, newspaper and magazine articles, appearances on Southland radio and TV shows, or books, they introduced their children to the wonders of nature. And my enthusiasm is boosted when I learn how fellow conservationists have managed to preserve another special place to walk and to give to future generations.

Although I've taken readers on journeys afoot around America, from the Olympic rain forest to the Florida Everglades, and around the world from the mountains of Greece to the beaches of Tahiti, the hikes around Southern California invariably prompt the most reader response. Let's face facts: it's easier, faster, and a whole lot cheaper to enjoy the alpine air of Mt. Baldy than to head off to Switzerland.

When you hike Southern California, you see the world—the Mediterranean in the Santa Monica Mountains, Santa Ynez Mountains and the Channel Islands; Little Switzerland atop Mt. San Jacinto and among the tall peaks of the San Gorgonio Wilderness; the Sahara Desert in the tall dunes of the Mojave Desert.

Included in this guide are many of my favorite Southern California mountain, coast and desert hikes. Experienced hikers will recognize some familiar terrain—Mts. Baldy, San Gorgonio and San Jacinto—but will find some new trails to travel. Newcomers to the Southland, and less experienced hikers, will find helpful introductions to the land—the major mountain ranges, the forests, deserts, and the coastline. Visitors from across the nation and around the world may discover that hiking is the best way to fully experience Southern California.

Between the covers of this book are the Southland's best hikes. I wanted to increase the odds of you having a great day in the great outdoors, so I left out many walkable but not-so-wonderful trails. As you may imagine, a "professional" hiker like myself encounters a lot of turkey trails; that is to say, paths that start nowhere and go nowhere, trails battered by nature or neglected by park officials to the point where I decided that they are too unsafe for you to use.

So with all this enthusiastic field-testing—mine, yours and that of park authorities—are you holding perfection in your hands?

Nope. Trails change over time. Like every hiker, I hate seeing a good trail go bad, but regrettably it happens. The ravages of fire and flood, rampant real estate development and bureaucratic neglect can ruin a favorite path. While out hiking, if you happen across a neglected, hazardous or overgrown trail, please report it to the relevant ranger or administrator. Only if you make your concerns known will conditions improve. It's up to all of us to preserve our trails—and the precious wild land they help us explore.

I hope that in some small way this book, in addition to suggesting some enjoyable hikes, contributes to a better understanding of the unique and fragile ecology of Southern California.

UNDERSTANDING DAY HIKING IN SOCAL

The land we call Southern California is an island, ecologically isolated from the rest of the continent by a combination of geographic and climatic factors. Helen Hunt Jackson once said of Southern California: "It's an island on the land." Carey McWilliams popularized the phrase in his definitive history of the region, *Southern California: An Island on the Land.* The land's island nature is apparent when you enter it from the north or east. When you round Point Conception and the north-south orientation of California becomes east-west, it is obvious that you have entered a unique geographical province. If you come to Southern California from the east through Cajon Pass or San Gorgonio Pass, the change is immediately evident. Light is softer, the climate more temperate.

The land includes seven counties: Santa Barbara, Ventura, Los Angeles, Orange, Riverside, San Bernardino and San Diego. Usually, only those parts of San Bernardino, Riverside and San Diego counties "west of the mountains" are in Southern California, but a case can be made for including all of them and adding Imperial County as well. Some boosters insist Southern California's northern boundary is San Luis Obispo or even the Monterey County line, but geographically and ecologically it's at Point Conception. Southern California is the land south of the Transverse Range, which knifes across California toward the Pacific just north of Santa Barbara.

Southern California is protected from the Mojave Desert by the San Bernardino and San Gabriel Mountain Ranges on the east and walled off from the San Joaquin Valley by other Transverse Ranges. The lowlands are covered with alluvial fans formed by earth washed down from the mountains.

Compass directions can be confusing to both newcomers and old-timers. "Up the coast" in other parts of the world is usually taken to mean north, but it's not north in Southern California.

To travel north from L.A., you head directly into the Mojave Desert, crossing east-west trending mountains in the process. If you traveled a straight line, as the crow flies, from San Bernardino to Santa Barbara, you would travel 137 miles west and only 27 miles north.

Carey McWilliams suggested, "The analyst of California is like a navigator who is trying to chart a course in a storm: the instruments will not work; the landmarks are lost; and the maps make little sense." California may be geographically cockeyed and Southern California even more so, but we day hikers ought to get our bearings before heading for the hills. We need to find a few landmarks and consult a map. Orienting yourself to Southern California isn't that difficult. Consult the map on the following pages, and try the accompanying geography exercise.

Santa Ynez Mts.

Santa
Barbara

Santa Monica Mts.

Channel Islands
National Park

Los
Angeles

Catalina
Island

SOUTHERN CALIFORNIA GEOGRAPHY MADE EASY

Use the locator map above or get yourself an Auto Club map of California or similar-sized map. Spread it on the floor.

Put your right thumb on Santa Barbara, your right pinkie on San Diego and spread your fingers in as wide a fan as you can manage. One of the first things you may notice is that your palm covers the L.A. Basin. Keep your palm firmly pressed down on L.A. to keep the metropolis from spreading into the wilderness. Look at your thumb. Above it is Pt. Conception, the northernmost point of Southern California. Above Santa Barbara are the Santa Ynez Mountains and beyond are those parts of Los Padres National Forest we call the Santa Barbara Backcountry.

Along your index finger are the San Gabriel Mountains and the Angeles National Forest. Your middle finger is in the San Bernardino Mountains, near

Mojave Desert

**SOUTHERN
CALIFORNIA**

San Gabriel Mts.

San Bernardino
Mts.

San Bernardino

Joshua Tree
National
Park

San Jacinto
Mts.

Santa Ana
Mts.

Santa Rosa
Mts.

Palomar
Mts.

Anza-Borrego
Desert State
Park

**San
Diego**

Cuyamaca
Mts.

MEXICO

Hélène Webb

the eastern terminus of this range is Mt. San Gorgonio, the highest peak in Southern California.

Between your middle and ring fingers, paralleling the coast in Orange Country are the Santa Ana Mountains, protected by the Cleveland National Forest. At the tip of your ring finger at the north end of Anza-Borrego Desert State Park lie the Santa Rosa Mountains. Take note of the Colorado Desert and farther to the north, the vast Mojave Desert.

Due east from your pinkie is the southern part of the Cleveland National Forest, as well as the Palomar and Cuyamaca mountain ranges.

Now that you're oriented, raise that right hand of yours and pledge to preserve, protect, and enjoy these places.

Best Hikes . . .

For Watching Whales
Pt. Dume above Zuma Beach
Cabrillo National Monument

For Sunset-Viewing
Crystal Cove State Park
Keys View, Joshua Tree National Park
Inspiration Point, Will Rogers SHP

To a Classic Peak
Mt. Wilson, Mt. Baldy, Mt. San Jacinto, Mt. San Gorgonio

For Romance
Any beach walk! Any island hike! Charmlee Wilderness Park,
Thousand Palms Oasis, Santa Barbara's Mission Canyon, Ojai Valley,
Antelope Valley California Poppy Reserve

Featuring Waterfalls
Switzer Falls, Eaton Canyon Falls, Sturtevant Falls, San Antonio Falls,
Holy Jim Falls, Tenaja Falls, Tahquitz Canyon Falls,

To Hot Springs
Deep Creek, Aqua Caliente Springs

For Tree-Huggers
Cheeseboro Canyon (oaks) Santa Rosa Plateau Preserve (Englemann oaks),
Joshua Tree National Park (Joshuas) Anza-Borrego Desert SP (elephant trees),
Palm Canyon (palms), Henninger Flats (tree nursery), San Bernardino National
Forest (Aspen Grove)

On the Beach
Carptinteria Beach, Zuma Beach, Crystal Cove, San Clemente State Beach

For Autumn Color
Placerita Canyon, Palomar Mountain State Park, Sycamore Canyon in Point
Mugu State Park

TO FIND WILDFLOWERS
Reagan Ranch area, Malibu Creek State Park, Charmlee Wilderness Park, Nicholas Flat in Leo Carrillo State Park, Limestone Canyon, Santa Rosa Plateau, Antelope Valley California Poppy Reserve, Anza-Borrego Desert State Park (several sites)

ALONG NATURE TRAILS
O'Neill Regional Park, Heaps Peak, Idyllwild County Park, Torrey Pines State Reserve, Devil's Punchbowl, The Living Desert, Borrego Palm Canyon

TO TAKE GUESTS FROM OUT-OF-TOWN
Rattlesnake Canyon, Big Santa Anita Canyon, Echo Mountain, Malibu Creek State Park, Solstice Canyon, Point Dume, Laguna Coast Wilderness Park

INTO HISTORY
Mt. Lowe Railway Trail, Arroyo Seco, Will Rogers State Historic Park, Cold Spring Canyon

WITH KIDS
Placerita Canyon, Malibu Creek State Park, Big Santa Anita Canyon, Rattlesnake Canyon, Carpinteria State Beach, San Clemente State Beach

TO PALM OASES
Palm Canyon (Palm Springs), Thousand Palms (Coachella Valley), Borrego Palm Canyon (Anza-Borrego Desert State Park) Forty-nine Palms (Joshua Tree National Park)

WITH EXCELLENT VISITOR CENTERS (LARGE ONES)
Joshua Tree National Park, Anza-Borrego Desert State Park, Channel Islands National Park

WITH EXCELLENT VISITOR CENTERS (SMALL ONES)
Catalina Island Conservancy, Santa Rosa Plateau Ecological Reserve, Chilao Visitor Center, Eaton Canyon Nature Center, Devil's Punchbowl County Park, Torrey Pines State Reserve, Idyllwild County Park

WITH MUSEUMS
The Living Desert, Cabrillo Marine Museum

GETTING THE MOST FROM
HIKING SOUTHERN CALIFORNIA

There are two tried-and-true approaches to selecting a hike. One is by mood (yours) and the other by scenery.

First decide on the kind of hike you'd like to enjoy. A walk for the whole family? A long solo trek in the wilderness where you can be alone to think and dream? An after-work workout? A first-date excursion? A scout or youth group outing?

Decide where you want to hike. About 150 hikes plus some options are described in this guide so it may be quite a challenge to select one.

Want some help narrowing the field? Check out my recommended "Best Hikes." Unsure of what to expect from the San Bernardino Mountains, Catalina Island or Joshua Tree National Park? Read the chapter introductions.

Pick a hike in your geographical area of interest. Next, turn to the corresponding trail description in the main body of the book.

Beneath the name of the trail is the distance from the trailhead to various destinations. Mileage, expressed in round trip figures, follows each destination. The hikes in this book range from one to sixteen miles. Gain or loss in elevation follows the mileage.

In matching a hike to your ability, consider mileage and elevation, as well as the condition of the trail, terrain and season. Hot, exposed chaparral, or a trail that roller-coasters steeply up and down can make a short walk seem long.

Use the following guidelines:

• A hike most suitable for beginners and children is under five miles long and requires an elevation gain less than 700 to 800 feet.

• A moderate hike is one in the five- to eight-mile range, with less than a 2,000-foot elevation gain. You should be reasonably fit for these. Pre-teens often find the going difficult.

• A hike longer than eight miles, particularly one with an elevation gain of 2,000 feet or more, is for experienced hikers in at least average condition. Those hikers in top form will enjoy these more challenging excursions.

Season is the next item to consider. Although Southern California is one of the few regions in the country that offers four-season hiking, some climactic restrictions must be heeded. You can hike some of the trails in this guide all of the time, all of the trails some of the time, but not all of the trails all of the time.

Snow closes the trails to Mt. Baldy and other high-country trails in the San Gabriel Mountains. Angeles Crest Highway is sometimes closed after a heavy snowfall. More-than-a-mile-high trails and trailheads located in the San

Bernardino Mountains and San Jacinto Mountains are usually inaccessible during winter, and often late into the spring.

Heavy rains can lead authorities to close trails to public use. State park rangers and rangers at the various county parks often close park trails after a heavy rain in order to protect the pathways from erosion by trail users—hikers and particularly mountain bikers.

For the hiker venturing out into flatland and mountain parks, heat, not moisture, is a more common challenge. Park authorities rarely close parks or trails in the summer so you won't be prevented from taking a hike; the question is: "Should you hike in the heat?"

Early mornings and late afternoons are the times for warm-weather jaunts in the low-elevation mountains and foothills, as well as in the county's various parks and reserves.

Years ago, portions of the SoCal's four national forests were closed automatically in the summer for fire-safety reasons and did not re-open until the first rains of the following rainy season. While fire closure is no longer a common Forest Service policy, do remember that low elevation trails in the Angeles, Cleveland, San Bernardino and Los Padres national forests are often too hot and dry to offer comfortable summer hiking.

Beneath the name of the hike at the top of the page is the trail name, plus the starting point and one or more destinations. Mileage, expressed in round trip figures, follows each destination. The hikes in this guide range from one to twenty miles, with the majority in the four to ten mile range. Gain or loss in elevation follows the mileage. In matching a hike to your ability, you'll want to consider mileage and elevation as well as condition of the trail, terrain, and season. Hot, exposed chaparral or miles of boulder-hopping can make a short hike seem long.

My introductions to the hikes describe what you'll encounter in the way of plants, animals and panoramic views and outline the natural and human history of the region. I'll also point out the good, the bad and the ugly and tell you straight out what's hot and what's not about a particular trail.

DIRECTIONS TO TRAILHEAD take you from the nearest major highway to trailhead parking. For trails having two desirable trailheads, directions to each are given. A few trails can be hiked one way, with the possibility of a car shuttle. Suggested car shuttle points are noted.

The Trailmaster's Southern California guides include many area maps to supplement the hiking maps; these maps help put a region into perspective and assist your journey to the trailhead.

THE HIKE describes the hike. The hike write-ups note important junctions and point out major sights. Options allow you to climb higher or farther or take a different route back to the trailhead. These trail descriptions, in combination with the superb maps created by my long-time collaborator at the Los Angeles Times, Hélène Webb, will help you stay oriented and get where you want to go. We haven't described and mapped every single feature, though; we've left it to you to discover the multitude of details that make a hike an adventure.

MAPS

The Automobile Club of Southern California publishes several maps useful to the hiker. Supplement the regional maps and trail maps in this guide with the Auto Club's county maps, including Santa Barbara County, Ventura County, Los Angeles County, Orange County, Riverside County, San Bernardino County and San Diego County. Add to your collection Los Angeles County Mountains & Deserts (a favorite of The Trailmaster because it highlights so many of the trail-heads in this guide) and the Auto Club's San Bernardino Mountains maps.

U.S. Forest Service maps to the Los Padres, Angeles, San Bernardino and Cleveland national forests help the hiker to get the big picture of these sprawling lands. I enthusiastically recommend Tom Harrison's maps of the San Gabriel Mountains, San Jacinto Mountains and Santa Monica Mountains. These maps, updated regularly, are very accurate and show all the hiking trails and dirt roads.

PERMITS AND FEES

NATIONAL FORESTS: The National Forest Adventure Pass is a parking permit that can be purchased for an annual fee that allows parking in Southern California's four national forest: Los Padres, Angeles, San Bernardino and Cleveland. An Adventure Pass is required for parking at "High Impact Recreational Areas," which covers most locales along the main forest highways and all the most popular trailheads.

Although an Adventure Pass is not required at every single trailhead, a pass is required at most of the major ones, as well at the more developed recreation areas and day-use sites. The annual pass currently costs $30 a year or $5 a day and can be purchased at Forest Service offices, outdoor retailers, and local outlets near or within the boundaries of the national forests.

COUNTY PARKS Parking/entrance costs for Ventura, Los Angeles, Orange and San Diego county parks ranges from free (usually at remote trailheads or "back-door" entrances to parks) to as high as $10 for some Orange County Parks on holidays.

Entry fees are often collected by an "Iron Ranger," particularly during the weekends when parks rarely have an employee staffing the entry kiosk.

Day-use entry fees for California state parks begin at $5 per vehicle. An Annual Day Use Pass is available for $125 per year and The Trailmaster heartily recommends that the state parks enthusiast get one for access to California's 275 state parks.

For an extensive discussion
of hiking techniques, apparel,
trail safety, and much more,
visit my website at

www.thetrailmaster.com

• The 10 essentials
• Hiking equipment
• Footwear and apparel
• Precautions and hazards
• Park contact information
• Nature essays and travel stories
• Lots more hikes from across the nation
and around the world

CHAPTER ONE

Santa Ynez Mountains

Some of the very best hiking in Southern California is along trails through the mountain canyons right behind Santa Barbara. The Santa Ynez Mountains, which range from 2,000 to 4,000 feet in elevation, extends about 50 miles from Matilija Canyon near Ojai to Gaviota Pass. Most of the fine trails start in lush canyon bottoms, zigzag up the hot, dry canyon walls, and follow rock ledges to the crest. From the top, enjoy sweeping views of the Pacific, Channel Islands and coastal plain. From the viewpoints, hikers can decipher Santa Barbara's sometimes confusing orientation; that is to say the east-west direction of the coastline and these mountains.

MISSION CANYON

TUNNEL TRAIL
From Tunnel Road to Seven Falls is 2 miles round trip with 400-foot elevation gain; to Inspiration Point is 4 miles round trip with 800-foot gain

"A pleasant party spent yesterday up Mission Canyon visiting noted Seven Falls and afterward eating a tempting picnic dinner in a romantic spot on the creek's bank. To reach these falls requires some active climbing, able-bodied sliding and skillful swinging...." –*Santa Barbara Daily Press*, 1887

Seven Falls has been a popular destination of Santa Barbarans since before the turn of the 20th century. The seven distinct little falls found in the bed of Mission Creek still welcome hikers.

Tunnel Trail was used by workers to gain access to a difficult city waterworks project launched by the city of Santa Barbara. Workers burrowed a tunnel through the Santa Ynez Mountains to connect the watershed on the backside of the mountains to the growing little city. Braving floods, cave-ins and dangerous hydrogen gas, a crew labored eight years and finished the project in 1912.

This easy family hike in the foothills follows Tunnel Trail, joins Jesusita Trail for an exploration of the Seven Falls along Mission Creek and ascends Inspiration Point for sweeping coastal views.

Mission Creek provided the water supply for Mission Santa Barbara. Near the mission, which you'll pass as you proceed to Tunnel trailhead, are some stone remains of the padres' waterworks system. Mission Creek also flows through the Santa Barbara Botanic Garden, which is well worth visiting because of its fine displays of native California flora. A ramble through the Santa Barbara foothills combined with a visit to the mission and botanic garden would add up to a very pleasant day's outing.

DIRECTIONS TO TRAILHEAD: From Highway 101 in Santa Barbara, exit on Mission Street. Turn east to Laguna Street, then left and drive past the historic Santa Barbara Mission. From the mission, drive up Mission Canyon Road, turning right for a block on Foothill Road, then immediately turning left back onto Mission Canyon Road. At a distinct V-intersection, veer left onto Tunnel Road and drive to its end. Park along the road.

THE HIKE: From the end of Tunnel Road, hike past a locked gate onto a paved road, which eventually turns to dirt as you leave the power lines behind and get increasingly grander views of Santa Barbara. The road makes a sharp left and crosses a bridge over the West Fork of Mission Creek.

Beyond the bridge, you'll hike a short distance under some handsome oaks to a junction. (Tunnel Trail angles northeast, uphill, leading three miles to "the sky road," East Camino Cielo.) You join Jesusita Trail and descend to Mission Creek.

At the canyon bottom, you can hike up creek into a steep gorge that was cut from solid sandstone. Geologically inclined hikers will recognize fossilized layers of oyster beds from the Oligocene Epoch, deposited some 35 million years ago. In more recent times, say for the last few thousands of winters, rainwater has rushed from the shoulder of La Cumbre Peak and cut away at the sandstone layers, forming several deep pools. If you decide to hike up Mission Creek, be careful; reaching the waterfalls–particularly the higher ones–requires quite a bit of boulder hopping and rock climbing. Even when there's not much water in the creek, it can be tricky going.

From the creek crossing, Jesusita Trail switchbacks steeply up the chaparral-cloaked canyon wall to a power line road atop a knoll. Although Inspiration Point is not all that inspiring, the view from the cluster of sandstone rocks at the 1,750-foot viewpoint is worth the climb. You can see the coastline quite some distance north and south, as well as Catalina and the Channel Islands, Santa Barbara and the Goleta Valley.

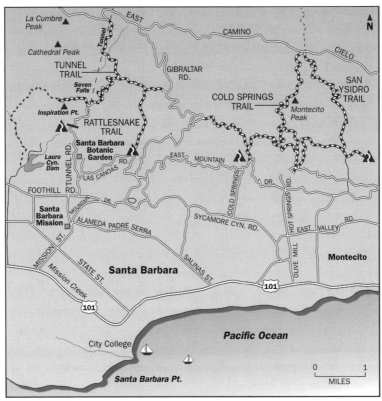

RATTLESNAKE CANYON

RATTLESNAKE CANYON TRAIL
From Skofield Park to Tin Can Meadow is 4.5 miles round trip with 1,000-foot elevation gain; to Gibraltar Road is 6 miles round trip with 1,500-foot gain

Rattlesnake Canyon Trail is serpentine, but otherwise far more inviting than its name suggests.

The joys of the canyon were first promoted by none other than the Santa Barbara Chamber of Commerce. Many a turn-of-the-20th-century visitor to Santa Barbara resorts enjoyed hiking and riding in the local mountains. Eager to keep the customers satisfied, in 1902 the chamber purchased easements from canyon homesteaders to develop a recreation trail.

"Chamber of Commerce Trail," as the Chamber called it, was an immediate success with both tourists and locals. However, to the chamber's consternation, both the trail and the canyon itself continued to be called Rattlesnake. Chamber of Commerce Canyon sounded a bit self-serving, so the Chamber tried to compromise with an earlier name, "Las Canoas Canyon," and adopted a 1902 resolution to that effect. "The name of Rattlesnake Canyon is unpleasantly suggestive of a reptile," it argued, "which is found no more plentifully there than elsewhere along the mountain range and may deter some nervous persons from visiting that most delightful locality."

In the 1960s, the city of Santa Barbara purchased the canyon as parkland. A handsome wooden sign at the foot of the canyon proudly proclaims: Rattlesnake Canyon Wilderness.

This trail explores Santa Barbara's little wilderness canyon. Red-berried toyon, manzanita with its white urn-shaped flowers, and purple hummingbird sage cloak the slopes and offer a variety of smells and textures. In the early spring ceanothus blooms, adding frosty whites and blues to the gray-green thickets. Shooting stars, larkspur, and lupine also spread their color over the slopes and meadows.

DIRECTIONS TO TRAILHEAD: From Highway 101 in Santa Barbara, go uptown (toward the mountains) on State Street to Los Olivos Street. Turn right and proceed a half mile, passing by the Santa Barbara Mission and joining Mission Canyon Road. Follow this road past its intersection with Foothill Road and make a right on Las Canoas Road. Follow Las Canoas to Skofield Park. Leave your car on the shoulder of the road or in the large parking area near the picnic grounds. The trail begins on Las Canoas Road near the handsome stone bridge that crosses Rattlesnake Creek.

Lunch Rock, a popular destination for generations of hikers.

THE HIKE: From the sandstone bridge across from Skofield Park, hike up a brief stretch of trail and join a narrow dirt road that parallels the east side of the creek. For lovely picnicking, take any of the steep side trails down to the creek. In the early 19th century, the mission padres built a dam in the bottom of the canyon. It channeled water into a stone aqueduct and diverted it into the mission's waterworks system. Portions of the aqueduct still exist and can be seen by the careful observer.

The trail zigs and zags across the creek, finally continuing along the west bank to open, grassy Tin Can Meadow. The triangular-shaped meadow gets its name from a homesteader's cabin constructed of chaparral framing and kerosene can shingles and sidings. Tin Can Shack once was an important canyon landmark and several guidebooks of that era mention it. It was a popular destination for picnickers who marveled at the inspired architecture and posed for pictures in front of it. In 1925, a brushfire destroyed the shack and it soon disintegrated into a pile of tin.

If you're feeling energetic, hike on toward the apex of the triangular meadow where you'll find a junction. The trail bearing left takes you 0.75 mile and climbs 500 feet to its intersection with the Tunnel Trail—and incidentally to many points of interest in the Santa Barbara backcountry. To the right, Rattlesnake Canyon Trail climbs about 0.75 mile and 500 feet to its intersection with Gibraltar Road. There you will be greeted by an unobstructed view of the South Coast.

COLD SPRING CANYON

COLD SPRING TRAIL

From Mountain Drive to Montecito Overlook is 4 miles round trip with 900-foot gain; return via Hot Springs Canyon is a 5.5-mile loop; to Montecito Peak is 7.5 miles round trip with 2,500-foot gain; to Camino Cielo is 9 miles round trip with 2,700-foot gain.

Cold Spring Canyon's near-wilderness nature is all the more surprising when considering its location—scarcely a mile as the orange-crowned warbler flies from the villas of the rich and famous, and just two miles from Montecito's boutiques and bistros.

When the Santa Ynez Forest Reserve was established in 1899, rangers used the trail up the West Fork of Cold Spring Canyon to patrol the Santa Barbara backcountry. Forest rangers soon realized that this tricky trail, which climbed around a waterfall and crossed shale slopes, was difficult to maintain. In 1905, the Forest Service built a trail up the East Fork of Cold Spring Canyon. West Fork lost its status as a government maintained transportation artery, and the pathway even disappeared from some maps over the years.(Local hikers, however, never forgot the wonders of West Fork Trail and today, while little used, it offers a fine hike. See West Fork Trail description.)

"Our favorite route to the main ridge was by a way called the Cold Spring Trail," wrote Stewart Edward White in his 1906 classic, *The Mountains.* "We used to enjoy taking visitors up it, mainly because you come on the top suddenly, without warning. Then we collected remarks. Everybody, even the most stolid, said something."

Cold Spring Trail begins by the alder-shaded, year-round creek, then rises out of the canyon for fine coastal views. Options abound for the ambitious hiker and several of them are described below.

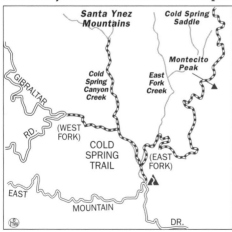

DIRECTIONS TO TRAIL-HEAD: From Highway 101 in Montecito, a few miles south of Santa Barbara, exit on Hot Springs Road and proceed toward the foothills for 2.5 miles to Mountain Drive. Turn left. A mile's travel on Mountain Drive brings you to the Cold Springs trailhead, which begins at a point where a creek flows over a cement drainage apron.

THE HIKE: The path rises briefly through oak woodland, then returns to the creek. On your left, 0.25 mile from the trailhead, is a junction with West Fork Trail. This century-old trail ascends 1.5 miles to Gibraltar Road.

Continuing past the West Fork trail junction, the East Fork Trail rises up the canyon wall and rejoins the creek 0.5 mile later. Look for a fine swimming hole below you to the right. The trail then switchbacks moderately out of the canyon to Montecito Overlook. Enjoy the view of the Santa Barbara coastline and the Channel Islands.

If you'd like to loop back to the trailhead via Hot Springs Canyon, you have two options. Easiest way is to take the Edison fire road and make a steep one-mile descent into that canyon. A more challenging route is to ascend Cold Springs Trail another 0.25 mile or so and look for an unsigned connector trail on the right. This path leads down to the ruins of the old Hot Springs Hotel (see Hot Springs Trail description). Once at the bottom of the canyon, you'll descend a fire road to a vehicle gate, then follow a footpath 0.5 mile around and through a residential area down to Mountain Drive. A mile's walk along one of Santa Barbara's more bucolic byways returns you to the Cold Spring trailhead.

(While the paths leading into and through Hot Springs Canyon are used by thousands of hikers per year, they are posted "private property".)

From the junction with the Hot Springs connector trail, Cold Spring Trail switchbacks up-canyon and offers fine coastal views. A one-mile climb brings you to two eucalyptus trees (about the only shade en route!) and another 0.75 mile of travel takes you to the unsigned junction with a side trail leading to Montecito Peak (3,214 feet). Enjoy the view!

Cold Spring Trail continues a last mile to Camino Cielo. From the Sky Road, many trails lead into the far reaches of the Santa Barbara backcountry.

West Fork, Cold Spring Canyon

WEST FORK TRAIL
From Mountain Drive to waterfall is 4 miles round trip with 1,000-foot elevation gain

Least known and certainly least traveled of Santa Barbara's foothill trails, the West Fork Trail ventures into some surprisingly wild terrain. Bold sandstone formations, clear springs, lush canyon vegetation and a 200-foot waterfall are few of the considerable charms of this branch of Cold Spring Canyon.

A good time to hike the West Fork is after the first heavy rain of winter. The creek's pools bubble over, innumerable newts take to the trail and the canyon's 200-foot waterfall is a sight to behold.

As Santa Barbara's foothill canyons go, West Fork is a bit of an odd duck; unlike most other canyons which have a north-south orientation, West Fork extends east-west.

An important note about that waterfall: For most hikers, Cold Spring Canyon's waterfall is a natural wonder to view, not visit. Experienced trekkers can follow a sketchy, soggy creekside route to the base of the falls and even beyond, but this is serious, time-consuming business—slow and often very wet going. Don't underestimate the time needed to complete this journey. Many hikers have been stranded up the creek after dark because they got a lot more hike than they bargained for.

If you have the time for another hike, I suggest the 4-mile round trip hike (with 900-foot elevation gain) up the east fork of Cold Spring Trail to Montecito Overlook.

DIRECTIONS TO TRAILHEAD: (See previous hike)

THE HIKE: The trail immediately crosses the creek to the east side of the canyon. It rises briefly through oak woodland, and returns to the creek. Look to your left, 0.25 mile out, for the signed West Fork Trail. A strategically placed bench allows contemplation of the creek bubbling through Cold Spring Canyon.

Cross the creek on West Fork Trail and begin a mellow ascent westward under a canopy of oak and bay laurel. Water pipes, historic and modern, parallel the trail.

After a short mile, look for an unsigned trail on the right leading down to the creek; this is the rough and sketchy path leading north up the canyon to the waterfall.

After this junction, West Fork Trail crosses and re-crosses the creek, then switchbacks in deep shade past ferns, alder and sycamore out of the creekbed onto more open slopes. The trail delivers a view of the waterfall then turns away from it as the canyon narrows and the going gets steeper. West Fork Trail ends at a hairpin turn of Gibraltar Road, one of the key access roads into the front country of Los Padres National Forest.

CHAPTER TWO

Los Padres National Forest

Hikers delight in the rugged mountain terrain arranged in a semi-circle around Santa Barbara and Ventura counties but face a difficult task in deciding what to call this million acres of Los Padres National Forest; there isn't one mountain range but many. Still, whatever this land of great gorges, sandstone cliffs and wide blue sky is called, it's guaranteed to please, as will the fine trail system that explores it. The Ojai area includes Sespe and Piru Creeks, wilderness areas and a sanctuary for the California condor. High in the Frazier Park area of Los Padres National Forest lies a splendid pine forest and the backcountry's highest peak, Mt. Pinos (8,831 feet).

MT. PINOS

MT. PINOS TRAIL
From Mt. Abel to Sheep Camp is 5 miles round trip with 500-foot elevation gain; to Mt. Pinos is 10 miles round trip with 900-foot gain.

The five-mile Mt. Pinos Trail offers the peak-bagger four opportunities to climb an 8,000-foot peak. Between Mts. Abel and Pinos, there are easy cross-country climbs to Grouse and Sawmill mountains. The trail passes through dense pine and fir hollows, visits historic Sheep Camp, and ascends Mt. Pinos, a blustery peak that offers views of the San Joaquin Valley, the Mojave Desert and the sprawling Los Padres National Forest high country.

You can travel from Mt. Pinos to Mt. Abel or vice versa; the Mt. Abel trailhead is much less visited.

DIRECTIONS TO TRAILHEAD: Exit Interstate 5 at the Frazier Park turnoff and drive west on Frazier Mountain Park Road, then Cuddy Valley Road. Five miles past the hamlet of Lake of the Woods is a junction. To reach Mt. Pinos trailhead, bear left and continue 9 miles to the Chula Vista Picnic Area. One more mile on a dirt road (closed in winter) takes you to the Condor Observation Site near the top of Mt. Pinos and the beginning (or end) of the Mt. Pinos Trail.

To reach the Mt. Abel trailhead, bear right at the above-mentioned junction and proceed 8 miles on Mil Potrero Road to Cerro Noroeste Road. Turn left and go 7 miles to the signed trailhead, 0.5 mile below the summit of Mt. Abel. Park in a safe manner along the road.

THE HIKE: Leaving the trailhead behind, you descend a draw into a forested hollow, 0.5 mile from the start. Bear left at the signed junction here. The trail ascends Grouse Mountain, named for the resident blue grouse. Soon the trail levels and reaches a saddle on the east slope of Grouse Mountain. To ascend to the summit, scramble a short distance up the slope to your right.

The trail continues following the saddle to a junction with North Fork Trail. To reach Sheep Camp, bear right on North Fork Trail and descend a pine-covered slope past a trickling little spring. Sheep Camp, 0.5 mile from the junction, is one of the highest trail camps in Los Padres National Forest. For the day hiker, it's a pleasant picnic spot.

Return to the main trail, which soon passes close to the summit of Sawmill Mountain. It's an easy cross-country climb to bag the peak.

Continuing on the main trail, you will descend the pine-covered slopes of Sawmill Mountain, then ascend an open slope via switchbacks up balding Mt. Pinos. Stand among the gnarled pine atop the 8,831-foot summit and enjoy the view from the highest peak in Los Padres National Forest.

CHUMASH WILDERNESS

MESA SPRING TRAIL
From Mt. Cerro Noroeste to Quatal Canyon Road is 10 miles one-way
with 2,400-foot elevation loss; Season: April-November

A small portion of the Chumash's ancestral land is now a wilderness area—about
36,000 acres of pine forest and juniper woodland, grasslands and badlands. A highlight is Quatal Canyon, a kind of Bryce Canyon-in-miniature, complete with dramatic pinnacles and weird eroded rock formations. It is rich in vertebrate fossils,
particularly from the Miocene Epoch (12 to 16 million years ago).

San Emigdio Mesa, a large, flat, alluvial fan forested with pinyon pine and
dwarf oak, is by far the most extensive of its kind in Southern California, and
recalls some of the mesas of the Great Basin.

This trail begins in a high pine forest, but passes through other ecosystems—
pinyon-juniper woodland, chaparral and grassland—as it descends from Mt. Abel
to Toad Spring Camp. It's a great introduction to the lay of the land, a fine
overview of the Chumash Wilderness.

DIRECTIONS TO TRAILHEAD: This trip requires a car shuttle—either
two cars or a nonhiking friend. Hikers will want to depart from the Mt. Abel
trailhead and arrive at the Toad Spring Campground trailhead.

From Interstate 5 in Frazier Park, exit on Frazier Mountain Park Road and
head west. The road, which becomes Cuddy Valley Road, continues to a Y-junction.
The left fork leads to Mt. Pinos, but you stay right and join Mil Potrero Road.
Drive 8.5 miles to Cerro Noroeste Road and turn left. Proceed 7 miles to the signed
trailhead 0.5 mile below the summit of Mt. Cerro Noroeste (Mt. Abel). Parking is
not plentiful right at the trailhead, so park in a safe manner along the road.

From the Cerro Noroeste Road/Mil Potrero Road junction, continue right

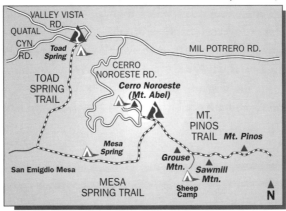

(west) on the latter road which, to make matters confusing, takes on the name Cerro Noroeste Road. Travel a mile to the signed turnoff for Toad Spring Campground, turning left on (Forest Road 9N09), continuing 0.3 mile to the camp, then another 0.4 mile to the unsigned trailhead on the left (south) side of the road.

THE HIKE: Leaving signed Mt. Abel trailhead, the path descends very steeply for 0.5 mile down a draw into a forested hollow. Here there's a signed junc-tion, with (incorrect) mileages for the trail leading left (southeast) to Mt. Pinos. You bear right on unsigned Mesa Spring Trail and descend past huge and widely spaced ponderosa pine. Scattered among the pines are silver fir, some of which are large enough and pretty enough to be the White House Christmas tree.

After a mile, you'll pass through a gate. (The Forest Service allows some cat-tle grazing on this land.) The path continues descending through a mixed transi-tion forest of pine and oak. The area has unusual botany. Inhabitants of dry lands—coffee berry and manzanita and scrub oak—mingle with subalpine species—pine, fir and snowplant.

The path drops a couple more miles through pinyon pine country to Mesa Spring Camp, at about 6,000 feet in elevation. It's a simple trail camp with picnic tables and water. A hundred yards from camp is a huge watering trough used by bovine forest users.

Mesa Spring, Mesa Spring Camp and Mesa Spring Trail are named for San Emigdio Mesa, the pinyon-pine covered territory that you skirt as the path leaves camp. Stay right at an unsigned trail junction just below camp and continue walk-ing for a couple miles on a flatland between the mesa on your left and the tall shoulder of Mt. Cerro Noroeste on your right.

At a (poorly) signed trail junction, you'll join Forest Service Trail 22W01, Toad Spring Trail, which leads northward 3.75 miles to Quatal Canyon Road.

The trail climbs and dips over pinyon pine- and juniper-dotted slopes. You'll get grand views west and south over the Chumash Wilderness and of the Cuyama Badlands to the northwest. Best view of all is the view right below of Quatal Canyon. The pinnacle rock formations resemble those in Southwest Utah.

Toad Spring Trail skirts the rim of Quatal Canyon. The last mile of the trail marches steeply up and down some minor hills before reaching its terminus (or trailhead, depending on how you look at it) at Quatal Canyon Road.

PINE MOUNTAIN

REYES PEAK TRAIL
From Reyes Peak Roadhead to Potrero John Overlook is 3.5 miles round trip with 300-foot elevation gain; to Haddock Peak is 7.5 miles round trip with 600-foot gain; to Haddock Trail Camp is 11 miles round trip with 800-foot gain

The invigorating scent of pine, great views, and a dramatic ridgetop trail are some of the highlights of a hike atop Pine Mountain. The mountain, which straddles the Mt. Pinos and Ojai Ranger Districts in Los Padres National Forest, is made up of several 7,000-foot-plus peaks, each offering a different backcountry panorama.

For most of its length, Reyes Peak Trail stays atop, or contours just below the ridgetop connecting Reyes to its sister peaks. The well-constructed footpath is shaded the whole way by white fir, Jeffrey, ponderosa and sugar pine. Inspiring views are offered from uninspiringly named Peaks 7091, 7114 and 7416, as well as from the saddles between the summits.

DIRECTIONS TO TRAILHEAD: From Highway 101 in Ventura, exit on Highway 33 and head north 47 miles (32 miles past Ojai) to the signed turnoff for Pine Mountain Recreation Area. Follow the narrow paved road past some campgrounds. After 6 miles the paved surface ends and you'll continue east one more mile on a dirt road to road's end, where there's a modest amount of parking.

THE HIKE: Follow the dirt road (closed to vehicles beyond the trailhead) about 150 yards. As the road curves southeast, join the unsigned eastbound trail that begins on the east side of the road. The trail descends slightly and soon passes below the pine- and boulder-covered summit of Reyes Peak (7,510 feet), high point of the Pine Mountain massif. Pine and fir shade the trail, which alternately follows the ridgeline and contours just below it.

You'll look down to the northwest at the farms and ranches of Cuyama Valley, and beyond to the stark Cuyama Badlands. Enjoy pine-framed views of Mt. Pinos (8,831 feet), highest peak in Los Padres National Forest. From the ridgetop, peer southwest into the Sespe River gorge.

After about 1.75 miles of travel, you'll be treated to a view of the canyon cut by Potrero John Creek. The eroded cliffs at the head of the canyon recall Utah's Bryce Canyon National Park.

Reyes Peak Trail continues east through pine and fir forest. After two more miles of travel, you'll drop into and switchback out of a hollow, and arrive at signed Haddock Peak. The peak offers good views to the south and west of the Ojai back-country. From the peak, the trail descends in earnest. Almost two miles of travel brings you to Haddock Trail Camp located on the banks of Piedra Blanca Creek.

REYES CREEK, BEARTRAP CREEK

BEARTRAP TRAIL

From Reyes Creek Camp to Upper Reyes Trail Camp is 6 miles round trip with 800-foot elevation gain; to Beartrap #1 Trail Camp is 10 miles round trip with 1,100-foot gain

Reyes and Beartrap creeks are two of the many pretty watercourses that spill from the northern slopes of Pine Mountain in Los Padres National Forest. The creeks run full speed in spring and even in dry years usually have water.

Upper Reyes is a cool canyon trail camp named for a local pioneer family. Farther up the trail is Beartrap Camp, where the Reyes and others settlers established hunting camps. The fierce grizzly was lord and sovereign over these mountains until hunters eliminated the animals from the area with guns and traps.

Near the trailhead is Camp Scheideck Lodge, established in the 1890s as a hunting lodge. Now the establishment is a funky country bar, where hikers may gather post hike to quench their thirst with a beer or soft drink.

DIRECTIONS TO TRAILHEAD: From Interstate 5, just north of Gorman, take the Frazier Park exit and follow Frazier Mountain Road west for 7 miles to Lockwood Valley Road. Turn left and proceed 24 miles to the signed turnoff for Reyes Creek Campground. A second sign advertising Camp Scheideck Lodge is also at this junction. Turn left and follow the paved road as it crosses the Cuyama River. Caution: Crossing can be difficult during times of high water. Park in the day-use area.

THE HIKE: From the trailhead, the path rises out of Reyes Creek Canyon. The trail leads through an interesting mixture of three life zones: chaparral, oak woodland and pine.

The trail switchbacks up to a saddle. Behind you, to the northwest, is a fine view of the tortured terrain of the Cuyama Badlands. In front of you, to the southeast, is the much more inviting forested canyon cut by Reyes Creek. From the saddle, a half-mile descent brings you to Upper Reyes Trail Camp. It's a pleasant stream-side camp, a good place to cool your heels or to take a lunch stop.

Energetic hikers will assault the switchbacks above Upper Reyes Trail Camp and climb to the ridge separating Reyes Creek from Beartrap Creek. The trail then descends to an oak- and pine-shaded camp on Beartrap Creek.

FISHBOWLS

CEDAR CREEK TRAIL
From Thorn Meadows to Cedar Camp is 4 miles round trip with 300-foot
elevation gain; to Fishbowls is 9 miles round trip with 1,000-foot gain

The Fishbowls of Piru Creek are a deep series of potholes dredged out of the sedimentary rock creekbed by the erosive power of rushing water. You'll enjoy basking on nearby flat rocks and dreaming your life away. When you awake from your dreams, a plunge into the cold water of the Fishbowls will quickly clear your head.

This hike is one of the nicest in the Mt. Pinos area of Los Padres National Forest. The trail climbs through cedar and pine forest to the headwaters of Piru Creek. The creek springs from the slopes of Pine Mountain and bubbles through a maze of mountains. Piru Creek pools were the site of gold mining at the turn of the century. Even today, you can sometimes spot weekend prospectors looking for a flash in the pan.

DIRECTIONS TO TRAILHEAD: From Interstate 5 just north of Gorman, take the Frazier Park exit and follow Frazier Mountain Road west for 7 miles to Lockwood Valley Road, a dirt road suitable for most passenger cars.

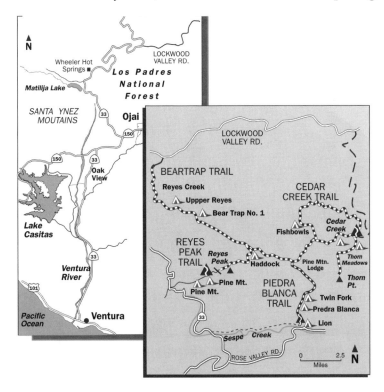

Proceed 7.5 miles, then turn right on signed Thorn Meadows Road (7N03B) and drive 0.5 mile to the beginning of Cedar Creek Trail on the right. Parking is along the road near the trailhead.

THE HIKE: From the trailhead, head up a dirt road that is closed to vehicles. The road soon narrows to a trail, which stays near Piru Creek. It's pleasant hiking through oak woodland and scattered pines. Wallflowers, scarlet buglers and Johnny jump-ups brighten the path. Watch for the chia with its small blue flowers. A staple food of local native Americans, a single teaspoon of chia seed was reported to have been able to sustain a traveler on a 24-hour walk.

After 2 miles of pleasant hiking, you arrive at peaceful Cedar Creek Camp on a south fork of Cedar Creek in a tiny basin ringed by cedar and big cone spruce. The camp is a wonderful place for a picnic and for soaking up some shade before the climb ahead.

The trail continues up forested slopes, along the backbone of a ridge and in a long mile reaches a signed junction. To the left, a trail leads to Pine Mountain Lodge Camp. Bear right, or north, to the Fishbowls on Fishbowls Trail (22W05). The trail swoops up and down two more ridges and offers great views of the sharp forested ridges of the Mt. Pinos high country. The trail then descends steeply to Fishbowls Trail Camp, 1.5 miles from the trail junction.

The camp occupies a quiet, shady canyon cut by the headwaters of Piru Creek. From the camp, the Fishbowls area is 0.25 mile upstream.

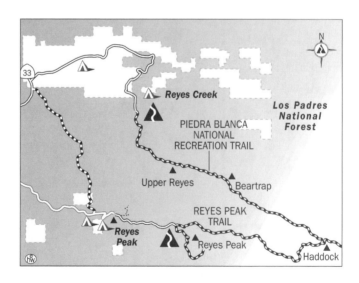

PIEDRA BLANCA

PIEDRA BLANCA NATIONAL RECREATION TRAIL
From Lion Campground to Piedra Blanca is 3 miles round trip with 200-foot elevation gain; to Twin Forks Camp is 6 miles round trip; 600-foot gain; to Pine Mountain Lodge Camp is 11 miles round trip with 3,000-foot gain

Sparkling Piedra Blanca (White Rock) is the sort of place where Castañeda's Don Juan might lurk. The sandstone formation extends for miles between the upper reaches of Sespe River and the mountains to the north. Most of the sandstone in the Sespe area, called the Sespe Formation, is distinguished by its red color. It's a land-laid formation, deposited in layers of mud and sand on land. Unlike the red rock that guards the mouth of Sespe Creek, Piedra Blanca's thick sequences of sedimentary rock are of marine origin. These marine deposits are particularly notable in the Santa Barbara backcountry. Perhaps the most spectacular formations are found at Piedra Blanca.

Piedra Blanca Trail ascends chaparral-cloaked hillsides and visits mighty Piedra Blanca. The path then follows Piedra Blanca Creek and climbs for some distance to Pine Mountain Lodge Camp, the site of a hunting and fishing lodge that once stood on the slopes of Pine Mountain.

DIRECTIONS TO TRAILHEAD: From Ojai, take Highway 33 north 14 miles. Turn right on signed Rose Valley Road and continue 6 miles to Lion Campground. Park in the special day-use lot near the campground. The some-times-signed trail begins across the creek.

THE HIKE: Cross Sespe Creek and join Piedra Blanca Trail. The trail cuts through chaparral and wastes no time heading for Piedra Blanca. These jumbo rocks are in your sight most of the way. Like clouds, the longer you gaze at the formations, the more they assume the shape of your imagination: dragons with missing teeth, the Washington Monument. . . .

From the rocks, the trail descends sharply to an unnamed tributary of Piedra Blanca Creek, finds the creek itself and follows it up the canyon. The trail dips in and out of the narrow oak woodland that lines the creek. You pass an attractive trail camp named for the dominant sandstone, Piedra Blanca, and soon come to Twin Forks Trail Camp, named for its location near the North and Middle Forks of Piedra Blanca Creek. Both Piedra Blanca and Twin Forks are fine picnic spots.

From Twin Forks, the trail twists along with the north fork of Piedra Blanca Creek. It ascends steeply for about 2 miles, then leaves the creek and climbs chaparral- and pine-covered slopes toward the top of Pine Mountain. Pine Mountain Lodge Trail Camp, located at an elevation of 6,000 feet, is cool and green, a good place to take off your shoes and sit awhile.

MATILIJA CREEK

MATILIJA TRAIL

Matilija Cyn. Rd. to Matilija Camp is 2 miles round trip with 200-foot elevation gain; to Middle Matilija Camp is 7 miles round trip with 900-foot gain; to Forest Road 6N01 is 15 miles round trip with 3,000-foot gain.

The meaning of Matilija is unknown, but it may have been the Chumash word to describe the showy Matilija poppy, prized by the Indians for its medicinal qualities. The poppy's botanical name, *Romneya coulteri* honors two Irish scientists and longtime friends, astronomer Romney Robinson and botanist Thomas Coulter.

Coulter first collected this outstanding flower in 1831. During the early years of this century, Ojai entrepreneurs dug up Matilija poppies by the thousands and sold them in Los Angeles.

The Matilija poppy is found along many Ojai backcountry trails and often alongside the road into and out of Ojai-Highway 33. It blooms from May to July, stands three to seven feet tall and is bushy at its base. The delicate flowers have six white crinkled petals and a golden center. Matilija poppies have a strong, sweet fragrance and hikers who near a stand may smell the flower before sighting it.

The Matilija Trail has the dubious distinction of being the flash point for some of the largest fires in Southern California history. In June of 1917 the Matilija-Wheeler Springs Fire burned for five days and nights and blackened more than 30,000 acres. The 1932 Matilija Fire burned nearly a quarter million acres. One of the fire lines was Highway 33, then under construction.

The 1985 Wheeler Fire scorched much of the Ojai backcountry, including the

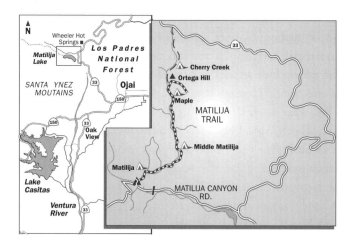

steep terrain watered by the many forks of Matilija Creek. The canyon bottoms have made a remarkable recovery.

Matilija Trail, at its lower end, offers an ideal family outing alongside the Upper North Fork of Matilija Creek. More experienced hikers will enjoy pushing on to the canyon's upper reaches for fine ocean and mountain views. Many nice pools, cascades and flat sunny rocks offer pleasant picnic spots. Some 30,000 acres of Ojai backcountry were set aside as the Matilija Wilderness.

DIRECTIONS TO TRAILHEAD: Continue on Highway 33 about four miles past Ojai, and past the leftward turnoff to Matilija Hot Springs. A short mile past the hot springs, turn left on Matilija Canyon Road (Forest Service Road 5N13) and proceed 5 miles to a locked gate across the road. A parking area is located just before the gate.

THE HIKE: Pass the locked gate and hike along the dirt road through Matilija Canyon Ranch and a private wildlife reserve. Please stay on the road and respect private property. After crossing two branches of Matilija Creek, the road turns left, but you will follow the unmarked spur that turns right and follows the creek. Within 50 yards, cross the creek twice more and begin hiking along the creek bank. A mile of nearly level walking brings you to Matilija Camp.

Matilija Camp is a nice picnic spot. Those geologically inclined will note how stream erosion in this area exposed areas of severe folding and faulting; past actions of the Santa Ynez Fault are very much in evidence.

Beyond the camp, the trail fords several small tributary creeks that feed the Upper North Fork of the Matilija, and crosses a wide meadow. The trail switchbacks above the creek for a while, then resumes again on the canyon bottom. Some level travel and few more crossings brings you to oak-shaded Middle Matilija Camp. You can lunch here and call it a day or push on upstream.

Beyond the camp, the trail crosses and re-crosses the creek half a dozen more times. The canyon floor is forested with big cone spruce, bay laurel and maple. You'll rise out of the canyon, then descend into the narrowing canyon and arrive at abandoned, but still serviceable, Upper Matilija Camp.

From this camp, the trail continues up-creek another mile, then rises steeply north out of the canyon. Switchbacks offer the hiker fine views of Old Man Mountain, the Santa Ynez range and the Pacific Ocean. The upper canyon slopes were severely burned in 1985. However, the maples at Maple Camp, the chokecherry, manzanita and scrub oak are recovering. A final steep climb brings you to the terminus of the trail at Forest Service Road 6N01 near Ortega Hill.

OJAI VALLEY

PRATT, FOOTHILL, SHELF ROAD TRAILS
Loop from Stewart Canyon to Gridley Canyon is 7 miles round trip with 600-foot elevation gain

Ojai, nestled in a little valley backed by the Topatopa and Sulphur Mountains, has meant tranquility to several generations of settlers and citrus growers, artists, musicians and mystics. Ojai Valley was the setting for Shangri-La in the 1937 movie *Lost Horizon.*

The 10-mile-long, 3-mile wide valley, surrounded by coastal mountain ranges has always had a sequestered feeling. Chumash Indians called this region Ojai, which means "nest." The meditative setting has spawned an artists colony, music festival and a number of health resorts. The environment has attracted the meta-physically-minded too; the hiker can look down on the Krotona Institute of Theosophy on one side of town and the Krishnamurti Foundation on the other.

Ancient geologic forces shaped the Ojai Valley that modern-day visitors find so attractive. This part of Ventura County lies in a region geologists call the Transverse Range Province. Transverse means lying across; mountains and valleys in these parts have been moved, by seismic and other forces, out of California's usual north-south orientation into an east-west configuration.

This east-west positioning means a lot of sunshine, with early morning light and long, lingering sunsets. Southern California locales with a southern expo-sure—Ojai, Malibu, Santa Barbara—often seem bathed in a magical light that is most bewitching.

Foothill Trail offers the best view of the town and valley. From the path,

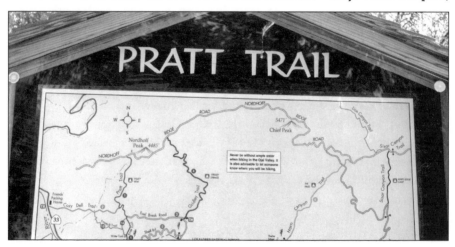

hikers get great views of the harmonious Spanish architecture of Ojai, sweet-smelling citrus groves and the sometimes misty, sometimes mystical Ojai Valley.

Amidst the charred ruins of Foothill Hotel

DIRECTIONS TO TRAILHEAD: From Highway 33 in the heart of downtown Ojai (the landmark arcade and the post office), turn north on North Signal and drive 0.8 mile to a water tank and a signed road on your left. Turn left and drive 0.3 mile on this road, past a Ventura County flood control works, the Stewart Canyon Debris Basin to a turnaround and parking.

THE HIKE: Join signed Pratt Trail and head west. The path dips into brushy, boulder-strewn Stewart Canyon, zigzagging beneath oaks and tangled understory of native and nonnative shrubs. A eucalyptus grove marks the site of the elegant Foothill Hotel, a casualty of an early 1900s fire. Turning north, the trail nears private homes and the hiker encounters signs, lots of them, clearly defining private property and public right-of-way.

A bit more than a mile from the trailhead, the trail becomes a fire road, passes a water tank and a junction with the west fork of Foothill Trail, and climbs to a plateau. Pratt Trail continues north, but you head east on Foothill Trail. The dirt road alternately dips and rises, and just as you're beginning to wonder if the trail will ever deliver a view, it finally climbs eastward out onto open slopes for great vistas of Ojai. From some vantage points you can see almost the whole Ojai Valley, Shangri-La indeed.

Nearly 3.5 miles (about half-way) into the hike, Foothill Trail continues as a footpath that leads 0.5 mile higgly-piggly around private property and through thick chaparral. The trail crosses then parallels a dirt road. You'll pass a gate, and continue another 0.1 mile to a junction, veering right on Gridley Canyon Trail.

Gridley Canyon Trail descends rather steeply, its route stabilized by railroad ties. The trail emerges at Gridley Road. Turn right on Gridley Road. Walk 0.4 mile downhill and look for Shelf Road and trailhead parking on the right. Shelf Road, very popular with local joggers and dog walkers, heads east and ascends moderately into the hills. Skirting citrus and avocado groves, Shelf Road serves up views that are just a little less-dramatic than those offered by higher Foothill Trail. Strategically placed benches offer rest for the weary.

Just after the road bends south, you'll reach a gate and Signal Road. Hike 0.2 mile down the road to the trailhead access road and return to the parking area.

Gridley Canyon & Nordhoff Peak

GRIDLEY TRAIL

From Gridley Road to Gridley Spring is 6 miles round trip with 1,400-foot elevation gain; to Nordhoff Peak is 12 miles round trip with 3,500-foot gain.

Prussian-born journalist Charles Nordhoff was one of the 19th century's biggest boosters of California and the California way of life. Nordhoff, an editor with the New York Evening Post, traveled extensively throughout the Golden State in 1870-1871, and wrote *California: for Health, Pleasure and Residence,* an enormously popular book that prompted much visitation and settlement.

The book had a profound effect on the nation's attitude toward California. No longer would California be regarded as the uncivilized far Western frontier, but as the perfect place in the sun — one that offered the chance to build a home or business, to raise crops or children in America's answer to the Mediterranean.

One of Nordhoff's favorite discoveries — quintessential Southern California as he saw it — was a beautiful valley located about 15 miles inland from Ventura. Nordhoff wrote about this valley for several Eastern magazines and newspapers, and as a result, the peaceful hamlet here quickly grew into a town. Grateful townspeople named it Nordhoff in 1874. Nordhoff it remained until 1916 when the anti-German sentiment of World War I prompted a change of name to Ojai.

Nordhoff's name remains on the 4,425-foot peak that forms a dramatic backdrop for the town of Nordhoff, er...Ojai. The summit offers splendid views of the Ojai Valley, the Ventura County coastline and the Channel Islands.

Ascending Nordhoff Peak is no picnic. The trail crosses steep, sun-baked slopes, but if you've picked a clear day for this trek, the views will reward your effort.

DIRECTIONS TO TRAILHEAD: From the intersection of Highways 33 and 150 in Ojai, proceed on the latter road, known as Ojai Avenue. You'll pass through town, and about 2 miles from the intersection, look for Los Padres National Forest Ojai Ranger Station on the left at 1190 Ojai Avenue. This is a good place to get the latest trail information. Proceed another half-mile and take the second left beyond the ranger station — Gridley Road. Follow Gridley 1.7 miles to its end. Signed Gridley Trail is on the left.

THE HIKE: Gridley Trail climbs a brushy draw, overhung with tall cean-othus. A half-mile's gentle ascent brings you to Gridley Fire Road (Forest Service Road 5N11). Turn right and follow this crumbling dirt road as it ascends above avocado groves planted on steep slopes. Leaving behind the "Guacamole Wilderness," the route enters Gridley Canyon, climbing to the northwest (and thankfully a bit cooler) side of the canyon.

Not much remains of Gridley Spring Camp, incinerated along with thousands of acres of the Ojai backcountry in the Wheeler Fire. Still, the vegetation in the area has made an astonishing recovery, and the spring named for an early homesteader, still flows.

Past Gridley Spring, peak-bound hikers will continue along the dirt road into an east fork of Gridley Canyon and join a switchbacking trail for the rigorous ascent. Notice the superb succession of sedimentary rocks displayed by the Topatopa mountains above you. Far below is the Pacific Ocean.

Two miles from the springs, you'll meet Nordhoff Fire Road (5N05). Turn left and follow this road a mile to Nordhoff Peak.

To the south is Ojai Valley, with Lake Casitas and the Pacific beyond. To the west rise the higher peaks of the Topatopa range, including the 6,210-foot signature peak, Topatopa. Also to the west is Sespe Condor Sanctuary. To the north is the Pine Mountain range and many more Los Padres National Forest peaks.

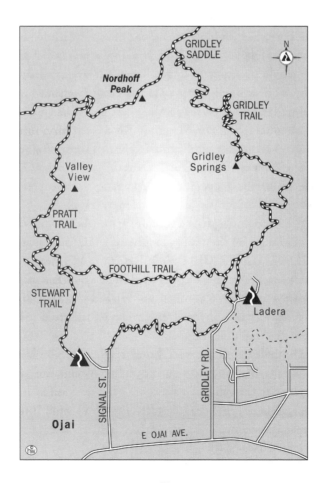

SULPHUR MOUNTAIN

SULPHUR MOUNTAIN ROAD RECREATION TRAIL
10 miles one way with 2,300-foot elevation loss

Once upon a time, Sulphur Mountain Road was one of the Southland's great Sunday drives. Motorists loved this curvy, dirt byway back of Ojai for the superb vistas it offered of the Ojai Valley, Topatopa Mountains, coast and Channel Islands.

These days, vehicles are banned from Sulphur Mountain but the sterling views remain to anyone willing to walk a crooked mile.

Make that 10 crooked miles. A substantial length of the road has been renamed Sulphur Mountain Road Recreation Trail, and traffic restricted to equestrians, cyclists, hikers and the occasional vehicle belonging to one of the local ranchers.

The Ojai backcountry is generally assumed to be the public lands of Los Padres National Forest, which borders Ojai to the east, west and north. But south of Ojai is more backcountry – Sulphur Mountain – almost all of which is private property. The mountain, occupying a 12-mile wide by 12-mile long block of land, is surrounded by highways: Highway 33 to the west, Highway 150 on the north and east, Highways 126 and 101 on the south. These highways approach, but do not cross, Sulphur Mountain. Sulphur Mountain Road Recreation Trail (maintained by Ventura County) is the only public crossing of this terra incognita.

The ridgeline traverse of Sulphur Mountain is a one-way hike, requiring either two vehicles or the cooperation of someone to drop you at the top of Sulphur Mountain and collect you at the bottom.

It's not difficult convincing friends or family members to provide shuttle service because, while you're on the trail (3 to 4 hours), they can enjoy nearby Ojai.

DIRECTIONS TO TRAILHEAD: Return to Highway 33 and follow it north to the outskirts of Ojai. Bear right onto Highway 150 and motor into downtown Ojai. Proceed another 6.5 miles on Highway 150 to signed Sulphur Mountain Road. Turn right and travel 4.75 miles on the steep and winding road to a locked gate at the trailhead.

To the pickup point at trail's end: From Highway 101 in Ventura, exit on Highway 33 and drive 7.5 miles to signed Sulphur Mountain Road. Turn right and proceed 0.4 mile to the vehicle gate.

THE HIKE: Join the road (paved at first) and hike west. Enjoy glimpses of the Ojai countryside at its most eclectic: a gazebo, a yurt, rusted farm implements, a huge red-tile-roofed hacienda.

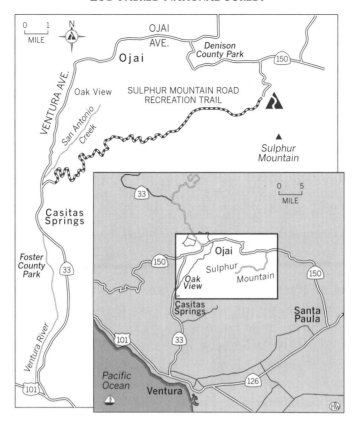

About 1.5 miles from the trailhead, the asphalt ends and you continue the descent on well-graded dirt road. Nearly three miles out, enjoy clear-day views of the Channel Islands and great blue Pacific.

At about mile 4, the trail delivers the first of several stunning, oak-framed panoramic vistas of the Ojai Valley. Particularly prominent in this aerial view is the Ojai Valley Inn & Country Club. Hikers growing a bit leg-weary as they approach the midpoint of this hike might start fantasizing about a massage and spa treatment at the resort.

In some years, Sulphur Mountain boasts fine spring wildflower displays—carpets of lupine and California poppies joining the profligate yellow mustard alongside the road.

The road continues dropping down the ridge and enters classic Southern California cattle country, where cows graze utterly undisturbed by passing hikers.

The last two miles of trail are steep—an elevation loss of more than 1,200 feet. All too soon, you might think, you hear the sound of traffic from Highway 33 and descend to trail's end.

SANTA PAULA CANYON

SANTA PAULA CANYON TRAIL
From Santa Paula Canyon to Big Cone Camp is 6.5 miles round trip with 800-foot elevation gain

Waterfalls, wading pools and swimming holes are some of the attractions of tranquil Santa Paula Canyon. A trail winds along the river bed through the canyon and visits some perfect-for-a-picnic trail camps.

The Y trail begins at St. Thomas Aquinas College, and near a malodorous oil field once owned by infamous oilman and Southern California booster Edward Lawrence Doheny. Doheny's black gold discoveries of 1892 made him an extremely wealthy man and began the first oil industry boom in Los Angeles. (Doheny's 30-room mansion is located behind iron gates just off Highway 150.)

During the Harding administration, Doheny received drilling rights on federal land in Elk Hills without undergoing the inconvenience of competitive bidding. A 1923 Senate investigation of the "Teapot Dome Scandal" uncovered Doheny's $100,000 loan to Secretary of the Interior Fall and led to Fall's conviction for accepting a bribe; Doheny, however, was acquitted of offering one.

Floods periodically sweep Santa Paula Canyon and wash out the trail. In recent years, erosion has been particularly severe and the trail is no longer an easy-

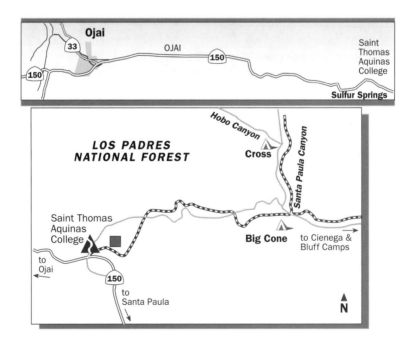

to-follow pathway. Humans, in the form of irresponsible local youth, have not been kind to the area either, and leave behind trash and graffiti.

Weekdays, hikers can find a measure of tranquility on the trail; on weekends, this no-longer-secret trail is one of the most popular in Ventura County.

DIRECTIONS TO THE TRAILHEAD: From the junction of Highways 33 and 150 in Ojai, head east from town on the latter road about 9.5 miles to the bridge spanning Santa Paula Creek. The trailhead is located at the entrance to St. Thomas Aquinas/Ferndale Ranch on the north side of the road, but you continue on Highway 150 across the Santa Paula Creek bridge to a wide turnout on the south side of the highway.

THE HIKE: Follow the asphalt drive onto the college grounds, sticking with the paved road leading north. At a fork in the road at the top of the campus, bear right and walk through a gate.

The paved road passes through Ferndale Ranch, leads past oil pumps and con- tinues as a dirt trail. About 1.5 miles from the trailhead, the path crosses to the north side of Santa Paula Creek and joins a retiring dirt road.

After another mile, the trail crosses the creek and begins a moderate to stiff climb up a slope bearing the less than lyrical name of Hill 1989. The trail gentles before descending to Big Cone Camp, perched on a terrace above Santa Paula Creek.

Just below the camp, the trail, now a narrow footpath, descends to the creek. As you descend, look up-canyon and spot a 25-foot waterfall and a deep pool some locals call "The Punchbowl." Resist the urge to practice the sport of extreme cliff-diving into the swimming hole; a broken neck and body (or worse) is the inevitable consequence.

You can continue past The Punchbowl, but know that the trails are often pretty awful. The trail crosses Santa Paula Creek and switchbacks up to an unsigned junction. A right at this junction leads above the east fork of Santa Paula Canyon 3.5 miles on poorly maintained trail to Cienega Camp. Hardy hikers will enjoy bushwhacking along to this camp set in a meadowland shaded by oak and big-cone spruce.

A left at the above-mentioned junction leads north up Santa Paula Canyon past some inviting pools. The path, sometimes called Last Chance Trail, climbs a mile to Cross, another big-cone spruce-shaded camp. Here Santa Paula Creek offers some nice falls and great swimming holes.

CHAPTER THREE

Ventura County Parks & Preserves

About half of fast-growing Ventura County is public land with lots of trails leading from the mountains to the valleys—or vice-versa depending on how you look at things. Perched on an elevated plateau above the Oxnard Plain lies the lovely oak-studded, mountain-surrounded Conejo Valley on the eastern edge of Ventura County. The hills and valley are a bit of pastoral Southern California, still inspiring today even after much suburban development. Orange- and tan-hued sandstone outcroppings of the once-lonely Simi Hills form a dramatic background behind Simi Valley suburbs. Oak woodlands and sweeping grasslands characterize the Santa Susana Mountains, which extend from Granada Hills westward into Ventura County.

WILDWOOD REGIONAL PARK

TO WILDWOOD CANYON, LIZARD ROCK
5 miles round trip; 400-foot elevation gain
Return via MountClef 7 miles round trip; 600-foot gain

Wildwood Park is a tranquil retreat on the outskirts of Conejo Valley. Hikers can explore two intriguing sections of the park—gentle Wildwood Creek and Canyon and the more rugged Mountclef Ridge.

This intriguing park with a trite name preserves 1,300 acres of canyonland and rocky cliffs. Wildwood Park is bounded by Conejo Creek and its two seasonal branches—Arroyo Santa Rosa and Arroyo Conejo. A special feature of the park is a waterfall called Paradise Falls.

Before the park came into being, it belonged to a development company that leased it out to MGM studios. The epic film *Spartacus* was filmed in Wildwood Canyon, and the sets for "Dodge City" and "The Rifleman" were located here.

The park boasts an extensive trail system. Hikers of all abilities will find a park trail to their liking. Families with small children can take a stroll along Wildwood Creek. Energetic hikers can trek to the park's high country—Lizard Rock and that Monument Valley in miniature, Mountclef Ridge. Grand valley views are yours from atop the ridge.

DIRECTIONS TO TRAILHEAD: From the Ventura Freeway (101) in Thousand Oaks, exit on Lynn Road. Drive 2.5 miles north to Avenida Los Arboles. Turn left and proceed a mile to the park entrance and a parking area. Leave your vehicle here or continue another half-mile down a dirt road to a second parking area.

THE HIKE: From the parking area, descend down the dirt fire road into Wildwood Canyon. You'll soon reach a junction. A left will take you to Meadows Cave and a picnic area. Turn right and follow the trail along oak-, willow- and cotton-wood-shaded Wildwood Creek. If you don't remember the names of the local flora, the park's placards will jog your memory.

After a short while, you'll reach a side trail on your right that leads up to Tepee Overlook. After taking a look at the teepee, which looks more like a picnic ramada than anything Native American, you can return to the creek trail the way you came or via a longer route by continuing on the dirt road past the teepee.

The creekside trail bends north with Wildwood Creek then climbs the sage- and lemonade berry-covered north canyon wall. Below is tiny Paradise Falls. Beyond the falls, both the creekside trail and Oak Grove Nature Trail meander through the oaks to a picnic area.

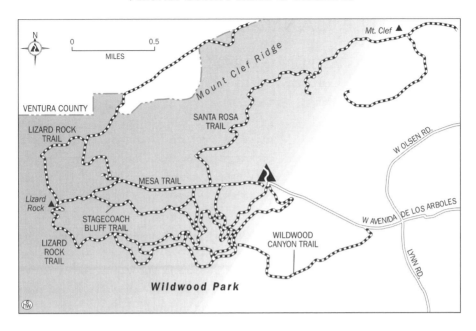

Beyond the picnic area, the trail heads west and crosses the creek a couple times. Approaching the park's western boundary you'll turn sharply north on signed Lizard Rock Trail. This path rises steeply over a wildflower-splashed grassy slope, then turns east and brings you to the base of a handsome cluster of rocks. The rock's resemblance to a lizard is dubious, but the lizard's-eye view from atop the rock is excellent.

Clear-day views are good from Lizard Rock and even better from the central and eastern portion of the Mount Clef Range. Far to the north you can see the Los Padres National Forest backcountry. More immediately to the north are the Las Posas Hills and to the south is Conejo Valley. To the northeast are the Santa Susana Mountains, and to the east are the Simi Hills. To the west are the Camarillo Hills and Oxnard Plain.

The trail heads east down the rocky ridgeline, passes an extensive prickly pear cactus patch and continues descending toward the main part of the park. Just before you return to familiar ground—the parking area and trails leading to it— you'll arrive at the signed junction with Santa Rosa Trail. For a nice option and some great views, follow this side trail as it ascends into rocky Mount Clef Range. Up-top are some lumpy, pudding-like conglomerate rocks and a panorama of both wild and suburban Ventura County.

OAK CREEK CANYON

OAK CREEK CANYON, LOS ROBLES TRAILS
From Oak Creek Canyon to Angel Vista Point is 8 miles round trip with 500-foot elevation gain

Perched on an elevated plateau that extends between Westlake and the Oxnard Plain lies the lovely, oak-studded, mountain-surrounded Conejo Valley. The valley, which crowns the eastern edge of Ventura County, certainly hosts its share of suburban developments, but retains a charming, pastoral side that offers some delightful hiking.

The network of pathways exploring the Conejo Valley's sometimes wide, sometimes narrow, open spaces is usually referred to as the Los Robles Trail System. Los Robles and companion trails link Conejo Valley with the extensive trail system in the Santa Monica Mountains. At the valley's west end, Los Robles Trail ties into Point Mugu State Park; an intrepid hiker could hike across the valley then over the mountains to the Pacific Ocean in the course of a day.

Los Robles Trail was developed—and is maintained—as a multi-use path, meaning the hiker can expect to see an occasional horseback rider and many mountain bikers. The trail, along with the terrain it traverses, is oriented east-west.

Just as the Santa Monica Mountains-crossing Backbone Trail links the scattered beauties of the mountains, Los Robles Trail unites the parks, preserves and open spaces of the Conejo Valley. Several connector trails extend from Westlake, Thousand Oaks and several neighborhoods to Los Robles Trail.

The middle section of Los Robles Trail offers a pleasant introduction to hiking the Conejo Valley and the region's trail system. Begin in pleasant Oak Canyon at the edge of Thousand Oaks and enjoy the winding path and the fine valley vistas it delivers.

DIRECTIONS TO TRAILHEAD: From Highway 101 (Ventura Freeway) in Thousand Oaks, exit on Moorpark Road and drive 0.5 mile south to Greenmeadow Avenue. Turn right (west) and proceed 0.4 mile to road's end at the parking lot for the Conejo Valley Arts Council Center and the signed trail.

THE HIKE: Walk among the oaks on Oak Creek Canyon Whole Access Trail, a footpath designed to assist the blind learn more about the great outdoors. Interpretive stations with text written in Braille describe the lovely surroundings.

After 0.25 mile, the path bends east and junctions. An eastern leg of the canyon trail loops back to the trailhead, but this hike heads briefly south to connect with Los Robles Trail.

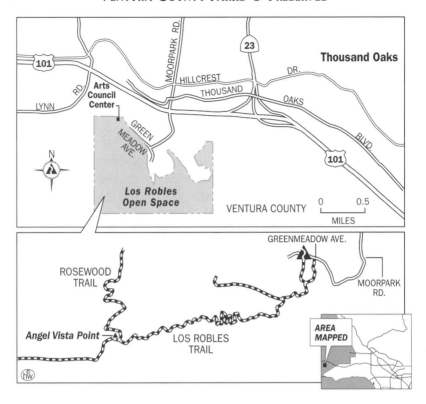

Stick with Los Robles Trail (West) at a couple of junctions. The path tunnels through the high chaparral and climbs gently. The first good Conejo Valley views come up at about the 2-mile mark on this hike.

The trail dips into a canyon, crosses a private road, then climbs again. Los Robles Trail meets Rosewood Trail (which descends to Lynn Road) at a signed junction. Stick with Los Robles Trail for another minute of hiking to reach Angel Vista Point, where a welcome picnic table offers a place to relax and enjoy Conejo Valley vistas.

Conejo Open Space

ROSEWOOD, LOS ROBLES TRAILS
From Lynn Road to Angel Vista Point is 4 miles round trip with 700-foot elevation gain; to Rancho Sierra Vista Satwiwa is 10 miles round trip

For 19th-century travelers, the Conejo Corridor was part of the stagecoach route connecting Los Angeles with Ventura. For today's hikers, the corridor is a trail network that extends west from Westlake Village all the way to Point Mugu State Park.

Offering bed and board to stagecoach passengers and horseback riders, the Grand Union Hotel (later the Stagecoach Inn) opened for business in 1876. The two-story, Monterey-style building featured a wrap-around balcony and fine dining. The inn was saved from the wrecking ball in the mid-1960s by the Conejo Valley Historical Society and moved to its present location. A 1970 fire completely destroyed the old inn but it was soon rebuilt and restored to its original appearance.

Museum displays illustrate Conejo Valley history. Outlying buildings include an old school house and a carriage house. Step out on the short nature trail that departs from the rear of the museum. For an enjoyable day, take a hike along the Conejo Corridor, picnic in Stagecoach Inn Park, then visit the museum. The trailhead for Rosewood Trail is located just south of the museum complex.

DIRECTIONS TO TRAILHEAD: From Highway 101 in Newbury Park, exit on Ventu Park Road. After 0.4 mile you'll notice the signed entrance to Stagecoach Inn Museum at 51 South Ventu Park Road, but keep going another block to an intersection with Lynn Road. Turn right (west), then make another right on Susan Drive (which looks more like a long driveway than a street) and park in the spaces along the perimeter of Stagecoach Inn Park. When the Stagecoach Inn Museum is open, you can walk from the park through a back gate onto the museum grounds. Carefully cross Lynn Road and join signed Rosewood Trail.

THE HIKE: The path crosses a little creek, leaves behind some residences and begins to climb the south slope of the hills. Better and better views are the reward for the climb, culminating in the best ridgetop view at Angel Vista Point, a somewhat grandiose name for a little flat spot with a single picnic table.

Catch your breath, and join the signed Los Robles Trail heading west. The path dips into a draw and crosses some private land (courtesy of a trail easement) as it meanders up and down the ridgeline to trail's end at a parking area at West Potrero Road. To extend your walk, cross West Potrero Road and join the connector trail that leads west 0.5 mile to the National Park Service's Rancho Sierra Vista/Satwiwa property. The ambitious hiker can continue a mile or so to a Native American cultural center, then connect with the extensive trail system in Point Mugu State Park.

HAPPY CAMP CANYON REGIONAL PARK

HAPPY CAMP CANYON, MIDDLE RANGE FIRE TRAILS
From Broadway Trailhead to eastern park boundary is 9 miles round trip with 700-foot elevation gain; return via Middle Ridge Fire Roads is 10 miles round trip with 1,000-foot gain

When viewed from the busy Simi Valley Freeway, the rapid suburbanization of Simi Valley can seem startling.

Not so, however, in the mountains bordering the north side of the valley. Here, working ranches and a rural lifestyle still prevail.

Happy Camp Canyon Regional Park, located in the eastern Ventura County city of Moorpark, preserves some 3,000 acres of rolling ranch land that looks as it did 100 years ago. The park preserves a part of the old Strathern Ranch, a huge spread owned by a pioneering family.

If you like your parks undeveloped, you'll appreciate Happy Camp; there's no camp, happy or otherwise, and no picnic ground. You'll find drinking water and restrooms at the trailhead, and that's about it.

The main trail leads along the bottom of oak- and sycamore-shaded Happy Camp Canyon, which lies between Oak Ridge to the north and Big Mountain to the south.

DIRECTIONS TO TRAILHEAD: From the Ventura Freeway (101) in Thousand Oaks, exit on Highway 23 and travel 10 miles north to Moorpark. Exit on New Los Angeles Avenue. (Or you can head west on the Ronald Reagan Freeway (118) to Moorpark and Highway 23 and exit on New Los Angeles Avenue.)

Head west on New Los Angeles Avenue a bit more than a mile to Moorpark Avenue and turn right. Travel north on 23 two miles to where the road makes a sharp left turn; continue straight ahead at this bend onto Happy Camp Road, then make an almost immediate right onto Broadway Road. Follow Broadway half a mile to its end at Happy Camp Park's parking lot. The trail into Happy Camp Canyon begins at the east end of the lot.

THE HIKE: The footpath heads north along the canyon wall, then swings east and drops to the bottom of the canyon. One mile of easy walking brings you to Happy Camp Road, which you'll follow to a locked gate. You'll pass a junction with Middle Ridge Fire Road (a possible return route for a longer hike) on your right.

Continue on Happy Camp Fire Road, past a large oak grove and colorful red and yellowish rock outcroppings, formed by underground fires fueled by the

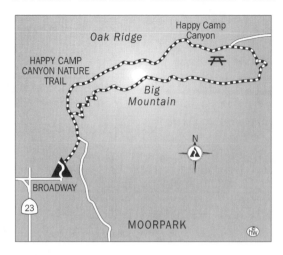

region's extensive oil deposits. Turn around at any time, or continue to a junction with a trail on your right that switchbacks steeply to Middle Ridge Fire Road on the canyon's south side.

Enjoy the great views of Big Mountain on the south side of the canyon, Oak Ridge to the north, and the Simi Valley below, as you hike along the ridge back to the canyon gate, and then retrace your steps a mile back to the trailhead.

CHAPTER FOUR

Simi Hills

On some maps the Simi Hills appear as little more than a narrow band between suburbs, but on the ground present some challenging territory to hike. In fact, the range's reddish-orange, sky-scraping sedimentary rock formations seem all the more awesome towering over flatland neighborhoods, and it's easy to see why these rugged hills were a popular setting for Western movies. The hills are known nationally as the locale for the Ronald Reagan Presidential Library and Museum, and known locally for a fine network of footpaths.

SIMI PEAK

CHINA FLAT TRAIL
5 mile loop with 1,000-foot elevation gain

China Flat Trail is an excellent (but not easy) introduction to the Simi Hills. It leads to China Flat, perched on the wild west side of the National Park Service's Cheeseboro Canyon Site. The trail's return loop contours high over the shoulder of 2,403-foot Simi Peak, highest summit in the Simi Hills.

Ambitious hikers will enjoy China Flat Trail as a backdoor entry along the ridgecrest to Cheeseboro and Palo Comado canyons, part of the Santa Monica Mountains National Recreation Area. Expect a 10- or 12-mile hike (or more), as well as a measure of solitude on this lightly traveled route.

China Flat Trail is a bit of a misnomer; the trail is anything but flat. And China Flat itself, while of more level relief than surrounding Simi peaks, will never be confused with one of those truly flat Flats found in other mountain ranges.

Still, China Flat Trail is a most enjoyable loop, requiring only a one-block neighborhood stroll to connect trail's end with the trailhead.

DIRECTIONS TO TRAILHEAD: From the Ventura Freeway (101) in Westlake Village, exit on Lindero Canyon Road and head north 4 miles. A few blocks from the trailhead, Lindero Canyon Road bends east. Look for the signed trailhead on the left (north) side of the road between King James Court and Wembly Avenue. Park on Lindero Canyon Road.

THE HIKE: Follow the trail north up a short, steep hill. Here a connector trail rising from King James Court meets the path. Continue on the main (China Flat) trail as it ascends past a sandstone formation. After climbing some more, the path gentles a bit and contours east to an unsigned junction. Keep to the left (north) and begin a stiff climb toward the ridgeline.

Finally the trail gains the ridge and you encounter another unsigned junction. Bear left and continue an ascent along the ridge to a saddle and yet another trail junction. (Ambitious trekkers bound for Cheeseboro Canyon will take the right fork.)

This hike uses the left fork and begins a moderate descent. Views from the shoulder of Simi Peak include Westlake Village, Agoura Hills and other communities clustered on the Ventura-Los Angeles County line, as well as the peaks of the Santa Monica Mountains.

The trail ends at a gate on King James Court. Follow this short street one block down to Lindero Canyon Road and your vehicle.

CHEESEBORO CANYON

CHEESEBORO CANYON TRAIL
From NPS Parking Lot to Sulfur Springs is 6 miles round trip with 100-foot elevation gain; to Sheep Corral is 9.5 miles round trip with 200-foot elevation gain

It's the old California of the ranchos: Oak-studded potreros, rolling foothills that glow amber in the dry months, emerald green in springtime. It's easy to imagine vaqueros rounding up tough Mexican range cattle.

For years this last vestige of old California faced an uncertain future, but thanks to the efforts of conservationists it was saved from golf course and suburban development.

From the days of the ranchos to 1985, Cheeseboro Canyon was heavily grazed by cattle. Grazing altered canyon ecology by displacing native flora and allowing

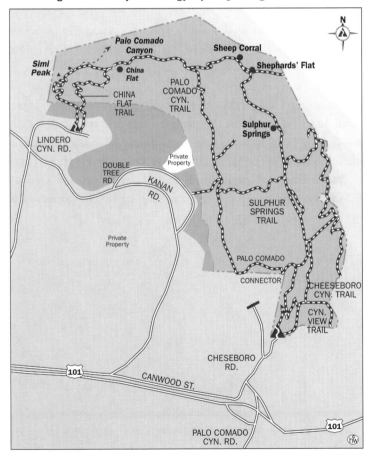

opportunistic plants such as mustard and thistle to invade. As you walk through the canyon, you'll see signs indicating research areas. The National Park Service is attempting to re-colonize native flora and eradicate nonnatives.

DIRECTIONS TO TRAILHEAD: From the Ventura Freeway (101) in Agoura, exit on Chesebro Road. Loop inland very briefly on Palo Comado Canyon Road, then turn right on Chesebro Road, which leads to the National Park Service's gravel entrance road and parking lot.

THE HIKE: Note your return route, Modello Trail, snaking north up the wall of the canyon, but follow the fire road east into Cheeseboro Canyon. The fire road soon swings north and dips into the canyon. You'll pass a signed intersection with Canyon Overlook Trail, a less-than-thrilling side trail that leads to a knoll overlooking the Lost Hills landfill.

After this junction, the main canyon trail, now known as Sulfur Springs Trail, winds through valley oak-dotted grassland and coast live oak-lined canyon. Watch for mule deer browsing in the meadows and a multitude of squirrels scurrying amongst the oaks.

The old road crisscrosses an (usually) all-but-dry streambed. A bit more than 3 miles from the trailhead, your nose will tell you that you've arrived at Sulfur Springs. You can turn around here or continue another 1.75 miles up a narrowing trail and narrowing canyon to an old sheep corral.

You can continue a bit farther on the trail to a junction with Palo Comado Canyon Trail and head south on this path back to the trailhead. Ranch Center Trail, a 1.1 mile long path, connects Palo Comado and Cheeseboro canyons, as does the 1.5 mile Palo Comado Connector Trail. The latter path leads to a junction 0.7 mile from the trailhead. Modelo Trail ascends a ridgetop for a good view of Cheeseboro Canyon and one of the finest remaining oak woodlands in Southern California.

UPPER LAS VIRGENES CANYON PRESERVE

EAST LAS VIRGENES CANYON TRAIL
From Las Virgenes Road to Laskey Mesa is 5.5 miles round trip with 500-foot elevation gain; many shorter and longer hikes possible

From atop the ridge on the southeastern corner of the former Ahmanson Ranch, commanding vistas of two competing visions of 21st-century Southern California are revealed to the hiker. Eastward and southward the San Fernando Valley suburb-anopolis sprawls across Los Angeles County. Westward beckons a magnificent, nearly untouched landscape of rolling grassland, oak dotted slopes and the dramatic summits of the Simi Hills, miles of wildland extending across Ventura County.

The preservationist vision prevailed after a decade-long battle that pitted conservationists and celebrity allies such as Rob Reiner and Martin Sheen against Washington Mutual with a $2 billion plan that called for construction of 3,000 homes, a golf course and a shopping mall on the ranch land. The enormous savings institution agreed to sell the land to the Santa Monica Mountains Conservancy in 2003.

Upper Las Virgenes Canyon Open Space Preserve's natural resources include some 4,000 valley and coastal live oak trees, as well as the ultra-rare San Fernando Valley spine flower, recently rediscovered after botanists believed it extinct for 70 years. The preserve is one of the state's prime raptor habitats and is home to Southern California's last viable population of the red-legged frog.

The rolling hills and broad mesas of the region have been a favorite location for filmmakers since the silent movie era. The Lasky Company owned the ranch, which boasted both a close proximity to studios and an almost complete lack of development. Among the movies filmed at Laskey Mesa, as it was then known, were *The Charge of the Light Brigade*, *They Died with Their Boots On*, and *Gone with the Wind*.

Few improvements are planned for the land, which will be preserved in an unaltered state as wildlife habitat and a nature park. Hikers can explore the 2,900-acre preserve on some 15 miles of trails and dirt roads.

More than one great trail awaits the hiker, so I've suggested four possible routes for your wanderings.

DIRECTIONS TO TRAILHEAD: From Highway 101 in Calabasas, exit on Las Virgenes Canyon Road and drive north 1.5 miles to road's end. Park on either side of the road. At road's end, you'll find the start of the main trail that leads into Upper Las Virgenes Canyon Open Space Preserve.

You can also enter the preserve from undeveloped trailheads located near the ends of Victory Boulevard and Vanowen Street.

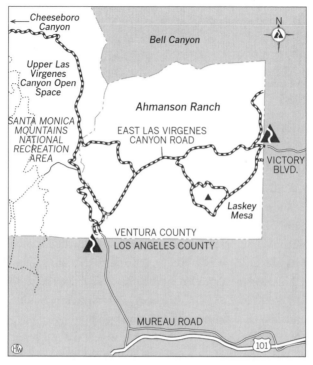

THE HIKE: One good introduction to the preserve's charms is the hike to Laskey Mesa. Head out along the park's main dirt entry road, branch right on East Virgenes Canyon Road and, about 1.75 miles from the trailhead, veer southward on the path to Laskey Mesa. Hike a mile loop around the 1,391-foot mesa and then return the way you came.

For a west-to-east traverse of the preserve, follow the entirety of East Las Virgenes Canyon Road from the trailhead to a pending trailhead near the end of Victory Boulevard. This route is a 6-mile round trip with modest elevation gain.

For a short (2 miles round trip), but nevertheless rewarding loop, walk a short way up the access road to the first intersection and bear left (northwest) up the main branch of Las Virgenes Canyon. After a mile, you'll intersect a footpath on your left. Return south on this trail, which travels the canyon west wall back to a trailhead located very close to the main trailhead.

Gung-ho hikers will ascend the road through Las Virgenes Canyon to wildland in the northwestern part of the preserve. About three miles from the trailhead, the road crosses the creek for a final time and arcs west. The ambitious can continue to the upper reaches of Cheeseboro Canyon and connect with many miles of national parkland trails.

ROCKY PEAK

ROCKY PEAK, CHUMASH TRAILS
To Rocky Peak via Rocky Peak Trail is 6 miles round trip with 1,200 foot elevation gain; to Rocky Peak via Chumash Trail is 7 miles round trip with 1,400-foot gain

One conservation success story is the preservation of Runkle Ranch, now Rocky Peak Park. The park, which straddles the Los Angeles-Ventura county line, sets aside some much-needed parkland for fast-growing Simi Valley.

The rocks of Rocky Peak are sandstone outcroppings that geologists say were formed some 65 million years ago during the Cretaceous Period of the Mesozoic Era. Besides its namesake promontory, 4,369-acre Rocky Peak Park includes Las Llajas and Blind canyons. These canyons have two of the most pleasant seasonal streams in the mountains. After a good rain, waterfalls cascade down the canyons. Until purchased by the Santa Monica Mountains Conservancy in 1991, the Rocky Peak area was owned by entertainer Bob Hope.

Chumash Trail begins in Chumash Park on the outskirts of Simi Valley and leads 2.5 miles to a junction with Rocky Peak Trail, which leads to the peak. Park trails provide access to Blind Canyon and the rolling meadowlands of the Santa Susana Mountains to the north. This hike is a good introduction to the charms of the Santa Susanas.

Rocky Peak area, Santa Susana Mountains.

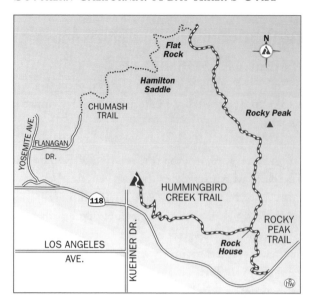

DIRECTIONS TO TRAILHEAD: To reach the Rocky Peak trailhead, take the Ronald Reagan Freeway (118) through the Simi Valley and exit on Rocky Peak Road (that's one exit west of Topanga Canyon Boulevard). The trailhead is immediately opposite the end of the freeway offramp. Caution: You can exit on Rocky Peak Road only by traveling west on Highway 118.

To Chumash trailhead: From the Ronald Reagan Freeway (118) in Simi Valley, exit on Yosemite Avenue. Head north 0.5 mile to Flanagan Drive, turn right, and drive 0.75 mile to road's end and Chumash Park.

THE HIKE: (Via Rocky Peak Trail) Begin at the locked gate of the fire road (closed to vehicles) and begin the ascent. Soon you'll get grand view (if you turn around, that is) across the freeway to the historic Santa Susana Pass, once crossed by stagecoaches.

The fire road continues up and up, with only a lone oak along the trail for shade. Rocky Peak is off to the right (east) of the trail. From the peak and related smaller peaks, you'll get vistas of the San Fernando Valley, Simi Valley, high peaks of Los Padres National Forest, Anacapa Island and the Santa Barbara Channel. Way off to the right (west) is the Ronald Reagan Presidential Library.

From Chumash Park, Chumash trailheads north from the end of Flanagan Drive: The path soon parallels a creek, makes a half-circle around a minor hill, then begins climbing in earnest high above Blind Canyon.

Some 2.5 miles of steady ascent brings you to an intersection with Rocky Peak Trail. If you turn right (south) on this trail, it's about a mile's walk to Rocky Peak. A left turn leads 2.5 miles to the park boundary and a large oak savanna.

CHAPTER FIVE

Santa Monica Mountains

The Santa Monica Mountains are the only relatively undeveloped mountain range in the U.S. that bisects a major metropolitan area. Large stretches are open and natural, covered with chaparral and oak trees, bright in spring with the Southlands best wildflower displays. A near-wilderness within reach of sixteen million people, the mountains extend from Griffith Park in the heart of the city to Point Mugu, fifty miles away. The largest areas of open space are in the western part of the mountains. Point Mugu State Park boasts a splendid native grass prairie and sycamore grove and the gorge cut by Malibu Creek (where the "M*A*S*H" TV series was filmed) is an unforgettable sight.

WILL ROGERS STATE HISTORIC PARK

WILL ROGERS TRAIL
To Inspiration Point is 2 miles round trip with a 300-foot elevation gain

Will Rogers, often called the "Cowboy Philosopher," bought a spread in the Santa Monica Mountains in 1922. He and his family eventually enlarged their weekend cottage to 31 rooms.

The Oklahoma-born Rogers toured the country as a trick roper, punctuating his act with humorous comments on the news of the day. His roping act led the humorist to later fame as a newspaper columnist, radio commentator and movie star.

Today, the ranch and grounds of the Rogers Ranch is maintained as Will Rogers State Historic Park, set aside in 1944. You can see a short film on Rogers' life at the park visitor center and tour the ranch house, still filled with his prized possessions.

Will Rogers and family

Rogers himself designed the riding trails that wind into the hills behind his ranch. The path to Inspiration Point is an easy family walk.

DIRECTIONS TO TRAILHEAD: From Sunset Boulevard in Pacific Palisades, 4.5 miles inland from Sunset's junction with Pacific Coast Highway, turn inland on the access road leading to Will Rogers State Historic Park. Park your car near the polo field or near Rogers' house.

THE HIKE: Join the path near the tennis courts west of park headquarters and begin ascending north into the mountains. (You'll see a couple of different trails; join the main, wide bridle path.)

Rogers Trail ascends a ridge overlooking nearby Rivas Canyon and leads to a junction, where you take the turnoff for Inspiration Point. Not really a point at all, it's actually more of a flat-topped knoll; nevertheless, clear-day views are inspiring: the Santa Monica Bay, the metropolis, the San Gabriel Mountains, and even Catalina Island.

Temescal Canyon

SUNSET, TEMESCAL CANYON, TEMESCAL RIDGE TRAILS
Canyon loop is 4.4 miles round trip with 700-foot gain; to Skull Rock is 5.4 miles round trip

Park agencies in the Santa Monica Mountains have combined forces to open a number of "gateways" to the mountains. For hikers (particularly those of us accustomed to beginning hikes at the end of dirt roads greeted by trail signs nailed to trees), these gateways are deluxe trailheads indeed: restrooms, picnic grounds, water fountains, native plant gardens and more.

I have a particular fondness for Temescal Gateway Park in Pacific Palisades. Not only does this park have it all, park pathways quickly leave it all behind.

Temescal Canyon is an ideal Santa Monica Mountains sampler. You get an oak- and sycamore-shaded canyon, a seasonal waterfall and terrific views from the ridge crest.

Temescal has long been a canyon that inspired nature-lovers and enlighten-ment-seekers. During the 1920s and 1930s, the canyon hosted Chatauqua assem-blies—large educational and recreational gatherings that featured lectures, concerts and stage performances. The canyon was purchased by the Presbyterian Synod in 1943 and used as a retreat center until 1995 when the Santa Monica Mountains Conservancy purchased the property.

DIRECTIONS TO TRAILHEAD: From Los Angeles, head west on the Santa Monica Freeway (10) to its end and continue up-coast on Pacific Coast Highway. Turn north (right) on Temescal Canyon Road and drive 1.1 miles. Just after the intersection with Sunset Boulevard, turn left into the (fee) parking area for Temescal Gateway Park.

(Sidewalks, picnic grounds, and an intermittent greenbelt along Temescal Canyon Road might tempt intrepid hikers to stride the mile from the beach to the trailhead.)

THE HIKE: Walk up-canyon on the landscaped path past the restrooms. The footpath takes on a wilder appearance and soon crosses a branch of Temescal Creek via a wooden footbridge.

At a signed junction, save Temescal Ridge Trail for your return route and con-tinue through the canyon on Temescal Canyon Trail. Travel among graceful old oaks, maples and sycamores to the "doggie turnaround" (no dogs beyond this point) and enter Topanga State Park.

The path ascends moderately to another footbridge and a close-up view of the small waterfall, tumbling over some large boulders. Leaving the canyon behind, the path steepens and climbs westward up Temescal Ridge to a signed junction with Temescal Ridge Trail.

I always enjoy heading uphill on this trail a half mile or so to distinctly shaped Skull Rock. The rock is a good place to rest, cool off, and admire the view.

As you return down Temescal Ridge Trail, you'll get excellent views of Santa Monica Bay, Palos Verdes Peninsula, Catalina Island, and downtown Los Angeles. The view to the southwest down at the housing developments isn't too inspiring, but the view of the rough, unaltered northern part of Temescal Canyon is.

After serving up fine views, the path descends rather steeply and tunnels into tall chaparral. Continue past junctions with Bienveneda and Leacock trails and follow the narrow ridgeline back to a junction with Temescal Canyon Trail. Retrace your steps on Sunset Trail back to the trailhead.

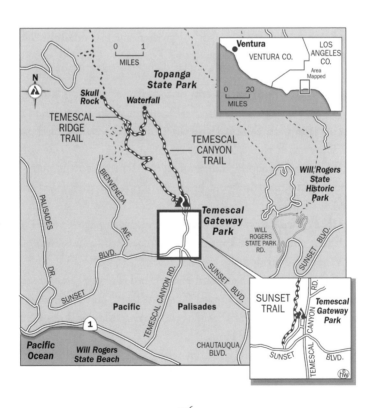

TOPANGA STATE PARK

EAGLE ROCK LOOP TRAIL (BACKBONE TRAIL)
To Eagle Rock via Eagle Rock/Eagle Springs Loop is 6.5 miles round trip
with 800-foot elevation gain; to Will Rogers SHP via Eagle Rock, Fire
Road 30, Rogers Road is 10.5 miles one way with a 1,800-foot loss

Topanga Canyon is a quiet retreat, surrounded by L.A. sprawl but retaining its
rural character. The state park is sometimes billed as "the largest state park within a city limit in the U.S."

The name Topanga is from the Shoshonean dialect. These people and their
ancestors occupied the canyon on and off for several thousand years until the
Spanish evicted them and forced them to settle at the San Fernando Mission.

Until the 1880s, there was little permanent habitation in the canyon. Early
settlers tended vineyards, orchards, and cattle ranches. In the 1920s, the canyon
became a popular weekend destination for Los Angeles residents. Summer cabins
were built along Topanga Creek and in subdivisions in the surrounding hills. For
one-dollar round-trip fare, tourists could board a Packard auto stage in Santa
Monica and be driven up Pacific Coast Highway and Topanga Canyon Road to
the Topanga Post Office and other, more scenic spots.

Most Topanga trails are good fire roads. On a blustery winter day, city and
canyon views are superb.

In the heart of the state park, the hiker will discover Eagle Rock, Eagle
Spring and get topographically oriented to Topanga. The energetic will enjoy the
one-way journey from Topanga to Will Rogers State Historic Park. The lower
reaches of the Backbone Trail offer a fine tour of the wild side of Topanga Canyon
while the ridgetop sections offer far-reaching inland and ocean views.

DIRECTIONS TO TRAILHEAD: From Topanga Canyon Boulevard,
turn east on Entrada Road; that's to the right if you're coming from Pacific Coast
Highway. Follow Entrada Road by turning left at every opportunity until you
arrive at Topanga State Park. The trailhead is at the end of the parking lot. (For
information about the end of this walk, consult the Will Rogers State Historic
Park write-up and directions to the trailhead in this guide.)

THE HIKE: From the Topanga State Park parking lot, follow the distinct
trail eastward to a signed junction, where you'll begin hiking on Eagle Springs
Road. You'll pass through an oak woodland and through chaparral country. The
trail slowly and steadily gains about 800 feet in elevation on the way to Eagle
Rock. When you reach a junction, bear left on the north loop of Eagle Springs
Road to Eagle Rock. A short detour will bring you to the top of the rock.

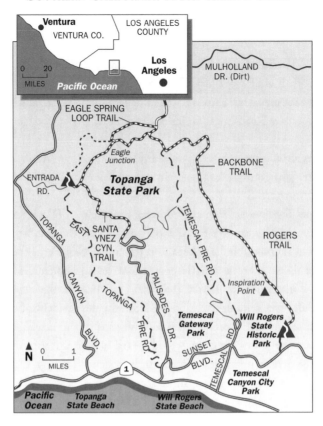

To complete the loop, bear sharply right (southwest) at the next junction, following the fire road as it winds down to Eagle Spring. Past the spring, you return to Eagle Spring Road and retrace your steps back to the trailhead.

Three-mile long Musch Ranch Trail, which passes from hot chaparral to shady oak woodland, crosses a bridge and passes the park pond, is another fine way to return to the trailhead.

To Will Rogers State Historic Park: Follow the loop trip directions to the northeast end of Eagle Rock/Eagle Spring Loop, where you bear right on Fire Road 30. In 0.5 mile you reach the intersection with Rogers Road. Turn left and follow the dirt road (really a trail) for 3.5 miles, where the road ends and meets Rogers Trail. Here a level area and solitary oak suggest a lunch stop. On clear days enjoy the spectacular views in every direction: To the left is Rustic Canyon and the crest of the mountains near Mulholland Drive. To the right, Rivas Canyon descends toward the sea.

Stay on Rogers Trail, which marches up and down several steep hills for about two more miles until it enters Will Rogers Park near Inspiration Point.

MALIBU CREEK

MALIBU CREEK TRAIL
To Rock Pool is 3.5 miles round trip with 150-foot elevation gain; to Century
Lake is 4.5 miles round trip with 200-foot elevation gain

Before land for Malibu Creek State Park was acquired in 1974, it was divided into
three parcels belonging to Bob Hope, Ronald Reagan and 20th Century-Fox.
Although the park is still used for moviemaking, it's primarily a haven for day
hikers and picnickers.

Today the state park preserves more than 7,000 acres of rugged country in the
middle of the Santa Monica Mountains. Malibu Creek winds through the park.
The creek was dammed at the dawn of the 20th century to form little Century
Lake.

The trail along Malibu Creek explores the heart of the state park. It's an
easy, nearly level walk that visits a dramatic rock gorge, Century Lake and several
locales popular with moviemakers.

The gorge of Malibu Creek.

DIRECTIONS TO TRAILHEAD: From Pacific Coast Highway, turn inland on Malibu Canyon Road and proceed 6.5 miles to the park entrance, 0.25 mile south of Mulholland Highway. If you're coming from the San Fernando Valley, exit the Ventura Freeway (101) on Las Virgenes Road and continue four miles to the park entrance.

THE HIKE: From the parking area, follow the wide fire road. You'll cross the all-but-dry creek. The road soon forks into a high road and a low road. Go right and walk along the oak-shaded high road, which makes a long, lazy left arc as it follows the north bank of Malibu Creek. You'll reach an intersection and turn left on a short road that crosses a bridge over Malibu Creek.

You'll spot the Gorge Trail and follow it upstream a short distance to the gorge, one of the most dramatic sights in the Santa Monica Mountains. Malibu Creek makes a hairpin turn through 400-foot volcanic rock cliffs and cascades into aptly named Rock Pool. The "Swiss Family Robinson" television series and some Tarzan movies were filmed here.

Return to the trailhead or retrace your steps back to the high road and bear left toward Century Lake. As the road ascends you'll be treated to a fine view of Las Virgenes Valley. When you gain the crest of the hill, you'll look down on Century Lake. Near the lake are hills of porous lava and topsy-turvy sedimentary rock layers that tell of the violent geologic upheaval that formed Malibu Canyon. The lake was scooped out by members of Crag's Country Club, a group of wealthy businessmen who had a nearby lodge.

Call it a day here, or continue on the fire road past Century Lake. You'll pass the location of the now-removed set for the "M*A*S*H" television series. The prominent Goat Buttes that tower above Malibu Creek were featured in the opening shot of each episode.

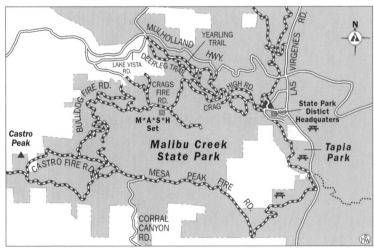

CASTRO CREST

BACKBONE TRAIL
From Malibu Canyon Road to Castro Crest is 7 miles one way with 2,000 foot gain; return via Bulldog Motorway, and Century Road is 14 miles round trip

The Backbone Trail route through Malibu Creek State Park is a splendid section of that 65-mile pathway across the Santa Monica Mountains. Both a primary and alternate route lead through the state park. The high "primary" route follows a dramatic ridgetop toward Castro Crest while the "alternate" route meanders along with Malibu Creek through the heart of the state park.

This day hike connects the two branches of the Backbone Trail and provides a grand tour of Malibu Creek State Park. Fine ocean and island views are offered along the first half of the hike and a chance to explore geologically and ecologically unique Malibu Creek Canyon on the second half.

DIRECTIONS TO TRAILHEAD: From Pacific Coast Highway, turn inland on Malibu Canyon Road and proceed 5 miles to Tapia County Park, located a short mile south of Malibu Creek State Park.

THE HIKE: Mesa Peak Motorway, as this dirt road is known, ascends steeply at first, gaining 1,500 feet in 2.5 miles. With the elevation gain comes sweeping panoramic views of Point Dume, Santa Monica Bay, and Palos Verdes Peninsula. On clear days, Catalina, Anacapa and Santa Cruz Islands float upon the horizon.

The trail veers left toward Mesa Peak (1,844 feet) and continues climbing in a northwesterly direction through an area rich in fossilized shells. Hillside roadcuts betray the Santa Monica Mountains' oceanic heritage. As you hike the spine of the range, a good view to the north is yours: the volcanic rocks of Goat Butte tower above Malibu Creek gorge and the path of Triunfo Canyon can be traced.

The road passes through an area of interesting sandstone formations and intersects paved Corral Canyon Road, which is termed Castro Motorway from this point. Continue west on Castro Motorway for one mile, reaching the intersection with Bulldog Motorway.

Clinging to life in the Castro Crest area is the humble Santa Susana tarweed, a plant only a botanist could love—or even find. *Hemizonia minthornii*, a low mass of woody stems and dull green herbage, was believed to exist only in the Santa Susana Mountains before its discovery in the late 1970s atop Castro Crest and in other isolated locales high in the Santa Monica Mountains.

Backbone Trail continues west toward the forest of antennae atop Castro Peak (2,824 feet).

Along the crest of the Santa Monicas

Return via Bulldog Motorway: For a nice loop trip back through Malibu Creek State Park, bear right on Bulldog Motorway. Descend steeply under transmission lines, veering east and dropping into Triunfo Canyon. In 3.5 miles, you reach Century Road. Turn right and soon pass what was once the location of the exterior sets used by the "M*A*S*H" television series. (The set is now on display in the Smithsonian Institution.) The prominent Goat Buttes that tower above Malibu Creek are featured in the opening shot of each episode.

The road passes Century Lake, crosses a ridge, then drops down to Malibu Creek and comes to a fork in the road. Take either the left (high road) or continue straight ahead over the bridge on the low road; the roads meet again downstream, so you may select either one. One-half mile after the roads rejoin, you approach the park's day use parking area.

Follow a dirt road that skirts this parking area, leads past a giant valley oak and approaches the state park's campground. Bear right on a dirt road that leads a short distance through meadowland to the park's Group Camp. Here you'll join a connector trail that will take you a mile up and over a low brushy ridge to Tapia Park. Hike through the park back to your car.

ZUMA CANYON

ZUMA LOOP, ZUMA RIDGE TRAILS
Around Zuma Canyon is 2-mile loop; via Zuma Ridge Trail is 9.8-mile loop with 1,700-foot elevation

At first, when you turn inland off Pacific Coast Highway onto Bonsall Drive and enter Zuma Canyon, the canyon looks like many others in the Santa Monica Mountains: huge haciendas perched on precipitous slopes, accompanied by lots of lots for sale. But the road ends and only footpaths enter Zuma Canyon.

Malibu, Topanga, Temescal and Santa Ynez—perhaps these canyons and others in the Santa Monica Mountains looked like Zuma a century ago: a creek cascading over magnificent sandstone boulders, a jungle of willow and lush streamside flora, fern-fringed pools and towering rock walls.

Hikers can partake of Zuma Canyon's grandeur via three routes: For an easy family hike join 2-mile Zuma Loop Trail, which explores the canyon mouth; hardy hikers will relish the challenge of the gorge—two miles of trail-less creek-crossing and boulder-hopping—one of the most difficult hikes in the Santa Monicas; Zuma Ridge Trail, lives up to the promise of its name. Hikers ascend Zuma Canyon's west ridge for grand ocean and mountain views, then follow a series of fire roads and footpaths to circle back to the trailhead.

This loop around Zuma Canyon's walls is a great workout and conditioning hike because of two major ascents and descents en route. Bring lots of water. Water is available at the Bonsall Drive trailhead but nowhere else on the hike.

DIRECTIONS TO TRAILHEAD: From Pacific Coast Highway in Malibu, head up-coast one mile past an intersection with Kanan-Dume Road and turn right on Bonsall Drive (this turn is just before the turnoff for Zuma Beach). Drive a mile (the last hundred yards on dirt road) to road's end at a parking lot.

To start the hike on Zuma Ridge Trail, continue very briefly up-coast past the Bonsall Drive turnoff on Pacific Coast Highway to the next major right turn—Busch Drive. Travel a bit over a mile to the small dirt parking lot and signed trail.

THE HIKE: Just before you join Zuma Ridge Trail (a dirt road, gated to prevent vehicle entry) note the signed footpath (Ridge Canyon Access Trail) just to the east. This path will return you to the trailhead on the very last leg of your long loop.

Begin your shadeless ascent, following the dirt road below some water tanks. Up, up, up you go along the ridge between Zuma Canyon on your right and Trancas Canyon on your left. Look behind you at the sparkling blue Pacific and the Malibu Riviera.

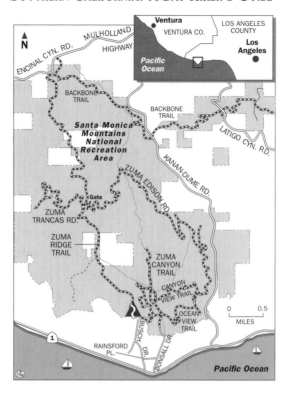

Three miles of vigorous ascent brings you to a junction with the right-forking Zuma Edison Road. What goes up must come down, and down east you go toward the floor of Zuma Canyon. After a mile's descent you'll pass a horse guzzler, then continue the steep descent another mile or so to the sycamore-shaded canyon bottom. By all means take a break here and marshal your energy for this hike's second major climb.

The road climbs southeasterly out of the canyon. Far below is Kanan-Dume Road, about a mile to the east. Zuma Edison Road bends north for 0.25 mile to intersect Zuma Canyon Connector Trail, a footpath that turns south to travel along a knife-edge ridge. This engaging path takes you 0.7 mile down to meet Kanan-Edison Road. Coast coastward as you descend this dirt fire road 1.3 miles to a junction with Canyon View Trail, a path that descends into the heart of Zuma Canyon. You could branch off on this pleasant trail, but in keeping with the ridge-route theme of this walk I prefer to continue on Kanan-Edison Road just 0.1 mile more to meet Ocean View Trail. This path descends westward 1.1 miles to the canyon bottom while serving up fine ocean views.

When you meet Zuma Canyon Trail, go left about 100 feet to meet Ridge-Canyon Access Trail. Join this 0.7 mile long footpath on a climb from the canyon bottom up and over a low hill to return to the Busch Drive trailhead.

SOLSTICE CANYON PARK

SOLSTICE CANYON TRAIL
3 miles round trip

Solstice Canyon Trail leads visitors along a year-round creek and introduces them to the flora and history of the Santa Monica Mountains. The path is a narrow country road—suitable for strollers and wheelchairs—which offers an easy family hike in the shade of grand old oaks and towering sycamores.

Solstice Canyon in the Santa Monica Mountains is enjoyable year-round, but autumn and winter are particularly fine times to ramble through the quiet canyon. In autumn, enjoy the fall color display of the sycamores and in winter, from the park's upper slopes, look for gray whales migrating past Point Dume.

Solstice Canyon Park opened on summer solstice, 1988. The Santa Monica Mountains Conservancy purchased the land from the Roberts family and transformed the 550-acre Roberts Ranch into a park. Ranch roads became foot trails. Milk thistle, castor bean and other assorted nonnative plants were almost eliminated (but since returned); picnic areas and a visitor contact station were built. Today National Park Service rangers are the stewards of Solstice Canyon.

Solstice Canyon's strangest structure resembles a futurist farm house with a

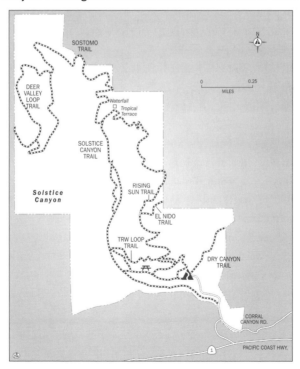

Light and shadow in Solstice Canyon

silo attached, and really defies architectural categorization. Bauhaus, maybe. Or perhaps Grain Elevator Modern. From 1961 to 1973 Space Tech Labs, a subsidiary of TRW used the building to conduct tests to determine the magnetic sensitivity of satellite instrumentation. The Santa Monica Mountains Conservancy was headquartered here for many years.

DIRECTIONS TO TRAILHEAD: From Pacific Coast Highway, about 17 miles up-coast from Santa Monica and 3.5 miles up-coast from Malibu Canyon Road, turn inland on Corral Canyon Road. At the first bend in the road, leave the road and proceed straight to the very small Solstice Canyon parking lot.

THE HIKE: Stop at the bulletin board, check out the latest park information and walk up the wide road.

About halfway along, you'll pass the 1865 Mathew Keller House and in a few more minutes, Fern Grotto. (A creek sidetrail offers an even more scenic alternative to the road.) The road travels under the shade of oak and sycamore to its end at the remains of the old Roberts Ranch House. Palms, agave, bamboo and bird of paradise and many more tropical plants thrive in the Roberts' family garden gone wild. A waterfall, fountain and an old dam are some of the other special features found in this paradisiacal setting known as Tropical Terrace.

Across the creek from Tropical Terrace is signed Rising Sun Trail, which climbs a ridge for rewarding canyon and ocean views. The two-mile trail offers an excellent, but more difficult return route.

CHARMLEE PARK

OCEAN VISTA TRAIL
3-mile loop

Charmlee, perched on the bluffs above Malibu, often has outstanding spring wild-flower displays. Most of the park is a large open meadow; the flower display, given timely rainfall, can be quite colorful. Lupine, paintbrush, larkspur, Mariposa lily, penstemon and California peony bust out all over.

Stop at Charmlee's small nature center and inquire about what's blooming where. Also pick up a copy of a brochure that interprets the park's Fire Ecology Trail. This nature trail interprets the important role of fire in Southern California's chaparral communities.

Good views are another reason to visit Charmlee. The Santa Monica Mountains spread east to west, with the Simi Hills and Santa Susana Mountains rising to the north. Down-coast you can see Zuma Beach and Point Dume and up-coast Sequit Point in Leo Carrillo State Park. Offshore, Catalina Island and two of the Channel Islands—Anacapa and Santa Cruz—can sometimes be seen.

Beginning in the early 1800s this Malibu meadowland was part of Rancho Topanga-Malibu-Sequit and was used to pasture cattle. For a century and a half, various ranchers held the property. The last of these private landholders—Charmain and Leonard Swartz—combined their first names to give Charmlee its euphonious name. Los Angeles County acquired the Charmlee property in the late 1960s and eventually opened the 460-acre park in 1981.

For the hiker, Charmlee is one of the few parks, perhaps even the only park, that actually seems to have a surplus of trails. Quite a few paths and old ranch roads wind through the park, which is shaped like a big grassy bowl.

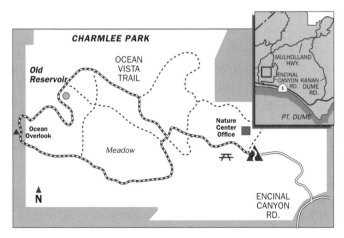

Because the park is mostly one big meadow fringed with oak trees, it's easy to see where you're going and improvise your own circle tour of Charmlee. Bring a kite and a picnic to this undiscovered park and take it easy for an afternoon.

DIRECTIONS TO TRAILHEAD: From Pacific Coast Highway, about 12 miles up-coast from the community of Malibu, head into the mountains on Encinal Canyon Road 4.5 miles to Charmlee Natural Area County Park.

THE HIKE: Walk through the park's picnic area on a dirt road, which travels under the shade of coast live oaks. The trail crests a low rise, offers a couple of side trails to the left to explore, and soon arrives at a more distinct junction with a fire road leading downhill along the eastern edge of the meadow. This is a good route to take because it leads to fine ocean views.

Follow the road as it skirts the eastern edge of the meadow and heads south. Several ocean overlooks are encountered but the official Ocean Overlook is a rocky outcropping positioned on the far southern edge of the park. Contemplate the coast, then head west to the old ranch reservoir. A few hundred yards away is an oak grove, one of the park's many picturesque picnic spots.

You may follow any of several trails back to the trailhead or join Fire Ecology Trail for a close-up look at how Southern California's Mediterranean flora rises phoenix-like from the ashes.

NICHOLAS FLAT

NICHOLAS FLAT TRAIL
From Leo Carrillo State Beach to Nicholas Flat is 7 miles round trip with 1,600-foot elevation gain

Leo Carrillo State Beach has always been a popular surfing spot. Surfers tackle the well-shaped south swell, while battling the submerged rocks and kelp beds. In recent years, the state added a large chunk of Santa Monica Mountains parkland, prompting a name change to Leo Carrillo State Park.

The park's Nicholas Flat area is one of the best spots in the Santa Monica Mountains for spring wildflowers because it's a meeting place for four different plant communities. Chaparral, grassland, coastal scrub and oak woodland all converge near the flat. Another reason for the remarkable plant diversity is Leo Carrillo's elevation, which varies from sea level to nearly 2,000 feet.

Along park trails, look for shooting star, hedge nettle, sugar bush, hollyleaf redberry, purple sage, chamise, blue dick, deer weed, burr clover, bush lupine, golden yarrow, fuschia-flowered gooseberry, and many more flowering plants. Around Nicholas Pond, keep an eye out for wishbone bush, encelia, chia, Parry's phacelia, ground-pink, California poppy, scarlet bugler and goldfields.

Even when the wildflowers fade away, Nicholas Flat is worth a visit. Its charms include a big meadow and a pond patrolled by coots. Atop grand boulders you can enjoy a picnic and savor Malibu coast views.

Nicholas Flat Trail can also be savored for one more reason: In Southern California, very few trails connect mountains to the sea. Get an early start. Until

Nicholas Flat, Santa Monica Mountains.

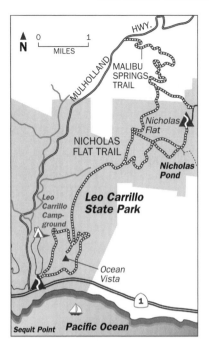

you arrive at oak-dotted Nicholas Flat itself, there's not much shade en route.

DIRECTIONS TO TRAILHEAD:

From the west end of the Santa Monica Freeway in Santa Monica, head up-coast on Pacific Coast Highway about 25 miles to Leo Carrillo State Beach. There's free parking along Coast Highway, and fee parking in the park's day use area. Signed Nicholas Flat trailhead is located a short distance past the park entry kiosk, opposite the day use parking area.

THE HIKE: Soon the trail splits. The right branch circles the hill, climbs above Willow Creek, and after a mile, rejoins the main Nicholas Flat Trail. Enjoy this interesting option on your return from Nicholas Flat.

Take the left branch, which immediately begins a moderate to steep ascent of the grassy slopes above the park campground. The trail switchbacks through a coastal scrub community up to a saddle on the ridgeline. Here you'll meet the alternate branch of Nicholas Flat Trail. From the saddle, a short side trail leads south to a hilltop, where there's a fine coastal view. From the viewpoint, you can see Point Dume and the Malibu coastline. During the winter, it's a good place to bring your binoculars and scout the Pacific horizon for migrating whales.

Following the ridgeline, Nicholas Flat Trail climbs inland over chaparral-covered slope. Keep glancing over your right shoulder at the increasingly grand coastal views, and over your left at the open slopes browsed by the park's nimble deer.

After a good deal of climbing, the trail levels atop the ridgeline and you get your first glimpse of grassy, inviting Nicholas Flat. The trail descends past a line of fire-blackened, but unbowed, old oaks and joins an old ranch road that skirts the Nicholas Flat meadows. Picnickers may unpack lunch beneath the shady oaks or out in the sunny meadow. The trail angles southeast across the meadow to a small pond. The man-made pond, used by cattle during the region's ranching days, is backed by some handsome boulders.

Return the way you came until you reach the junction located 0.75 mile from the trailhead. Bear left at the fork and enjoy this alternate trail as it descends into the canyon cut by Willow Creek, contours around an ocean-facing slope, and returns you to the trailhead.

SANDSTONE PEAK

MISHE MOKWA TRAIL
From Circle X Ranch to Sandstone Peak is 5 miles round trip with 1,100-foot elevation gain

Sandstone Peak, highest peak in the Santa Monica Mountains, is one of the high-lights of a visit to Circle X Ranch, 1,655 acres of National Park Service land on the border of Los Angeles and Ventura counties. The park boasts more than 30 miles of trail plus a much-needed public campground.

Half a century ago the land belonged to a number of gentlemen ranchers, including movie actor Donald Crisp, who starred in *How Green Was My Valley*. Members of the Exchange Club purchased the nucleus of the park in 1949 for $25,000 and gave it to the Boy Scouts. The emblem for the Exchange Club was a circled X—hence the name of the ranch.

During the 1960s, in an attempt to honor Circle X benefactor Herbert Allen, the Scouts petitioned the United States Department of the Interior to rename Sandstone Peak. The request for "Mt. Allen" was denied because of a long-standing policy that prohibited naming geographical features after living persons. Nevertheless, the Scouts held an "unofficial" dedication ceremony in 1969 to honor their leader.

Sandstone Peak—or Mt. Allen if you prefer—offers outstanding views from its 3,111-foot summit. If the five-mile, up-and-back hike to the peak isn't suffi-ciently taxing, park rangers can suggest some terrific extensions.

DIRECTIONS TO TRAILHEAD: Drive up-coast on Pacific Coast Highway past the outer reaches of Malibu, a mile past the Los Angeles County line. Turn inland on Yerba Buena Road and proceed five miles to Circle X Ranch. You'll pass the park's tiny headquarters building and continue one more mile to the signed trailhead on your left. There's plenty of parking.

THE HIKE: From the signed trailhead, walk up the fire road. A short quar-ter-mile of travel brings you to a signed junction with Mishe Mokwa Trail. Leave the fire road here and join the trail, which climbs and contours over the brushy slopes of Boney Mountain.

Breaks in the brush offer good views to the right of historic Triunfo Pass, which was used by the Chumash to travel inland to coastal areas. Mishe Mokwa Trail levels for a time and tunnels beneath some handsome red shanks.

The trail then descends into Carlisle Canyon. Across the canyon are some striking red volcanic formations, among them well-named Balanced Rock. The path, shaded by oak and laurel, drops into the canyon at another aptly named rock formation—Split Rock.

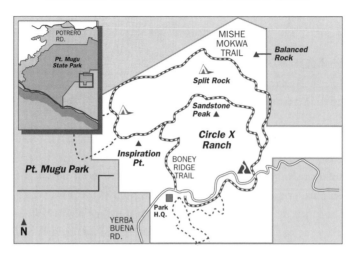

Split Rock is the locale of a trail camp, shaded by oak and sycamore. An all-year creek and a spring add to the camp's charm. It's a fine place for a picnic.

From Split Rock, begin your ascent out of Carlisle Canyon on an old ranch road. From the road's high point, look straight ahead up at a pyramid-like volcanic rock formation the Boy Scouts call Egyptian Rock. To the northwest is Point Mugu State Park. You are walking on the Backbone Trail.

The fire road turns south and you'll pass a trail camp located amidst some cottonwoods. Past the camp, the fire road angles east. Look sharply to the right for a short, unsigned trail that leads to Inspiration Point. Mt. Baldy and Catalina are among the inspiring sights pointed out by a geographical locator monument.

Continue east on the fire road and you'll soon pass the signed intersection with Boney Peak Trail. This trail descends precipitously to park headquarters. If for some reason you're in a hurry to get down, this bone-jarring route is for you.

Continue ascending on the fire road. After a few switchbacks look for a steep trail on the right. Follow this trail to the top of Sandstone Peak. "Sandstone" is certainly a misnomer; the peak is one of the largest masses of volcanic rock in the Santa Monica Mountains. Sign the summit register and enjoy commanding, clear-day views: the Topatopa Mountains, haunt of the condors, the Oxnard Plain, the Channel Islands, and the wide blue Pacific.

After you've enjoyed the view, you'll descend a bit more than a mile on the fire road back to the trailhead.

RANCHO SIERRA VISTA/SATWIWA

SATWIWA LOOP TRAIL
Loop Trail is 1.5 miles round trip with 200-foot elevation gain; to Waterfall is 5.6 miles round trip From parking area, add 0.5 mile round trip to all hikes

Satwiwa Native American Natural Area offers a chance to explore a place where Chumash walked for thousands of years before Europeans arrived on the scene. A visitor center helps moderns learn the habits of birds and animals, the changes the seasons bring, and gain insight into the ceremonies that kept—and still keep—the Chumash bonded to the earth.

For hunter-gatherers, as anthropologists call them, this land on the wild west end of the Santa Monica Mountains was truly bountiful with seeds, roots, bulbs, berries, acorns and black walnuts. Birds, deer and squirrel were plentiful, as were fish and shellfish from nearby Mugu Lagoon. It was this abundant food supply that helped the Chumash become the largest tribal group in California at the time of Cabrillo's arrival in 1542.

Chumash territory ranged from Topanga Canyon near the east end of the Santa Monica Mountains all the way up the coast to San Luis Obispo and out to the Channel Islands. Satwiwa means "The Bluffs" and was the name of a Chumash settlement located at this end of the Santa Monica Mountains.

The name of this park site, Rancho Sierra Vista/Satwiwa reflects its history as both a longtime (1870s to 1970s) horse and cattle ranch and ancestral land of the Chumash. Many visitors are surprised to learn of the extent of Chumash settlement and even more surprised to be greeted by a living Chumash and find out they're not just museum relics.

The National Park Service prefers to call Satwiwa a culture center rather than a museum in order to keep the emphasis on living Native Americans. The park service decided not to interpret the loop trail through Satwiwa with plant ID plaques and brochures; instead of the usual natural history lessons, it's hoped that hikers will come away with a more spiritual experience of the land.

DIRECTIONS TO TRAILHEAD: From Highway 101 in Newbury Park, exit on Wendy Drive and head south a short mile to Borchard Road. Turn right and travel 0.5 mile to Reino Road. Turn left and proceed 1.2 miles to Lynn Road, turn right and continue another 1.2 miles to the park entrance road (Via Goleta) on the south side of the road opposite the new Dos Vienta housing development.

The paved park road passes an equestrian parking area on the right and a small day use parking lot on the left before it dead-ends at a large parking lot 0.7 miles from Lynn Road.

THE HIKE: From the parking lot, follow the signed footpath a short quarter-mile to the Satwiwa Native American Indian Culture Center. Signed Satwiwa Loop Trail begins its clockwise journey by leading past an old cattle pond, now a haven for waterfowl and wildlife.

The path then crosses a landscape in transition—from grazing land back to native grasses and wildflowers. You'll pass a junction with Wendy Trail, a pathway that connects the Satwiwa area with Wendy Drive.

Next the trail traverses a narrow, oak-filled ravine, then ascends to an old windmill. From the trail's high point near the windmill, the hiker gains excellent vistas to the north of Conejo Valley and scattered suburbs. To the west lies a landmark, cone-shaped prominence, 1,814-foot Conejo Mountain.

Dominating the view to the south is Boney Mountain, a series of sheer cliffs and some of the highest peaks in the Santa Monica Mountains. Shamans gathered some of their power from Boney Mountain, still considered a sanctuary by the Chumash.

Satwiwa Loop Trail descends to a junction with Hidden Valley Connector Trail (an opportunity to extend your hike to a waterfall or other destinations in Pt. Mugu State Park). The loop trail descends back to the culture center.

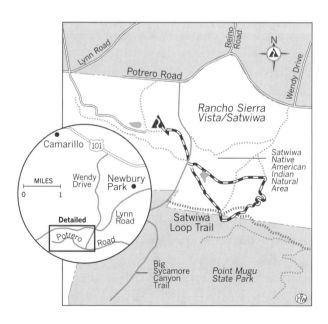

SYCAMORE CANYON

SYCAMORE CANYON TRAIL

From Big Sycamore Canyon to Deer Camp Junction is 6.5 miles round trip with 200-foot elevation gain; return via Overlook Trail is 10 miles round trip with 700-foot gain

Every fall, millions of monarch butterflies migrate south to the forests of Mexico's Transvolcanic Range and to the damp coastal woodlands of Central and Southern California. The monarch's awe-inspiring migration and formation of what entomologists call over-wintering colonies are two of nature's most colorful autumn events.

All monarch butterflies west of the Rockies head for California in the fall; one of the best places in Southern California to observe the arriving monarchs is the campground in Big Sycamore Canyon at Point Mugu State Park.

Sycamore Canyon Trail takes you through a peaceful wooded canyon, where a multitude of monarchs dwell, and past some magnificent sycamores. The sycamores that shade the canyon bearing their name are incomparable. The lower branches, stout and crooked, are a delight for tree-climbers. Hawks and owls roost in the upper branches.

The trail follows the canyon on a gentle northern traverse across Point Mugu State Park, the largest preserved area in the Santa Monica Mountains. This trail, combined with Overlook Trail, gives the hiker quite a tour of the park. During October and November, Sycamore Canyon offers the twin delights of falling autumn leaves and fluttering butterflies. (Ask park rangers where the monarchs cluster in large numbers.)

DIRECTIONS TO TRAILHEAD: Drive up-coast on Highway 1, 32 miles from Santa Monica, to Big Sycamore Canyon Campground in Point Mugu State Park (day-use fee). Walk past the campground entrance through the campground to a locked gate. The trail begins on the other side of the gate.

THE HIKE: Take the trail up-canyon, following the creek. Winter rains cause the creek to rise, and sometimes keeping your feet dry while crossing is difficult. Underground water keeps much of the creekside vegetation green year-round—so this is fine hike in any season.

One-half mile from the campground you'll spot Overlook Trail, which switchbacks to the west up a ridge and then heads north toward the native tall grass prairie in La Jolla Valley. Make note of this trail, an optional return route. A second half-mile of nearly level canyon walking brings you to another major hiking trail that branches right—Serrano Canyon Trail, an absolute gem.

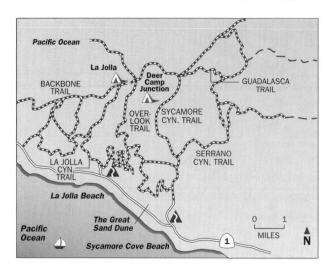

Another easy mile of walking beneath the sycamores brings you to a picnic table shaded by a grove of large oak trees. The oaks might be a good turnaround spot for a family with small children. The total round trip distance would be a little over 4 miles.

Continuing up the canyon you'll pass beneath more of the giant sycamores and soon arrive at Wood Canyon Junction, the hub of six trails which lead to all corners of the park. Bear left on signed Wood Canyon Trail and in a short while you'll reach Deer Camp Junction. Drinking water and picnic tables suggest a lunch stop. Oak trees predominate over the sycamores along Wood Canyon Creek; however, the romantic prefer the sycamores, some of which have large clumps of mistletoe in the upper branches.

You can call it a day here and return the way you came. As you hike down the canyon back to the campground, the large and cranky scrub jay population will scold you, but don't let the squawking birds stop you from enjoying one of California's finest sycamore savannas.

To return via Overlook Trail: Continue past the junction with Wood Canyon Trail and Deer Camp Junction on the Wood Canyon Trail, which becomes Pumphouse Road. You'll climb over the divide between Sycamore Canyon and La Jolla Valley. Upon reaching a junction, you'll head south on the Overlook Trail, staying on the La Jolla Canyon side of the ridge. True to its name, Overlook Trail offers good views of grassy mountainsides, Boney Peak and Big Sycamore Canyon.

You'll pass an intersection with Scenic Trail, a rough path that hugs the ridge separating La Jolla and Big Sycamore Canyon, where you'll bear right and follow the fire road one-half mile back to the trailhead.

LA JOLLA VALLEY

LA JOLLA VALLEY LOOP TRAIL

From Ray Miller Trailhead to La Jolla Valley is 7 miles round trip with 700-foot elevation gain; return via Overlook Trail, Ray Miller Trail is 7 miles round trip with 800-foot gain

Ringed by ridges, the native grassland of La Jolla Valley welcomes the walker with its drifts of oak and peaceful pond. This pastoral upland in the heart of Point Mugu State Park is unique: it has resisted the invasion of non-native vegetation. It's rare to find native grassland in Southern California because the Spanish introduced oats and a host of other foreign grasses for pasture for their cattle. In most cases, the imported grasses squeezed out the natives; but not in La Jolla Valley.

La Jolla Valley Loop Trail passes a small waterfall and tours the beautiful grasslands of the valley. This is a fine pathway to follow during the spring when wildflowers and numerous coastal shrubs are in bloom; this fragrant trail smells as good as it looks.

Another way to loop through the park is to make use of Ray Miller Trail. Sometimes called Overlook Fire Road, this trail is the beginning (or the end, depending on how you view the mountains) of the Backbone Trail. The path offers terrific coastal views and nicely complements the park's interior trails.

The trailhead was named the Ray Miller Trailhead in 1986, a tribute to volunteer ranger Ray Miller. The first official camp host in the state park system, Miller spent his retirement years, from 1972 until his death in 1989, welcoming visitors to Point Mugu State Park.

DIRECTIONS TO TRAILHEAD: Drive up the coast on Pacific Coast Highway from Santa Monica (21 miles up from Malibu Canyon Road if you're coming from the Ventura Freeway and the San Fernando Valley). The turnoff is 1.5 miles north of Big Sycamore Canyon Trailhead, which is also part of Point Mugu State Park. From the turnoff, bear right to the parking area. The signed trailhead, near an interpretive display, is at a fire road that leads into the canyon.

THE HIKE: The fire road leads north up the canyon along the stream bed. As the canyon narrows, some tiny waterfalls come into view. Past the falls, the trail passes some giant coreopsis plants. In early spring the coreopsis, also known as the tree sunflower, sprouts large blossoms. Springtime travel on this trail takes the hiker past the dainty blue and white blossoms of the ceanothus and the snowy white blossoms of the chamise. Pause to take in the sight (and pungent aroma!) of the black sage with its light-blue flowers and hummingbird sage with its crimson flowers.

At the first trail junction, bear right on the La Jolla Valley Loop Trail. In a little less than a half mile, you'll arrive at another junction. Leave the main trail and you will descend the short distance to a lovely cattail pond. The pond is a nesting place for a variety of birds including the redwing blackbird. Ducks and coots paddle the perimeter.

Returning to the main trail, you'll skirt the east end of La Jolla Valley, enjoy an overview of waving grasses and intersect a T junction. To the right 0.7 mile away, is Deer Camp Junction, which provides access to trails leading to Sycamore Canyon and numerous other destinations in the state park.(To return via Overlook and Ray Miller Trails, bear right toward Deer Camp Junction. See instructions below.)

To continue with La Jolla Valley Loop Trail, bear left and in half a mile you'll arrive at La Jolla Valley Camp. The camp, sheltered by oaks and equipped with piped water and tables, is an ideal picnic spot. The valley is a nice place to spend a day. You can snooze in the sun, watch for deer, or perhaps stalk the rare and elusive chocolate lily, known as the Cleopatra of the lily family— the darkest and the loveliest.

After leaving the camp, you could turn left on a short connector trail that skirts the pond and takes you back to La Jolla Valley Loop Trail, where you retrace your steps on that trail and La Jolla Canyon Trail.

To complete the circle on La Jolla Valley Loop Trail, however, continue a half mile past the campground to the signed junction, where you'll bear left and follow a connector trail back to La Jolla Canyon Trail.

Those returning via Overlook and Ray Miller Trails will find that bearing right (west) at the above-described junction will soon bring you to Overlook Trail, a dirt road. Bear right (south) here, descending south along the ridge that separates Big Sycamore Canyon to the east from La Jolla Canyon to the west.

At a fork, bear right, continuing your descent to a junction with Ray Miller Trail. Join this trail, which descends over some red rock, then parallels the coast and coast highway.

Listen carefully and you can hear the distant booming of the surf. Enjoy the stunning ocean views. The Channel Islands—particularly Anacapa and Santa Cruz—are prominent to the northwest. Farther south is Catalina Island. During the winter months, you might sight a migrating California gray whale on the horizon.

The path works its way west, squeezing through a draw dotted with prickly pear cactus. The trail leads down a brushy hill past a group camp and returns you to the trailhead.

CHAPTER SIX

San Gabriel Mountains

Most of the San Gabriel Mountains are included
within the 700,000 acres of the Angeles National Forest,
one of the most heavily used national forests in America,
and one that for more than a century has delighted Southland
residents seeking quiet retreats and tranquil trails.
Big Santa Anita Canyon, Arroyo Seco and Mt. Baldy
have been renowned hiking destinations since the first
Great Hiking Era and are popular one hundred years later
in the second Great Hiking Era. The range's front country
offers the hiker inviting arroyos, fine vista points and
relatively easy-to-access trailheads from the metropolitan
flatlands. Angeles Crest Highway offers a scenic byway
to the high country, grand mountain peaks
and a wealth of taller trees.

PLACERITA CANYON COUNTY PARK

PLACERITA CANYON TRAIL
From Nature Center to Walker Ranch Picnic Area is 4 miles round trip
with 300-foot elevation gain

Placerita Canyon has a gentleness that is rare in the steep, severely faulted San Gabriel Mountains. A superb nature center, plus a walk through the oak- and sycamore-shaded canyon adds up to a nice outing for the whole family.

In 1842, seven years before the '49ers rushed to Sutter's Mill, California's first gold rush occurred in Placerita Canyon. Legend has it that herdsman Francisco Lopez awoke from his nap beneath a large shady oak tree, during which he had dreamed of gold and wealth. During the more mundane routine of fixing his evening meal, he dug up some onions to spice his supper and there, clinging to the roots, were small gold nuggets. Miners from all over California, the San Fernando Placers, as they became known, poured into Placerita Canyon. The prospecting was good, though not exceptional, for several years. The spot where Lopez made his discovery is now called the Oak of the Golden Dream. A plaque marks his find.

Placerita Canyon has been the outdoor set for many a Western movie and 1950s television series, including "The Cisco Kid" and "Hopalong Cassidy." Movie companies often used the cabin built in 1920 by Frank Walker. Walker, his wife, Hortense, and their twelve children had a rough time earning a living in what was then a wilderness. The family raised cows and pigs, gathered and sold leaf-mold fertilizer, panned for gold, and hosted movie companies. The family cabin, modified by moviemakers, stands by the nature center.

Placerita Canyon's nature center has some very well-done natural history exhibits and live animal displays. Pamphlets, available at the center, help visitors enjoy park nature trails including: Ecology Trail, which interprets the canyon bottom and chaparral communities; Hillside Trail which offers a view of Placerita Canyon; Heritage Trail, which leads to the Oak of the Golden Dream.

DIRECTIONS TO TRAILHEAD: From Highway 14 (Antelope Valley Freeway) in Newhall, exit on Placerita Canyon Road and turn right (east) two miles to Placerita Canyon County Park. Park in the large lot near the Nature Center.

THE HIKE: From the parking lot, walk up-canyon, following the stream and enjoying the shade of oaks and sycamores. A 1979 fire scorched brush within a hundred feet of the nature center, but remarkably spared the oak woodland on the canyon bottom. Nature regenerates quickly in a chaparral community; some of the chamise on the slopes may be a hundred years old and veterans of dozens of fires.

The canyon narrows and after a mile the trail splits. Take your pick: the right branch stays on the south side of the canyon while the left branch joins the north side trail. The two intersect in a half-mile, a little short of the Walker Ranch Group Campground. Here you'll find a picnic ground with tables, water and restrooms.

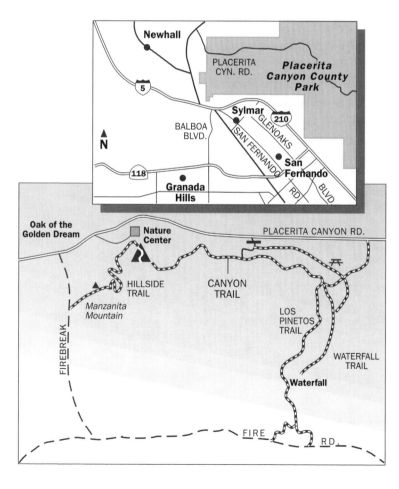

MT. LUKENS

STONE CANYON TRAIL
From Vogel Flats to Mt. Lukens is 8 miles round trip with 3,200-foot elevation gain

Mt. Lukens, a gray whale of a mountain beached on the eastern boundary of Los Angeles, is the highest peak within the city limits. A hike up this mile-high mountain offers a great aerobic workout and terrific clear-day views of the metropolis.

Theodore P. Lukens, for whom the mountain is named, was a Pasadena civic and business leader, and an early supporter of the first scientific reforestation effort in California. A self-taught botanist, Lukens believed that burnt-over mountainsides could be successfully replanted. During 1899 alone, Lukens and fellow mountaineers planted some 65,000 seeds in the mountains above Pasadena.

After the death of Lukens in 1918, a 5,074-foot peak was named to honor the one-time Angeles National Forest Supervisor and Southern California's "Father of Forestry." Stone Canyon Trail is by far the nicest way to ascend Mt. Lukens. (Other routes are via long wearisome fire roads.) The trail climbs very steeply from Big Tujunga Canyon over the north slope of Lukens to the peak. (Another way to climb Mt. Lukens is via Haines Canyon Road. Consult the Deukmejian Wilderness Park trail description.)

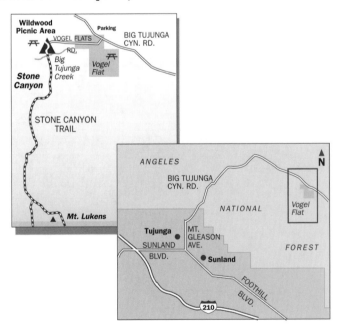

Carry plenty of water on this trail; none is available en route. It's fun to unfold a city map on the summit to help you identify natural and man-made points of interest.

One warning: In order to reach the beginning of the Stone Canyon Trail, you must cross the creek flowing through Big Tujunga Canyon. During times of high water, this creek crossing can be difficult and dangerous—even impossible. Use your very best judgement when approaching this creek.

DIRECTIONS TO TRAILHEAD: From Foothill Boulevard in Sunland, turn north on Mt. Gleason Avenue and drive 1.5 miles to Big Tujunga Canyon Road. Turn right and proceed 6 miles to Doske Road and make another right. Descend to Stonyvale Road, then left and drive 0.5 mile to a parking area at road's end.

THE HIKE: After carefully crossing the creek, begin the vigorous ascent, which first parallels Stone Canyon, then switchbacks to the east above it. Pausing now and then to catch your breath, enjoy the view of Big Tujunga Canyon.

The trail leads through chamise, ceanothus and high chaparral. Fires have scorched the slopes of Mt. Lukens. Stone Canyon Trail could use a few more shady conifers and a little less brush. Theodore Lukens and his band of tree planters would today be most welcome on the mountain's north slopes!

About 3.5 miles from the trailhead, you'll intersect an old fire road and bear left toward the summit. Atop the peak is a forest of radio antennae.

Old maps called the summit "Sister Elsie" before the peak was renamed for Lukens. As the story goes, Sister Elsie Peak honored a beloved Roman Catholic nun who was in charge of an orphanage for Native American children located in the La Crescenta area.

Enjoy the sweeping panorama of the Santa Monica and Verdugo mountains, Santa Monica Bay and the Palos Verdes Peninsula, and the huge city spreading from the San Gabriel Mountains to the sea.

ARROYO SECO

ARROYO SECO TRAIL
(GABRIELINO NATIONAL RECREATION TRAIL)
From Windsor Avenue to Teddy's Outpost is 3 miles round trip; to Gould Mesa Campground is 4 miles round trip; to Paul Little Picnic Area is 6.5 miles round trip with a 400-foot elevation gain; to Oakwilde Trail Camp is 10 miles round trip with a 900-foot gain

During the early decades of the 20th century, Arroyo Seco was an extremely popular place for a weekend outing. About halfway up the wild section of the canyon stood Camp Oak Wilde, a rustic resort constructed in 1911. Hikers and horsemen stayed a night or two or used the hostelry as a rest stop on the way up to Mt. Wilson. During the 1920s, a road was constructed and automobilists traveled the arroyo to Camp Oak Wilde.

Southern California's "flood of the century" wiped out Oak Wilde in 1938. The awesome torrent also washed away the road and many vacation cabins. A few stone steps and foundations, ivy-covered walls and bridges give today's hiker hints of a time gone by.

Besides the Southern California history lesson, oak-, sycamore- and bay-filled Arroyo Seco has much to offer. The modern-day traveler can walk the old 1920s auto road and newer Forest Service trails to quiet picnic areas. Because the path up the Arroyo Seco is officially part of the Gabrielino National Recreation Trail, it's usually kept in very good condition.

This is a great morning walk. On hot afternoons, however, you might want to exercise elsewhere; smog fills the Arroyo Seco.

DIRECTIONS TO TRAILHEAD: From the Foothill Freeway (210) in Pasadena, take the Arroyo Boulevard/Windsor Avenue exit. Head north on Arroyo, which almost immediately becomes Windsor, and travel 0.75 mile. Just before Windsor's intersection with Ventura Street, turn into the parking lot on your left. From the small lot you can look down into the bottom of the Arroyo Seco and see the Jet Propulsion Laboratory.

THE HIKE: As you walk up Windsor you'll spot two roads. The leftward road descends to JPL. You head right on a narrow asphalt road, closed to vehicle traffic. You'll pass some fenced-off areas and facilities belonging to the Pasadena Water Department and a junction with Lower Brown Mountain Road. A short mile from the trailhead are some Forest Service residences.

The road, dirt now, penetrates the arroyo and enters a more sylvan scene, shaded by oaks and sycamores. Often you can't help but chuckle at the "No

Fishing" signs posted next to the creekbed; most of the time the arroyo is quite "seco" and if there are any fish around, they must've walked here.

Teddy's Outpost Picnic Area is your first destination. In 1915, Theodore Syvertson had a tiny roadside hostelry at this site. A half-mile beyond Teddy's is large Gould Mesa Campground, with plenty of picnic tables. Next stop, a short distance past the campground, is a small picnic area called Nino. A mile beyond Gould Mesa Campground is Paul Little Picnic Area.

Now you leave the bottom of the arroyo and climb moderately to steeply up the east wall of the canyon. After curving along high on the wall, the trail then drops back to the canyon floor, where oak-shaded Oakwilde Trail Camp offers a tranquil rest stop. A few stone foundations remind the hiker that Arroyo Seco was once Pasadena's most popular place for a weekend outing.

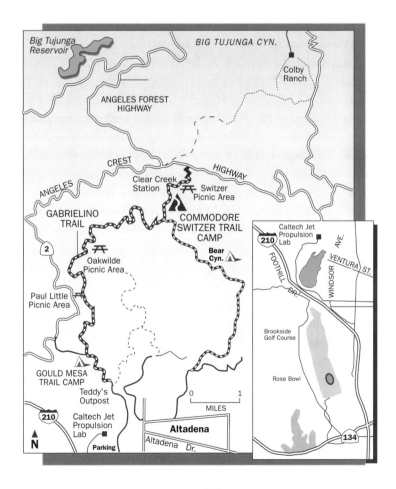

ECHO MOUNTAIN

SAM MERRILL TRAIL
From Cobb Estate to Echo Mountain is 5 miles round trip with 1,400-foot elevation gain

Professor Thaddeus Sobieski Coulincourt Lowe's Echo Mountain Resort area can be visited not only by retracing the tracks of his "Railway to the Clouds" (See Mt. Lowe Railway hike), but also by way of a fine urban edge trail that ascends from the outskirts of Altadena.

This historic hike visits the ruins of the one-time "White City" atop Echo Mountain. From the steps of the old Echo Mountain House are great clear-day views of the megalopolis. Energetic hikers can join trails leading to Inspiration Point and Idlehour campground.

Pasadena and Altadena citizens have been proud to share their fascination with the front range of the San Gabriels. This pride has extended to the trails ascending from these municipalities into the mountains.

Local citizens, under the auspices of the Forest Conservation Club, built a trail from the outskirts of Altadena to Echo Mountain during the 1930s. During the next decade, retired Los Angeles Superior Court clerk Samuel Merrill over-hauled and maintained the path. When Merrill died in 1948, the trail was named for him.

Sam Merrill Trail begins at the former Cobb Estate, now a part of Angeles National Forest. A plaque placed by the Altadena Historical Society dedicates the estate ground as "a quiet place for people and wildlife forever."

DIRECTIONS TO TRAILHEAD: From the Foothill Freeway (210) in Pasadena, exit on Lake Avenue and travel north 3.5 miles to its end at Loma Alta Drive. Park along Lake Avenue.

THE HIKE: From the great iron gate of the old Cobb Estate, follow the trail along the chain-link fence. The path dips into Las Flores Canyon, crosses a seasonal creek in the canyon bottom, then begins to climb. As you begin your earnest, but well-graded ascent, enjoy good, over-the-shoulder views of the San Gabriel Valley and downtown Los Angeles. Two long, steep and mostly shadeless miles of travel brings you to a signed junction. Bear right and walk 100 yards along the bed of the old Mt. Lowe Railway to the Echo Mountain ruins. Just before the ruins is a drinking fountain, very welcome if it's a hot day.

Up top, you'll spot the railway's huge bull wheel, now embedded in cement, and just below is a pile of concrete rubble, all that remains of the railway depot.

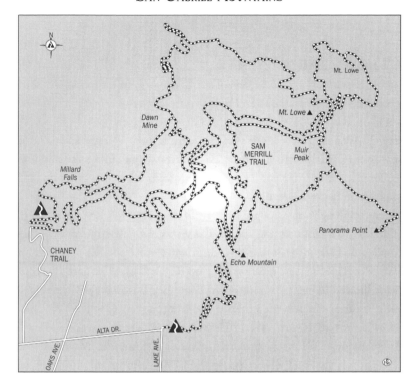

Energetic hikers can join signed trails that lead to Mt. Lowe Camp and to Inspiration Point and Idlehour Campground.

The steps and foundation of the Echo Mountain House are great places to take a break and enjoy the view straight down precipitous Rubio Canyon, the route of Lowe's railway. A bit down the mountain to the east stood another hotel—the Chalet—but nothing remains of it.

Echo Mountain takes its name from the echo that supposedly bounces around the semicircle of mountain walls. I've never managed to get very good feedback; perhaps even echoes fade with time.

MT. LOWE

MT. LOWE RAILWAY TRAIL
From Sunset Ridge to Mt. Lowe Trail Camp is 10 miles round trip with
2,700-foot gain; to Inspiration Point is 11 miles round trip

Professor Thaddeus Lowe, Civil War balloonist, man of fame and fortune, was
the quintessential California dreamer. His dream was to build a railway into—and
a resort complex atop—the San Gabriel Mountains high above Pasadena. In the
1890s, his dream became a reality.

During the height of its popularity, millions took Professor Lowe's "Railway
to the Clouds" to fine hotels and spectacular views of Southern California. Until it
was abandoned in the 1930s, it was the Southland's most popular tourist attraction.

From Pasadena, visitors rode a trolley up Rubio Canyon, where a pavilion and
hotel were located. After taking refreshments, they boarded the "airships" of the
great cable incline, which carried them 3,000 feet (gaining 1,300 feet) straight up to
the Echo Mountain Resort Area. "Breathtaking" and "hair-raising" were the
most frequent descriptions of this thrilling ride. Atop Echo Mountain was the
White City, with a hotel, observatory, and a magnificent searchlight purchased
from the Chicago World's Fair. When the searchlight swept the mountaintop,
the white buildings of the resort were visible from all over Los Angeles. From
Echo Mountain, tourists could board a trolley and ride another few miles to Mt.
Lowe Tavern at the end of the line.

This historic walk follows the old railway bed, visits the ruins of the White
City and Mt. Lowe Tavern, and concludes with some fine views of Los Angeles
from Inspiration Point. The old railway bed with its gentle seven percent grade
makes for easy walking. An interpretive brochure is (sometimes) available from
Angeles National Forest headquarters in Arcadia. Begin this hike as described
below or from Echo Mountain (see my account of this trail).

DIRECTIONS TO TRAILHEAD: Exit the Foothill Freeway (210) at
Lake Avenue and follow it north to its end. Turn left on Loma Alta Drive. Go
one mile to Chaney Trail Road and turn right. At a Y in the road, take the right
fork to the Sunset Ridge parking area. The trailhead is located at the locked gate,
which bars vehicles from Sunset Ridge Fire Road.

THE HIKE: The trail begins just past the locked gate. Follow the paved
Sunset Ridge Fire Road. You may follow the fire road two miles to the junction
with Echo Mountain Trail, but a more attractive alternative is described here.

Follow the road 0.25 mile to the signed Sunset Ridge Trail on your left. Join
this trail, which parallels the fire road, and leads into peaceful Millard Canyon.

Mt. Lowe "Railway to the Clouds."

Near the canyon bottom, the trail forks at a signed junction. Bear right and ascend back up to Sunset Ridge Fire Road. Follow the fire road about 75 yards, and on your right you'll spot the signed junction with Echo Mountain Trail.

To Echo Mountain: Bear right on Echo Mountain Trail, which leads one-half mile over the old railway bed to Echo Mountain. Echo Mountain takes its name from an echo that bounces around the semicircle of mountain walls.

On Echo Mountain are the foundations of Echo Mountain House and the chalet. The most prominent ruin is the large iron bull wheel that pulled the cars up the steep incline from Rubio Canyon. A fire swept Echo Mountain in 1900, leveling all of the White City except the observatory. Picnic tables suggest a lunch stop among the ruins. Leave behind the ruins of the White City, return to Sunset Ridge Fire Road and bear right.

The paved road soon becomes dirt and an interpretive sign at "Cape of Good Hope" lets you know you've joined the Mt. Lowe Railway tour. Continue along the railway bed, passing the attractions that impressed an earlier generation of travelers: Granite Gate, Horseshoe Curve, and the site of the Great Circular Bridge.

Near the top, you'll come to the site of Mt. Lowe Tavern, which burned in 1936. Almost all signs of the tavern are gone, but this peaceful spot under oaks and big cone spruce still extends its hospitality. In its place is Mt. Lowe Trail Camp, which welcomes hikers with shade, water, restrooms and picnic tables.

Before heading down, follow the fire road east and then south for 0.5 mile to Inspiration Point. Where the fire road makes a hairpin left to Mt. Wilson, go right. At Inspiration Point, you can gaze through several telescope-like sighting tubes aimed at Santa Monica, Hollywood and the Rose Bowl. After locating a sight that inspires you, return the same way.

EATON CANYON

EATON CANYON TRAIL
From the Nature Center to Eaton Falls is 3 miles round trip with 200-foot gain

Late one August afternoon in 1877, John Muir set out from Pasadena to begin his exploration of the San Gabriel Mountains. The great naturalist was very impressed with Eaton Falls, as he wrote in his book, *The Mountains of California:* "It is a charming little thing, with a low, sweet voice, singing like a bird, as it pours from a notch in a short ledge, some thirty-five or forty feet into a round mirror-pool."

After enjoying Eaton Falls, Muir followed bear trails, sometimes on all fours, up the chaparral-smothered ridges of the mountains.

Judge Benjamin Eaton channeled and piped the canyon's waters to nearby ranches. The judge's neighbors laughed when he planted grapevines, but the vines were quite successful and commanded a high price. Soon many other San Gabriel Valley farmers planted vineyards.

Much of the canyon named for Judge Eaton is now part of Eaton Canyon County Park. A nature center has exhibits which emphasize Southern California flora and fauna. Nature trails explore a variety of native plant communities—chaparral, coastal sage, and oak-sycamore woodland.

Eaton Canyon County Park is a busy place on weekends. Family nature walks are conducted by docent naturalists; the park also has birdwalks, natural history classes and children's programs.

The walk up Eaton Canyon to the falls is an easy one, suitable for the whole family. Eaton Canyon Trail leads through a wide wash along the east side of the canyon to a junction with Mt. Wilson Toll Road. In fact, Eaton Canyon Trail was once a toll road itself; fees were collected from 1890 to 1911. The hiker seeking strenuous exercise can join Mt. Wilson Road for a steep, eight-mile ascent of Mt. Wilson.

DIRECTIONS TO TRAILHEAD: From the Foothill Freeway (210) in Pasadena, exit on Altadena Drive. Proceed north 1.75 miles to the signed entrance of Eaton Canyon County Park. Turn right into the park and leave your car in the large lot near the nature center.

THE HIKE: From the parking lot, hike through the attractive grounds of the nature center. Cross the creek, then meander beneath the boughs of large oak trees and pass a junction with a connector trail that leads to the Mt. Wilson Toll Road. Check on conditions before hiking.

To the east, you'll spy the plateau overlooking Eaton Canyon. A hundred years ago, this land belonged to the wealthy capitalist and pioneer forester and builder of Venice Beach, Abbott Kinney, and his Kinneloa Ranch. Kinney loved this area and was a bit miffed when a nearby peak was named Mt. Harvard for the university that built an observatory atop the mountain, rather than for him.

The trail leads along the wide arroyo. Eaton Canyon was widened considerably by a 1969 flood that washed away canyon walls. This flood, and the many floods before and since, have spread alluvium, or water-transported sand and rock, across the canyon floor. It takes a hearty group of drought-resistant plants to survive in this soil and Southern California's sometimes not-so-benign Mediterranean climate. Notice the steepness of the canyon's walls. Early Spanish settlers called the canyon "El Precipio."

A mile's travel from the nature center brings you to the Mt. Wilson Toll Road bridge. A right turn on the toll road will take you on a long, steep ascent to the top of Mt. Wilson. A left turn on Mt. Wilson Toll Road will bring you a very short distance to the unsigned junction with Altadena Crest Trail. This rather dull trail travels two miles above the reservoirs and backyards of residential Altadena. Walking 0.5 mile on Altadena Crest Trail to a vista point will reward you with great clear-day views of the Los Angeles Basin.

To reach Eaton Falls, continue straight up Eaton Canyon wash. You'll rock-hop across the creek several times as you walk to trail's end at the falls.

The "round mirror-pool," described by John Muir, enjoyed by hikers more than a century later.

HENNINGER FLATS

MT. WILSON TOLL ROAD
From Altadena to Henninger Flats is 6 miles round trip with 1,400-foot elevation gain

Consider the conifers. A wind-bowed limber pine clinging to a rocky summit. A sweet-smelling grove of incense cedar. The deep shade and primeval gloom of a spruce forest.

Where do trees come from?

I know, I know. "Only God can make a tree."

Keep your Joyce Kilmer. Hold the metaphysical questions. Our inquiry here is limited to what happens in the aftermath of a fire or flood, when great numbers of trees lie dead or dying.

Fortunately for California's cone-bearing tree population—and tree lovers—there is a place where trees, more than 120,000 a year, are grown to replace those lost to the capriciousness of nature and the carelessness of humans. The place is Henninger Flats, home of the Los Angeles County Experimental Nursery.

Perched halfway between Altadena and Mt. Wilson, Henninger Flats is the site of Southern California's finest tree plantation. On the flats you'll be able to view trees in all shapes and sizes, from seedlings to mature stands. It's a small museum with reforestation exhibits.

After careers as a gold miner, Indian fighter and first Sheriff of Santa Clara County, Captain William Henninger came to Los Angeles to retire in the early 1880s. While doing a little prospecting, Henninger discovered the little mesa that one day would bear his name. He constructed a trail over which he could lead his burros.

Atop the flats he built a cabin, planted fruit trees, raised hay and corn. His solitude ended in 1890 when the Mt. Wilson Toll Road was constructed for the purpose of carrying the great telescope up to the new observatory. Captain Henninger's Flats soon became a water and rest stop for hikers, riders and fishermen who trooped into the mountains.

After Henninger's death in 1895, the flats were used by the U.S. Forest Service as a tree nursery. Foresters emphasized the nurturing of fire- and drought-resistant varieties of conifers. Many thousands of seedlings were transplanted to fire- and flood-ravaged slopes all over the Southland. Since 1928, Los Angeles County foresters have continued the good work at Henninger Flats.

The Pasadena and Mt. Wilson Toll Road Company in 1891 fashioned a trail to the summit of Mt. Wilson. Fees were 50 cents per rider, 25 cents per hiker. A 12-foot wide road followed two decades later. During the 1920s, the road was the

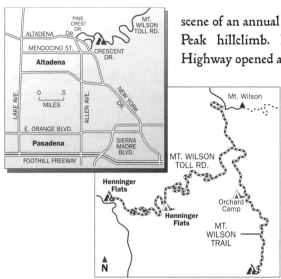

scene of an annual auto race, similar to the Pike's Peak hillclimb. In 1936 the Angeles Crest Highway opened and rendered the toll road obsolete. Since then the toll road has been closed to public traffic and maintained as a fire road.

A moderate outing of just under 6 miles, on good fire road, the trail up to Henninger Flats is suitable for the whole family. The flats offer a large picnic area and fine clear-day city views.

At this writing, a 2005 landslide covered a portion of the old road and prompted authorities to close it. A trail bypass has been constructed but the road remains officially closed. Call the Eaton Canyon Nature Center for the latest trail conditions.

DIRECTIONS TO TRAILHEAD: From the Foothill Freeway (210) in Pasadena, exit on Altadena Drive. Proceed north 1.75 miles to the signed entrance of Eaton Canyon County Park. Turn right into the park and leave your car in the large lot near the nature center.

THE HIKE: From the parking lot, hike through the attractive grounds of the Nature Center. Cross the creek, then meander beneath the boughs of large oak trees to a junction with the signed connector trail leading to the Mt. Wilson Toll Road. Ascend this steep, long footpath to the toll road and turn right. The road begins a series of switchbacks up chaparral-covered slopes. Occasional painted pipes mark your progress.

Henninger Flats welcomes the hiker with water, shade, and two campgrounds where you may enjoy a lunch stop. Growing on the flats are some of the more common cone-bearing trees of the California mountains including knobcone, Coulter, sugar, digger and Jeffrey pine, as well as such exotics as Japanese black pine and Himalayan white pine.

After your tree tour, return the same way.

Ultra-energetic hikers will continue up the old toll road to Mt. Wilson; the journey from Altadena to the summit is 9 miles one-way with an elevation gain of 4,500 feet.

MT. WILSON

MT. WILSON TRAIL
From Sierra Madre to Orchard Camp is 9 miles round trip with a 2,000-foot elevation gain; to Mt. Wilson is 15 miles round trip with a 4,500-foot gain

The tale of the Old Mt. Wilson Trail begins with Benjamin Davis Wilson, who gazed up at the commanding peak located high above his San Gabriel Valley vineyard and figured those abundant stands of pine and cedar on the mountain's shoulders would be an ideal source of timber. He built the first trail to "Wilson's Peak" in 1864.

As the communities located at the base of the San Gabriel Mountains grew in population during the 1880s, the townspeople began hiking up Mt. Wilson for weekend recreation. Eager to keep the hiking customer refreshed and satisfied, local entrepreneurs constructed trail resorts on the mountain.

The trail struggled with a rival thoroughfare when the Mt. Wilson Toll Road Company opened a wide, well-graded route in 1891 for a charge of 25 cents per hiker. But by the dawn of the 20th century, the old trail made a big-time comeback when a hiking fervor known as the Great Hiking Era swept the Southland.

In 1905 the Pacific Electric Railway extended its trolley service to Sierra Madre, reaching within a quarter-mile of the trailhead. Hikers came in droves on the weekend to tramp the path; others took the easy way by renting a mule or burro. Some 40,000 travelers passed through the trail's mid-point, Orchard Camp, in 1911.

Benjamin Wilson

After the passing of the Great Hiking Era in the 1930s, the trail was all but abandoned until the late 1950s when rebuilding efforts began. Sierra Madre citizens, aided by Boy Scout troops, rebuilt the trail all the way up-canyon to its junction with the old Mt. Wilson Toll Road.

Sierra Madre citizens also prevented county flood control engineers from bulldozing and check-damming Little Santa Anita Canyon. The aroused citizenry established Sierra Madre Historical Wilderness Area to preserve the canyon.

This hike takes you up Little Santa Anita Canyon, visits Orchard Camp, and climbs to the top of Mt. Wilson. It's a classic climb, one of the nicest all-day hikes in the Southland.

DIRECTIONS TO TRAILHEAD: From the Foothill Freeway (210) in Arcadia, exit on Baldwin Avenue and head north. Turn right on Miramonte Avenue near the junction of Mt. Wilson Trail Road, which is on your left. The trail begins 150 yards up this road and is marked by a large wooden sign. After passing some homes, the trail shortly intersects the main trail.

THE HIKE: After trudging 1.5 miles up Santa Anita Canyon you reach a junction with a side trail, which leads to the nearby canyon bottom. Here you can lean against an old oak, cool your heels in the rushing water, relax and watch the river flow.

Continue hiking on the ridge trail as it climbs higher and higher above the canyon floor onto sunny, exposed slopes. A hot 3 miles of hiking brings you to Decker Spring and another 0.5 mile to Orchard Camp, a shady glen dotted with oak and spruce trees. When Wilson was building his trail, a construction camp called Halfway House was built here. Later homesteaders tried their hand planting apple and cherry trees—hence the name Orchard Camp.

During the Great Hiking Era, a succession of entrepreneurs utilized Orchard Camp as a trail resort and welcomed thousands of hikers. Hikers traveling through the canyon in the 1920s reported seeing "The Nature Man of Mt. Wilson," a tall bronzed hermit who looked like he stepped out of the pages of the Old Testament. The nature man carried a stone axe and worked on the trail for his keep. Some say he's still around, protecting the canyon—though he no longer springs out of the brush and greets every hiker who passes.

Orchard Camp is a nice place to picnic. You might want to call it a day here and return the same way.

The trail continues through thick chaparral up Santa Anita Canyon to its head. It contours on the shelf-like trail, heads east on a firebreak and crosses over a steep manzanita-covered ridge. At the intersection with Winter Creek Trail, turn left (west) and ascend steeply to Mt. Wilson Toll Road, 2 miles from Orchard Camp.

Turn right on the Toll Road and follow it a mile as it ascends through well-spaced spruce to Mt. Wilson Road, just outside Skyline Park.

BIG SANTA ANITA CANYON

GABRIELINO NATIONAL RECREATION TRAIL
From Chantry Flat to Sturtevant Falls is 3.5 miles round trip with 500-foot gain; to Spruce Grove Camp is 8 miles round trip with 1,400-foot gain; to Mt. Wilson is 8 miles one-way with 4,000-foot gain

Cascades, a waterfall and giant woodwardia ferns are a few of the many delights of historic Big Santa Anita Canyon. The bucolic canyon has been popular with Southern California hikers for a hundred years.

William Sturtevant, known to his friends as "Sturde," pioneered many miles of San Gabriel Mountains trails. He traveled from California to Colorado in the early 1880s with forty burros. A packer par excellence, he soon found his services to be in great demand in the San Gabriels.

Sturtevant hewed out a trail over the ridge from Winter Creek to the top of the canyon and in 1898 opened Sturtevant Camp. The rustic resort consisted of a dining hall, tents, and a store and was a popular trail resort well into the 1930s.

In Santa Anita Canyon today some eighty-odd cabins are serviced by a burro train from Chantry Flats, named for another early packer, Charlie Chantry. One of the more colorful sights in the local mountains—and a look backward into a bygone era—is a glimpse at the pack animals plodding up the trail to Sturtevant Camp, now a Methodist Church retreat.

Sturtevant's trail is now a section of the 28-mile long Gabrielino National Recreation Trail. The trail to Sturtevant Falls is very popular on weekends—but not as popular as it was on Fourth of July weekend 1919 when 5,000 people tramped into the canyon and signed the trail register! The ambitious hiker may continue past the falls to Spruce Grove Camp and even as far as the top of Mt. Wilson.

DIRECTIONS TO TRAILHEAD: From the Foothill Freeway (210) in Arcadia, exit on Santa Anita Avenue and drive six miles north to its end at Chantry Flat. (Unfortunately, this road is often closed for repair.) The trail begins across the road from the parking area. A tiny store at the edge of the parking lot sells maps and refreshments.

THE HIKE: Descend on the paved fire road, part of the Gabrielino Trail, into Big Santa Anita Canyon. At the bottom of the canyon you'll cross a footbridge near the confluence of Big Santa Anita and Winter Creeks. Here a small sign commemorates Roberts Camp, a resort camp founded in 1912. Owner Otto Lyn Roberts and other canyon boosters really "sold" the charms of the canyon to Southern Californians in need of a quiet weekend. As you follow the path up-canyon along the oak-and alder-shaded creek, you'll soon determine that the canyon "sells" itself.

The only blemish on the pristine scene is a series of check-dams construct-ed of giant cement "Lincoln logs," by the Los Angeles County Flood Control District and the Forest Service in the early 1960s. In their zeal to tame Big Santa Anita Creek, engineers apparently forgot that fast-moving water is sup-posed to erode canyon bottoms; floods are what originally sculpted this beauti-ful canyon. Today, thanks to the check-dams, the creek flows in well-organized fashion, lingering in tranquil pools, then

Early hiker, Big Santa Anita Canyon

spilling over the dams in fifteen-foot cascades. Over the years, moss, ferns, alders and other creekside flora have softened the appearance of the dams and they now fit much better into the lovely surroundings.

The trail passes some private cabins and reaches a three-way trail junction. To visit Sturtevant Falls, continue straight ahead. You'll cross Big Santa Anita Creek, then re-cross where the creek veers leftward. Pick your way along the boul-der-strewn creek bank a final hundred yards to the falls. The falls drops in a silver stream fifty feet to a natural rock bowl. (Caution: Climbing the wet rocks near the falls can be extremely hazardous to your health. Stay off.)

Return the same way, or hike onward and upward to Spruce Grove Trail Camp. Two signed trails lead toward Spruce Grove. The leftward one zigzags high up on the canyon wall while the other passes above the falls. The left trail is easier hiking while the right trail heads through the heart of the canyon and is prettier. Either trail is good walking and they rejoin in a mile.

After the trails rejoin, you'll continue along the spruce-shaded path to Cascade Picnic Area. You can call it a day here or ascend another mile to Spruce Grove Trail Camp. Both locales have plenty of tables and shade.

Still feeling frisky? Hikers in top condition will charge up the trail to Mt. Wilson—an 8-mile (one way) journey from Chantry Flat. Continue on the trail up-canyon a short distance, cross the creek and you'll find a trail junction. A left brings you to historic Sturtevant Camp, now owned by the Methodist Church. The trail to Mt. Wilson soon departs Big Santa Anita Canyon and travels many a switchback through the thick forest to Mt. Wilson Skyline Park.

WINTER CREEK

WINTER CREEK TRAIL
From Chantry Flat to Hoegees Camp is 6 miles round trip with 300-foot elevation gain; return via Mt. Zion Trail, Gabrielino Trails is 9 miles round trip with 1,500-foot gain

Before the dawn of the 20th century, packer/entrepreneur William Sturtevant set up a trail camp in one of the woodsy canyons on the south-facing slope of Mt. Wilson. This peaceful creekside refuge from city life was called Sturtevant's Winter Camp. In later years the name Winter was given to the creek whose headwaters arise from the shoulder of Mt. Wilson and tumble southeasterly into Big Santa Anita Canyon.

In 1908, Arie Hoegee and his family built a resort here that soon became a popular destination for Mt. Wilson-bound hikers; it remained so until it was battered by the great flood of 1938. A trail camp named for the Hoegees now stands on the site of the old resort and offers the modern-day hiker a tranquil picnic site or rest stop.

A hike along Winter Creek is a fine way to greet the arrival of winter. One of a half-dozen trails accessible from the popular Chantry Flat trailhead located just above Altadena in the Angeles National Forest, Winter Creek Trail offers a pleasant family hike in the front range of the San Gabriel Mountains.

DIRECTIONS TO TRAILHEAD: From the Foothill Freeway (210) in Arcadia, exit on Santa Anita Avenue and drive six miles north to its end at Chantry Flat. (Unfortunately, this road is often closed for repair.) The trail begins across the road from the parking area. A tiny store at the edge of the parking lot sells maps and refreshments.

THE HIKE: Descend 0.75 mile on the paved fire road, part of the signed Gabrielino Trail, into Big Santa Anita Canyon. At the bottom of the canyon, you'll cross a footbridge near the confluence of Big Santa Anita and Winter Creeks.

After crossing the bridge, look leftward for the signed Lower Winter Creek Trail. Following the bubbling creek, the trail tunnels beneath the boughs of oak and alder, willow and bay. The only blemish on the pristine scene is a series of check dams constructed of giant cement "Lincoln logs" by the Los Angeles County Flood Control District and Forest Service in the early 1960s. Fortunately, moss, ferns and other creekside flora have softened the appearance of the dams over the years and they now fit much better into the lovely surroundings.

You'll pass some cabins, built early in the 20th century and reached only by trail. Ever since, the needs of the cabin owners have been supplied by pack train.

When you see man and beast moving through the forest, it's easy to imagine that you've stepped a century back in time, back into Southern California's Great Hiking and Trail Resort Era.

After crossing Winter Creek, you'll arrive at Hoegees Camp. A dozen or so tables beneath the big cone spruce offer fine picnicking. Almost all signs of the original Hoegees Camp are gone, with the exception of flourishing patches of ivy. (In later years, Hoegees was renamed Camp Ivy.)

Walk through the campground until you spot a tiny tombstone-shaped trail sign. Cross Winter Creek here and bear left on the trail. In a short while you'll pass a junction with Mt. Zion Trail, a steep trail that climbs over the mountain to Sturtevant Camp and Big Santa Anita Canyon.

After recrossing the creek, you'll pass a junction with a trail leading to Mt. Wilson and join the Upper Winter Creek Trail. This trail contours around a ridge onto open chaparral-covered slopes. This stretch of trail offers fine clear-day views of Sierra Madre and Arcadia. The trail joins a fire road just above Chantry Flat and you follow this road through the picnic area back to the parking lot where you left your car.

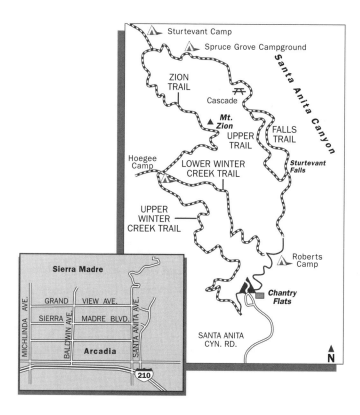

SAN GABRIEL WILDERNESS

DEVIL'S CANYON TRAIL
From Chilao to Devil's Canyon Trail Camp is 7 miles round trip with 1,500-foot elevation loss; to Devil's Canyon Waterfall is 11 miles round trip with 2,300-foot loss

Los Angeles residents, while inching along on some crowded interchange, may be comforted by knowing that no other metropolis has a wilderness area so close. When you hike the primeval canyons of the San Gabriel Wilderness Area, you won't believe you're only eighteen as-the-crow-flies miles from downtown L.A.

The 36,137-acre wilderness is rough and rugged country, the bulk of which is contained in two canyons, Devil's and Bear. Chaparral coats the sunny canyon slopes while pine and fir reach from the ridges to the sky. In spring, this is color country: the laurels glow yellow with flowers, the willows fluff up, the ceanothus blossoms blue and white.

The wilderness area is surrounded on three sides by roads: on the north and west by Highway 2, on the east by Highway 39. Picnickers and campers crowd its edges, skiers peer down at it from nearby ridges. But despite its accessibility, most people only look at this wilderness. The view down from the brink of Devil's Canyon, the sharp descent, and the thought of the walk back up, scare off casual walkers.

Devil's Canyon Trail, from Chilao to the trail camp, is the most pleasant path in the wilderness. It takes you through the middle third of the canyon, past willow-shaded pools and dancing cascades, to spots that make the Big City seem hundreds of miles away.

DIRECTIONS TO TRAILHEAD: From La Canada, drive 27 miles up the Angeles Crest Highway, 0.25 mile past the entrance to Upper Chilao Campground. Look for a parking lot on the left side of the highway. The signed trailhead, which is usually below snowline, is across the highway from the parking lot.

THE HIKE: Remind yourself, as you begin descending steeply into Devil's Canyon, that the tough part of this trip comes last. Pace yourself accordingly. The trail steps back and forth from pine and spruce on the shady slopes to thick chaparral on sunny slopes.

After two miles, the trail meets a pleasant little creek and descends with its bubbling waterway down into the canyon. At trail's end is Devil's Canyon Trail Camp, a primitive creekside retreat, where the only sounds you hear are the murmur of the creek and the rustling of alder leaves.

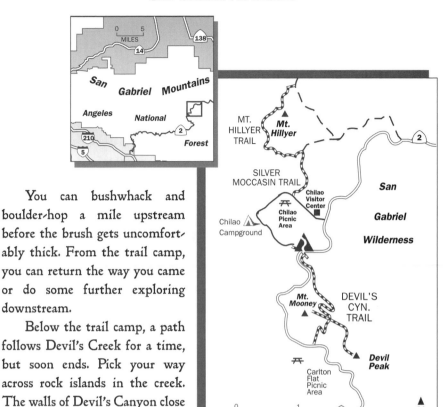

You can bushwhack and boulder-hop a mile upstream before the brush gets uncomfortably thick. From the trail camp, you can return the way you came or do some further exploring downstream.

Below the trail camp, a path follows Devil's Creek for a time, but soon ends. Pick your way across rock islands in the creek. The walls of Devil's Canyon close in and you find yourself in trackless boulder-hopping country; pleasant, but slow-going. You continually cross the creek, decipher routes around deep pools and descend gingerly down misty boulders.

Blackened alder leaves cover the surface of still eddies, where pan-sized trout may lurk. The canyon narrows, its steep rock walls pinching Devil's Creek into a series of cascades. As the canyon narrows further, the cascades grow more spectacular and waterfalls occur. The first falls come from side creeks and 0.25 mile farther down-creek you arrive at the first mainstream falls, which plunge 20 feet to a bubbling pool.

Expert mountaineers sometimes continue downstream from the falls, but it's a precarious route and is recommended only for the very skilled. Your return to Devil's Canyon Trail Camp may be faster than your descent, because it's easier to pick routes and climb up rocks, than down them. Your climb from the trail camp to the highway will, of course, be slower.

CHILAO

SILVER MOCCASIN TRAIL

From Chilao to Horse Flats Campground is 2 miles round trip with 200-foot elevation gain; to Mt. Hillyer is 6 miles round trip with 1,000-foot gain

Even on the Angeles National Forest map, the trail looks intriguing: a red dashed line zigs and zags through the heart of the San Gabriel Mountains and connects Chantry Flat and Shortcut Station, Chilao, Cloudburst and Cooper Canyon. Designed by the Los Angeles Area Council of the Boy Scouts of America, the 53-mile long Silver Moccasin Trail, extends from Chantry Flat to the mountain named for the founder of the Boy Scouts, Lord Baden-Powell. Scouts who complete the week-long trek earn the prized Silver Moccasin award.

One pretty stretch of the Silver Moccasin Trail tours the Chilao country, a region of giant boulders and gentle, Jeffrey pine-covered slopes. Another path—Mt. Hillyer Trail—leads to the top of 6,162-foot Mt. Hillyer. From the top, you'll get views to the north of the desert side of the San Gabriels.

Located just off Angeles Crest Highway near the trailhead, the Angeles National Forest Chilao Visitor Center is well worth a visit. Exhibits interpret flora, fauna and forest history. Behind the station are three short nature trails.

DIRECTIONS TO TRAILHEAD: From the Foothill Freeway (210) in La Canada, exit on Angeles Crest Highway (2) and wind 27 miles up the mountain road to the signed turnoff for the Chilao Visitor Center. Turn left and follow the paved road past the visitor center a half-mile to signed Silver Moccasin Trail. Parking at the trailhead is limited, but there's a wide turnout located just up the road.

THE HIKE: The trail ascends a manzanita- and yucca-covered slope to the top of a minor ridge. A mile from the trailhead, the trail widens and you reach a signed junction. Here Silver Moccasin Trail swings southeast toward the highway and Cooper Canyon, but you go right with a retiring dirt road one hundred yards to Horse Flat Campground. The camp, with plenty of pine-shaded picnic tables, is a good rest stop.

Just as you reach the gravel campground road, head left with the signed Mt. Hillyer Trail. The path switchbacks up pine-, incense cedar- and scrub oak-covered slopes. Some big boulders suggest a perfect hideout, whether you're fleeing the sheriff or the stresses of modern life.

Up top, Mt. Hillyer may remind you of what Gertrude Stein said of Oakland: "There's no there there." The summit is not a commanding pinnacle, but a forested flat. With all those trees in the way, you'll have to walk a few hundred yards along the ridgeline to get your view of the green country to the south and the brown, wrinkled desert side of the San Gabriels to the north.

MT. WILLIAMSON

MT. WILLIAMSON TRAIL
From Islip Saddle to Mt. Williamson is 5 miles round trip with 1,600-foot elevation gain

Mt. Williamson stands head and shoulders above other crests along Angeles Crest Highway. The 8,214-foot peak offers grand views of earthquake country—the Devil's Punchbowl, San Andreas Fault and the fractured northern edges of the San Gabriel Mountains.

The summit of Mt. Williamson is the high point and culmination of well-named Pleasant View Ridge, a chain of peaks that rises from the desert floor to Angeles Crest Highway. It's quite a contrast to stand atop the piney peak, which is snow-covered in winter, and look down upon Joshua trees and the vast sand-scape of the Mojave Desert.

The mountain's namesake is Major Robert Stockton Williamson, who first explored the desert side of the San Gabriels in 1853. Williamson, a U.S. Army map-maker, led an expedition in search of a railroad route over or through the mountains. Certainly Williamson found no passable route through the Mt. Williamson area or any other place in the San Gabriel Mountains high country, but the major did find a way around the mountains, so his mission was definitely a success. Williamson's Pacific Railroad Survey report to Congress detailed two railroad routes: Cajon Pass on the east end of the San Gabriels and Soledad Canyon on northwest.

Two fine forest service trails ascend Mt. Williamson from Angeles Crest Highway. One trail leads from Islip Saddle, the other from another (unnamed) saddle 1.5 miles farther west. Both are well-graded, well-maintained routes, part of the Pacific Crest Trail.

Possibly, after a glance at a map, the idea of linking the east and west Mt. Williamson trails with a walk along Angles Crest Highway, in order to make a loop trip, will occur to you. Don't be tempted. The problem is that between the two trails, Angeles Crest Highway passes through a couple of tunnels—a definite no-no for pedestrians.

Both Mt. Williamson trails are winners; you can't go wrong. Mt. Williamson is a great place to beat the heat, and offers fine hiking in all seasons but winter, when snow covers the trail.

DIRECTIONS TO TRAILHEAD: From the Foothill Freeway (210) in La Canada, exit on Angeles Crest Highway (2) and drive about 38 miles, or 2.5 miles past (east of) the Snowcrest Ski Area. Look for the (sometimes) signed trail to Mt. Williamson on the left (north) side of the highway.

The Mt. Williamson east trail is easier to find. Continue 4 mile east of the Snowcrest Ski Area and, after you pass through the highway tunnels, you'll see the parking area at Islip Saddle on the left (north) side of the highway.

THE HIKE: At Islip Saddle, you'll spot South Fork Trail (remember this fine trail for another day) heading northeast down to South Fork Camp near Devil's Punchbowl County Park. But you'll join the trail to Mt. Williamson and begin ascending through a forest of Jeffrey and ponderosa pine.

Two miles of steep, but not brutal climbing brings you to a junction with the westerly ascending Pacific Crest Trail.

Hike north on the ridgeline along an unmaintained trail, which gets a little fainter as it nears the summit of Mt. Williamson. From the peak, savor the dramatic views of the desert below. If you have a good map along, you can pick out the many playas (dry lake beds), buttes and mountain ridges of the dry lands below. At the base of Mt. Williamson is that greatest of earthquake faults—the San Andreas Rift Zone. Most striking of all is the view of Devil's Punchbowl and its jumbled sedimentary strata.

Remember that this isn't a loop hike; return the way you came.

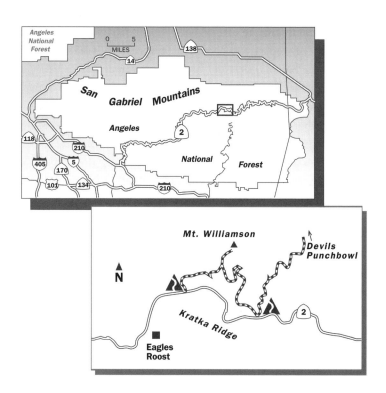

MT. ISLIP

PACIFIC CREST, MT. ISLIP TRAILS
From Angeles Crest Highway to Little Jimmy Trail Camp is 3 miles round trip with 500-foot elevation gain; to Mt. Islip is 5.4 miles round trip with 1,300-foot gain

Mt. Islip, (pronounced eye-slip) is not named, as you might guess, for a clumsy mountaineer, but for Canadian George Islip, who homesteaded in San Gabriel Canyon a century ago. The mountain is by no means one of the tallest San Gabriel mountain peaks, but its relatively isolated position on the spine of the range makes it stand out. The summit offers the hiker fine views of the middle portion of the Angeles National Forest high country and of the metropolis.

Mt. Islip has long been a popular destination for hikers. The mountain was particularly popular with Occidental College students who built a huge cairn (heap of boulders), dubbed the "Occidental Monument," atop the summit in 1909. The monument, which had the name Occidental on top, stood about two decades, until the Forest Service cleared the summit of Mt. Islip to make room for a fire lookout tower. Today, the monument and the fire lookout are long gone, but the stone foundation of the fire lookout's living quarters still remains.

One early visitor to the slopes of Mt. Islip was popular newspaper cartoonist Jimmy Swinnerton (1875-1974), well known in the early years of the 20th century for his comic strip "Little Jimmy." By the time he was in his thirties, hard-working, hard-drinking Swinnerton was suffering from the effects of exhaustion, booze, and tuberculosis. His employer and benefactor, William Randolph Hearst, sent Swinnerton to the desert to dry out. Swinnerton, however, found the summer heat oppressive so, loading his paintbrushes onto a burro, he headed into the San Gabriel Mountains.

Swinnerton spent the summers of 1908 and 1909 at Camp Coldbrook on the banks of the north fork of the San Gabriel River. Often he would set up camp high on the shoulder of Mt. Islip near a place called Gooseberry Spring, which soon became known as Little Jimmy Spring. During the two summers Swinnerton was encamped in the San Gabriels, entertained passing hikers with sketches of his Little Jimmy character. His campsite, for many years known as Swinnerton Camp, now bears the name of Little Jimmy Trail Camp.

You can reach Mt. Islip from the south side of the mountains, the way Jimmy Swinnerton did, or start from the north side from Angeles Crest Highway. This hike follows the latter route, which is a bit easier than coming up from Crystal Lake.

DIRECTIONS TO TRAILHEAD: From the Foothill Freeway (210) in La

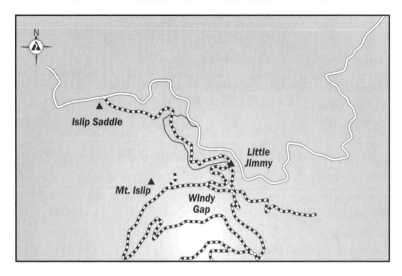

Canada, exit on Angeles Crest Highway (2) and proceed some 41 miles to signed Islip Saddle. At the saddle, on the north side of the highway, is a large parking area.

THE HIKE: Your trail, at first, is a dirt road (closed to all but Forest Service vehicles). Jeffrey and sugar pine shade the route. A half-mile ascent brings you to a three-way junction. To your right is the old crest trail coming up from Islip Saddle.

Both the forest road and the trail lead toward Little Jimmy, but hikers will prefer the trail. The trail stays just below and parallel to the road as it ascends a mile over forested slopes to Little Jimmy Trail Camp. The camp, popular with scout troops, has tables, stoves and restrooms. A side trail leads 0.25 mile southeast to all-year Little Jimmy Spring.

At the west end of camp, pick up the signed trail to Mt. Islip. A half-mile of switchbacks through piney woods brings you up to a sharp ridgeline. From atop the ridge, you'll enjoy great views of Crystal Lake, the San Gabriel Wilderness, and the canyons cut by Bear Creek and the San Gabriel River. The trail turns east and follows the ridge for another half-mile to the 8,250-foot peak. Summit views include the ski areas of Snowcrest and Mt. Waterman to the west and Mt. Baden-Powell to the east.

MT. BADEN-POWELL

MT. BADEN-POWELL TRAIL
From Vincent Gap to summit is 8 miles round trip with 2,800-foot
elevation gain; Season: May-October

This trail and peak honor Lord Baden-Powell, a British Army officer who founded the Boy Scout movement in 1907. The well-engineered trail, grooved into the
side of the mountain by the Civilian Conservation Corps in the mid-1930s,
switchbacks up the northeast ridge to the peak.

The peak was once known as North Baldy, before Southern California Boy
Scouts lobbied the Forest Service for a name change. Mt. Baden-Powell is the terminus of the scouts' 53-mile Silver Moccasin Trail, a rugged week-long backpack through
the San Gabriels. Scouts who complete the long trail earn the Silver Moccasin Award.

The trail follows a moderate, steady grade to the top of the mountain, where
there's a monument honoring Lord Baden-Powell. On the summit, you'll meet
those ancient survivors, the limber pines, and be treated to superb views across the
Mojave Desert and down into the Iron Fork of the San Gabriel River.

DIRECTIONS TO TRAILHEAD: Take the Angeles Crest Highway (2)
for 53 miles from La Cañada to the Vincent Gap Parking Area. The signed trail-

Limber Pines cling to the summit of Mt. Baden-Powell.

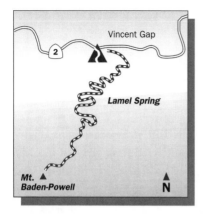

head is at the northwest edge of the parking area.

If you're coming from the east, take Interstate 15 to the Wrightwood exit, three miles south of Cajon Pass. Proceed 8 miles west on Highway 138 to its intersection with Highway 2. Turn left on Highway 2 and follow it for 14 miles to the trailhead.

THE HIKE: The trail immediately begins ascending from Vincent Gulch Divide, a gap which separates the upper tributaries of the San Gabriel River to the south from Big Rock Creek to the northwest. You begin switchbacking southwest through Jeffrey pine and fir. The trail numbers more than three dozen of these switchbacks, but so many beautiful attractions compete for the hiker's attention that it's hard to get an accurate count.

In 1.5 miles, a side trail (unmarked) leads a hundred yards to Lamel Spring, an inviting resting place and the only dependable water en route.

With increased elevation, the switchbacks grow shorter and steeper and the vegetation changes from fir to lodgepole pine. Soon, even the altitude-loving lodgepoles give way to the heartiest of pines, the limber pine. A half-mile from the summit, around 9,000 feet in elevation, the first of these squat, thick-trunked limber pines come into view. Shortly, you'll intersect a side trail to the limber pine forest.

To Limber Pine Forest: A tiny sign points right (southwest) to the limber pine stand, 0.125 mile. These wind-loving, subalpine dwellers are one of the few living things that can cope with the rarefied atmosphere. *Pinus flexilis,* botanists call the species, for its long, droopy, flexible branches. They bow and scrape like hyperextended dancers and appear to gather all their nourishment from the wind.

Back on the main trail, a few more switchbacks bring you atop the ridge where Mt. Baldy can be glimpsed. You walk along the barren crest and intersect the Pacific Crest Trail. PCT swoops off to Little Jimmy Spring.

You continue past the limber pines to the summit. A concrete monument pays homage to Lord Baden-Powell. Enjoy the superb view out across the Mojave to the southern Sierra and east to Baldy, San Gorgonio and San Jacinto.

SAN GABRIEL RIVER'S EAST FORK

EAST FORK TRAIL
From East Fork Station to the "Bridge to Nowhere" is 9 miles round trip with 1,000-foot elevation gain; to Iron Fork is 12 miles round trip with 1,400-foot gain

Sometimes you'll see a weekend gold miner find a flash in the pan, but the real treasure of this section of the San Gabriel River lies in its beauty, its alders and tumbling waters. It's wet going; you'll be doing a lot of wading as well as walking, but you'll be well rewarded for all your boulder-hopping and stream-crossing.

This day hike takes you through the monumental middle section of the East Fork of the San Gabriel River, into the Sheep Mountain Wilderness. The dizzy chasm of the Narrows is awesome, the steepest river gorge in Southern California.

Road builders of the 1930s envisioned a highway through the East Fork to connect the San Gabriel Valley with Wrightwood and the desert beyond. The great flood of 1938 interrupted these plans, leaving a handsome highway bridge stranded far up-river, the so-called "Bridge to Nowhere." You'll pass the cracked asphalt remains of the old East Fork Road and gain access to the well-named Narrows. Expect to get wet at the numerous river crossings. High water during winter or spring means these crossings will likely be unsafe. A 2006 wildfire dubbed the "Nowhere Fire" charred the slopes of the canyon near the Bridge to Nowhere.

"The Bridge to Nowhere," East Fork of San Gabriel River.

In the early years of the 20th century, at the junction of Iron Fork with the main river, miner George Trogden had a home and angler's headquarters, where miners and intrepid fishermen gathered to swap tales. Up-river from Iron Fork is Fish Fork, whose waters cascade from the shoulders of Mt. Baldy. It, too, has been a popular fishing spot for generations of anglers.

DIRECTIONS TO TRAILHEAD: From the San Bernardino Freeway (10) exit on Azusa Avenue (Highway 39) and head north. Ten miles up Highway 39, turn right (east) on East Fork Road and continue eight more miles to the East Fork Ranger Station. Park below the station.

THE HIKE: Follow the service road above the east side of the river 0.5 mile. Next, descend to the canyon floor and begin crossing and re-crossing the river. A bit more than two miles from the trailhead is Swan Rock, a mighty wall west of the river with the faint outline of a gargantuan swan.

As the canyon floor widens and twists northward, you'll climb up the right side of the canyon and continue up-river on the remains of East Fork Road, high above the rushing water. After ascending north a ways, you'll reach the "Bridge to Nowhere." No road meets this bridge at either end; the highway washed away in the flood of 1938.

Cross the bridge and join a slim trail that soon drops you into The Narrows. A quarter-mile from the bridge, Narrows Trail Camp is a fine place to picnic and view the handsome gorge.

Hardy hikers, like the river, will squeeze their way between towering granite walls. Iron Fork joins the river from the left, six miles from the trailhead.

Yet another mile up-river is Fish Fork, where another abandoned camp offers good picnicking. You can slosh up Fish Fork for another mile before a falls and the sheer canyon walls halt your progress.

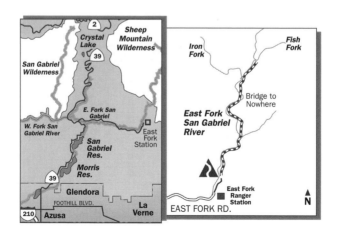

ICEHOUSE CANYON

ICEHOUSE CANYON TRAIL

From Icehouse Canyon to Icehouse Saddle is 8 miles round trip with 2,600-foot gain

Icehouse Canyon Trail, leading from Icehouse Canyon to several 8,000-foot peaks, is an ideal introduction to the high-country delights of the Cucamonga Wilderness. The precipitous subalpine slopes of the wilderness, thickly forested with sugar pine, ponderosa pine and incense cedar, offer fresh mountain air and a network of good footpaths. The 4,400-acre wilderness, set aside by Congress in 1984, includes the Three T's—Timber Mountain, Telegraph Peak and Thunder Mountain—as well as 8,859-foot Cucamonga Peak, easternmost sentinel of the San Gabriel Mountains.

Icehouse Canyon is the hiker's only easy entry into the Cucamonga high country. The saddle and nearby peaks offer fine views to the hiker. Sierra Club peak-baggers like this trail because several peaks are within "bagging distance" of Icehouse Saddle, an important trail junction.

Icehouse Canyon was for many years known as Cedar Canyon because, as the story goes, the great cedar beams for Mission San Gabriel were logged here. The name Icehouse originated in the 1860s when ice was cut in the lower canyon and shipped to San Gabriel Valley residents.

The Chapman Trail, constructed in 1980, was named for the family that built the Icehouse Canyon resort and numerous cabins in the 1920s. The well-constructed trail heads up Cedar Canyon to Cedar Glen. The trail climbs out of Cedar Canyon, then contours on a steady grade back over to Icehouse Canyon.

DIRECTIONS TO TRAILHEAD: From the San Bernardino Freeway (10) in Upland, exit on Mountain Avenue. Head north on Mountain, which joins Mt. Baldy Road in San Antonio Canyon and winds its way to Mt. Baldy Village. Stop at the Mt. Baldy Visitor Center to obtain a free Wilderness Permit in order to enter the Cucamonga Wilderness. Go 1.5 miles past the village to Icehouse Canyon parking area.

THE HIKE: The trail leads east along the floor of the canyon. The path stays close to the oak- and spruce-shaded creek and passes some cabins. After 1.5 miles, the trail forks. You may take the "high route," the Chapman Trail, one mile to Cedar Flats and then three miles up to Icehouse Saddle, or continue straight ahead on the shorter and steeper Icehouse Canyon Trail directly up the canyon.

If you decided to continue on the Icehouse Canyon Trail, you'll pass a few more cabins. The trail climbs up the north slope of the canyon, before dropping down again and crossing the creek. The trail switchbacks steeply through pine and spruce. The tall trees frame a nice picture of Old Baldy. The Chapman Trail and the Icehouse Canyon Trail intersect and a single trail ascends a steep 0.75 mile to the top of Icehouse Saddle.

You can enjoy the view and return the same way, or pick one of the fine trails that lead from Icehouse Saddle and add to your day hike. You can continue eastward and drop down the Middle Fork Trail to Lytle Creek. A right (southeast) turn puts you on a trail that climbs two miles to Cucamonga Peak. A sharp right southwest leads 2.5 miles to Kelly's Camp and Ontario Peak. And a left on the Three T's Trail takes you past Timber Mountain, Telegraph Peak and Thunder Mountain, then drops to Baldy Notch.

"Old Baldy" wearing a snowy cap.

SAN ANTONIO CANYON

SKI HUT TRAIL

To San Antonio Falls is 2.5 miles round trip with 200-foot elevation gain; to San Antonio Canyon Overlook is 6.5 miles round trip with 2,600-foot gain; to Mt. Baldy summit is 8.5 miles round trip with 3,800-foot gain

This day hike utilizes an attractive, but not-so-well-known trail that leads up San Antonio Canyon to the top of Baldy. Hikers of all ages and abilities will enjoy the 0.5-mile walk to San Antonio Falls. After a little rain, the three-tiered, 60-foot waterfall is an impressive sight.

Hikers who want more than the "leg stretcher" walk to the falls but aren't quite up for an assault on the peak can choose two intermediate destinations: the Sierra Club ski hut, where there's a cool spring, or a high ridge overlooking San Antonio Canyon. Hikers in top form, with good trail sense (the last mile of trail

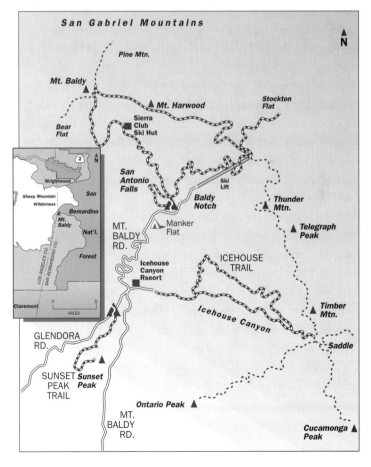

is rough and tentative), will relish the challenge of the summit climb. A clear-day view from the top offers a panorama of desert and ocean, the sprawling Southland and the southern High Sierra.

DIRECTIONS TO TRAILHEAD: From the San Bernardino Freeway in Claremont, exit on Mountain Avenue and head north, joining Mt. Baldy Road in San Antonio Canyon and winding about 11 miles to Manker Campground. About 0.3 mile past the campground entrance, look to the left for an unsigned paved road with a vehicle barrier across it. Park in the dirt lot just below the beginning of the road.

THE HIKE: Walk up the fire road, which is closed to all motor vehicles except those belonging to ski-lift maintenance workers. After a modest ascent, you soon behold San Antonio Falls. If you decide to hike down to the base of the falls, watch for loose rock and use caution on the rough trail. Resume walking along the road (unpaved beyond the falls). Soon look sharply left for an unsigned trail.

The trail ascends very steeply along the side of San Antonio Canyon. Trail connoisseurs will appreciate this path which, despite its steepness, has a hand-hewn, unobtrusive look and follows the natural contours of the land. Jeffrey pine, ponderosa pine and fir shade the path.

From the ski lift road it's 1.75 miles by trail to Sierra Club ski hut. Near the hut, constructed in 1935, is a cool and refreshing spring. Just past the ski hut the trail crosses a tiny creek, then snakes through a boulder field. Beyond the boulders the trail ascends via a 0.5-mile series of steep switchbacks to a ridgetop overlooking the headwaters of San Antonio Canyon. There's a great view from the tree-shaded ridgetop and, if you aren't up for a summit climb, this is a good picnic spot or turnaround point.

Peak-baggers will continue up the extremely rugged trail for another mile to the summit. The trail is rough and tentative in places, but rocks piled in cairns help you stay on course. You'll get a good view of Devil's Backbone, the sharp ridge connecting Mt. Harwood to Mt. Baldy.

Boulders are scattered atop Baldy's crown. Some rock windbreaks offer shelter. Enjoy the view of an assortment of San Gabriel and San Bernardino mountain range peaks, the Mojave and the metropolis.

Depending on energy or inclination, you can either return the same way or take Devil's Backbone Trail to Mt. Baldy Notch. From the Notch, follow the fire road down Manker Canyon back to the trailhead or ride down the ski lift.

MT. BALDY

DEVIL'S BACKBONE TRAIL
From Baldy Notch via ski lift, then to Mt. Baldy summit is 7 miles round trip with 2,200-foot gain; without ski lift is 13 miles roundtrip with 3,800-foot gain

Three saintly mountains—San Gorgonio, San Jacinto and San Antonio—tower over the City of the Angels. Lowest of the three, but by far the best-known is Mt. San Antonio, more commonly known as Mt. Baldy. The 10,064-foot peak, highest in the San Gabriel Mountains, is visible from much of the Southland. Its summit gleams white in winter and early spring, gray in summer and fall. Old Baldy is so big and bare that it seems to be snow-covered even when it's not.

Legend has it that the padres of Mission San Gabriel, circa 1790, named the massive stone bulwark after Saint Anthony of Padua, Italy. The 13th-century Franciscan friar was evidently a favorite of California missionaries; a number of geographical features, both in Monterey County and around Southern California, honor San Antonio. In the 1870s, San Antonio Canyon and the nearby high country swarmed with gold-seekers, who dubbed the massive peak a more earthly "Old Baldy."

Surely one of the most unique resorts in the San Gabriels was the Baldy Summit Inn, perched just below the summit of the great mountain. Gale-force winds battered the above-timberline camp, which consisted of two stone buildings and a cluster of tents. William Dewey, the owner-guide, and Mrs. Dewey, the chef, welcomed guests to their resort during the summers of 1910 through 1912. Advertised rates were one dollar a meal, one dollar a bed. The camp burned in 1913 and never reopened.

A moderate (compared to other routes up Baldy), but certainly not easy, ascent follows the Devil's Backbone Trail from Baldy Notch to the summit. This is a popular trail and the one most hikers associate with Mt. Baldy. A clear-day view from the top offers a panorama of desert and ocean, the sprawling Southland and the Southern high Sierras.

Baldy is a bit austere from afar, but up-close, the white granite shoulders of the mountain are softened by a forest of pine and fir. Dress warmly for this trip and keep an eye out for rapidly changing weather conditions.

DIRECTIONS TO TRAILHEAD: From the San Bernardino Freeway (10), exit on Mountain Avenue. Head north on Mountain, which joins Mt. Baldy Road in San Antonio Canyon and winds 12 miles to road's end just beyond Manker Campground.

If you're hiking Baldy, sans ski lift, park on the left (west) side of Mt. Baldy Road, about 0.5 mile below the ski lift parking area. Your trailhead is the gated Baldy fire road.

Purchase a ticket and ride the ski lift up to Baldy Notch. The lift is operated weekends and holidays all year.

An alternative is to walk up a fire road to Baldy Notch. This option adds three miles each way and a 1,300-foot gain to the walk. The fire road switchbacks up the west side of the steep San Antonio Canyon, offers a good view of San Antonio Falls, then climbs northward to the top.

THE HIKE: From Baldy Notch, a wide gravel path leads to a commanding view of the desert. You then join a chair lift access/fire road, and ascend a broad slope forested in Jeffrey pine and incense cedar. The road ends in about 1.25 miles at the top of a ski lift, where a hiker's sign-in register beckons.

From the top of the ski lift, a trail leads out onto a sharp ridge known as the Devil's Backbone. To the north, you can look down into the deep gorge of Lytle Creek, and to the south into San Antonio Canyon. You'll then pass around the south side of Mt. Harwood, "Little Baldy," and up through scattered stands of lodgepole pine.

The trail reaches a tempestuous saddle. (Hold onto your hat!) From the saddle, a steep rock-strewn pathway zigzags past a few wind-bowed limber pine to the summit.

Boulders are scattered atop Baldy's crown. A couple of rock windbreaks offer some shelter. Enjoy the view of San Gabriel and San Bernardino mountain peaks, the Mojave and the metropolis, and return the same way.

CHAPTER SEVEN

Orange County Parks & Preserves

Old stereotypes die hard, and the prevailing opinion of far too many Southlanders is that there is nowhere to hike in Orange County. Nothing could be further from the truth. While California's most densely populated county, Orange is also its second-most biologically diverse and boasts an excellent regional park system and a fine trail network.

The county's wilderness parks, including Caspers, Aliso & Wood Canyons and Laguna Coast, are particularly compelling places to take a hike, and offer plenty of room to roam.

For an outing to remember, take a naturalist-guided hike through Limestone Canyon or one of the other splendid locales in the Irvine Ranch Reserve.

SANTIAGO OAKS REGIONAL PARK

WINDES, PACIFICA, WILDERNESS LOOP TRAILS
0.7 mile loop and 2.5-mile loop of the park

Santiago Oaks Regional Park preserves 350 acres of pastoral Orange County, including its splendorous signature oak woodland, groupings of mature ornamental trees and even a grove of Valencia oranges. Such a diversity of environments attracts many species of birds, both common and unusual to the area.

The name of the park, creek and canyon are derived from the old Rancho Santiago de Santa Ana. During the 1930s, Dorment Winde, CFO for Bixby Ranch Company, purchased land along Santiago Creek and planted an orange grove. The ranch house built by the Winde family in 1938 is now the park's nature center.

Stop at the engaging nature center before hitting the trail—lots of park trails, in fact. Sure bets are aptly named Santiago Creek Trail and other footpaths that meander near the creek.

Historic Dam Trail leads to . . . an old dam. With the aid of Chinese laborers, the Serrano and Carpenter Water Company built a clay dam here in 1879. This dam was destroyed by floods, and replaced in 1892 with a more substantial structure of river rock and cement. The dam looks particularly tiny when compared to the huge Villa Park Flood Control dam a short distance upstream.

Sample the park's ecosystems with Windes Nature Trail. The 0.75-mile trail and its Pacifica Loop offer clear-day glimpses of the county's coastline. As nature trails go, this one is definitely on the steep side. Reward for following the trail on the ascent up 770-foot Rattlesnake Ridge are good views of the park and beyond.

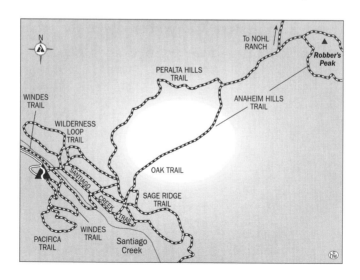

A view of pastoral OC from days gone by.

For a longer (2.5 mile) loop of the park, in a counterclockwise direction, begin with Santiago Creek Trail and follow it to the eastern boundary of the park. Take Sage Ridge Trail and Wilderness Loop Trail westbound back to reconnect with Santiago Creek Trail.

For great views of the Anaheim Hills, Chino Hills and a whole lot of Orange County, take a hike up to the rocky knob known as Robbers Peak and steal a look at what remains of rural Orange County. The 3-mile round trip hike (with a 700-foot elevation gain) begins amongst the oaks in the regional park, ascends the park's brushy ridges and travels to the 1,152-foot peak via Anaheim Hills Trail.

Cross Santiago Creek and follow Santiago Creek Trail amongst the oaks along the north side of the creek. At a signed junction with Oak Trail turn left (northeast).

As you ascend, you'll leave the regional park behind and get a grand view from suburbia to the Pacific. Nearing the sandstone peak, Anaheim Hills Trail peels off to the right, but you keep following the ridge, curving north then west to the summit. Not so long ago, the view would have taken in hundreds of cattle, orange groves, and barley fields. Nowadays the panorama is considerably less pastoral.

DIRECTIONS TO TRAILHEAD: From the Costa Mesa Freeway (55) in Orange, exit on Katella Avenue and head east. Katella undergoes a name change in a half-mile to Villa Park Road, then a second name change to Santiago Canyon Road. About three miles from the freeway, turn left on Windes Drive and drive 0.75 mile to Santiago Oaks Regional Park.

Weir Canyon Wilderness Park

WEIR CANYON LOOP TRAIL
From Hidden Canyon—a 4-mile loop with 300-foot elevation gain.

From the trail high on the west wall of Weir Canyon, the hiker gets a view of Orange County that's both stereotypical and surprising. The view westward is that of Orange County to the max: houses perched everywhere on the slopes of the Anaheim Hills, several freeways, the city of Anaheim, plus many more cities sprawling toward the coast. In contrast to this 21st-century vista, the view east is minimalist Orange County; that is to say, mostly parkland, a pastoral landscape of hills and canyons that in the right light looks like a plein-air painting made during the late 19th century.

Weir Canyon Wilderness Park (the name wilderness might be stretching the definition a bit, but it's certainly a wilderness compared to the developed areas of the Anaheim Hills) is one of those great so-near-yet-so-faraway places in Orange County to take a hike. It's a pleasure to report it's the park—not nearby subdivisions—that's been extending its boundaries farther into the hills toward the toll road (Highway 241).

Geographers say the Anaheim Hills comprise a long, low ridge extending west from the Santa Ana Mountains and rising above Santa Ana Canyon and the Santa Ana River. Weir Canyon Trail offers a gentle introduction to the considerable pleasures of these hills.

The hills are alive with flowers and their fans—among them, the author.

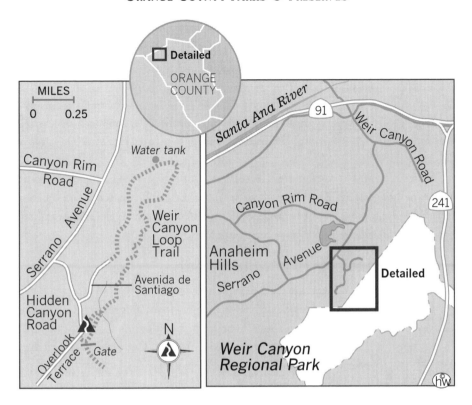

DIRECTIONS TO TRAILHEAD: From the Riverside Freeway (91) in Anaheim Hills, exit on Weir Canyon Road. Head south 0.7 mile to Serrano Avenue. Turn right (west) and proceed 2 miles to Hidden Canyon Road. Turn left (south) and follow it a half-mile to its end at Overlook Terrace and the signed trailhead. Park along Hidden Canyon Road.

THE HIKE: From the park sign, the trail leads northeast. Ignore a path descending toward the canyon bottom and continue on the main path as it rises and then levels. Enjoy eastward views into Weir Canyon and westward ones of some intriguing sandstone outcroppings.

The path dips into and climbs out of some minor side canyons, skirts some residences at about the 2.5 mile mark, then U-turns and begins heading south. After leading you a mile along the western rim of Weir Canyon, the path drops to the end of Avenida de Santiago. Walk down the steep residential street to Hidden Canyon Road, turn left, and return to the trailhead.

PETERS CANYON REGIONAL PARK

LAKE VIEW, LOWER CANYON, EAST RIDGE TRAILS
2 to 6 mile loops

In 1899, "green space," in these parts had an entirely different meaning than it does today. Here in a remote canyon, local sportsmen introduced golf to Orange County.

Santa Ana and Orange duffers leased land from the Irvine Company and laid out a nine-hole course. The "greens" were oil-soaked earthen patches and the fairways were little more than brush-cleared canyon bottom. It must have been hard to make par in Golf Canyon, as it became known.

Today Golf Canyon is the site of Peters Canyon Park, located on the edge of more suburbs-in-the-making on the eastern frontier of the communities of Orange and Tustin. The Irvine Company donated the park land in 1992.

Park highlight is a reservoir, gathering place for many migratory and resident waterfowl. Bring binoculars and watch for herons and egrets along the willow-lined shores. Also watch the skies for the red-tailed and Cooper's hawks circling above the eucalyptus groves located in lower Peters Canyon.

A network of old Irvine Ranch roads and footpaths explore the canyon and its east wall. Most popular is Lake View Trail, a 2-mile path that loops around the reservoir. It's a 6-mile round trip walk to the eucalyptus groves at the park's south end.

DIRECTIONS TO TRAILHEAD: From Highway 55 in Orange, exit on Chapman Avenue and head east 4.5 miles to Jamboree Road. Turn right and proceed a half-mile to Canyon View Avenue, then turn right again. The park is a short distance up the road on your left.

THE HIKE: Join signed Lake View Trail as it meanders along the northern edge of Upper Peters Canyon Reservoir, built in 1931 by the Irvine Company to hold water for its agricultural operations. A lower reservoir was built in 1940, but as you'll see when you visit the lower canyon, it's dry these days, and serves as an emergency flood control basin.

The trail joins a dirt road on the west side of the lake, passes a couple of side trails leading down to the lake, then skirts the dam. Loop back along the east side of the reservoir to the parking area or continue along the canyon bottom on Lower Canyon Trail. As you near the south end of the park, you'll pass a World War II "battlefield." This part of Peters Canyon was used by the U.S. Army during the war to train troops and stage mock battles.

Visit the eucalyptus groves at the park's south end then, if you wish, join East

Ridge View Trail for the return back up the canyon. The views promised by this trail's name are of the length of Peters Canyon as well as semi-suburban, semi-pastoral Orange County.

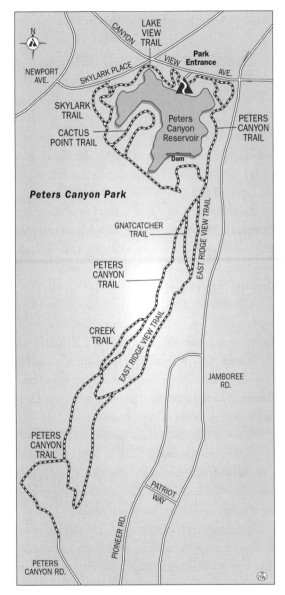

LIMESTONE CANYON

LIMESTONE CANYON TRAILS
To The Sinks is 2.5 miles round trip; to Dripping Springs is 6 miles round trip

For more than a century, Irvine Ranch cowboys were the only ones to roam scenic Limestone Canyon, one of the wildest lands remaining in Orange County. Now, hikers can experience what is now known as Limestone Canyon Reserve by taking a guided hike.

Limestone Canyon, located in southeastern Orange County, borders Cleveland National Forest and Limestone-Whiting Ranch Wilderness Park. The 5,000-acre reserve encompasses coastal sage scrub, chaparral and grassland communities, as well as oak and sycamore woodlands and even fern-surrounded dripping springs.

Limestone Canyon's name came from the cement-making operation of early Santiago Canyon settler Samuel Shrewsbury. Limestone rock was melted, hammered into a powder, then mixed with sand and used as mortar.

Eventually, "cluster developments"—residential communities concentrated in distinct areas to maximize remaining open space, will be constructed off Santiago Canyon Road. In coming years, Limestone Canyon may become accessible to the public and open for self-guided adventures.

Currently, public access includes The Nature Conservancy-led tours oriented to specific user groups, including hikers, cyclists and equestrians, as well as to children, artists, and bird-watchers. Once a month, Limestone Canyon is open to the public. Call The Nature Conservancy at (714) 832-7478 or check the hike schedule at www.irvineranchlandreserve.org

The hiking in Limestone Canyon ranges in distance from a 2.5 mile out-and-back to an overlook of The Sinks to a 15-mile loop. Depending on the hike, guides offer a range of nature interpretation from a little to a lot.

The 10-mile Limestone Canyon & Loma Ridge hike takes in a lot of the reserve and gets high on the ridgelines for spectacular views of Orange County. The 6-mile round trip jaunt to Dripping Springs is a particularly fine hike as is the 6-mile hike to Bolero Spring via "Hangman's Tree" Canyon.

"The Grand Canyon of Orange County" overstates the case a bit for Limestone Canyon, though The Sinks area of Limestone Canyon, where magnificent sandstone cliffs tower above a ravine, does resemble a mini-Grand Canyon. Hikers get great views of The Sinks, gloriously eroded, multi-layered formations with rugged river rock deposited layers on top and soft ancient marine layers on the bottom.

The Sinks are part of the Sespe Vaqueros Formation, formed 20 to 40 million years ago during a time of lowered sea levels and a more arid climate. The bottom layers (the whitish part) was deposited during humid times. Creeks deposited the top (reddish part) of the Sespe formation; its red color is form the oxidation (rust) of the iron present in the rock.

Another attraction for the hiker is Limestone's lovely and dense oaksycamore woodlands. The woodlands, along with nearby rock caves, are the favored haunts of several species of bat. Oaks and cliff outcrops offer habitat for a range of raptors: red-tailed hawk, red-

Limestone Canyon: Make your reservation for a great hike.

shouldered hawk, Cooper's hawk, turkey vulture, great horned owl, barn owl and Western screech owl.

Limestone Canyon is a great place for bird-watching. Look for raptors circling over the native grassland (wild eye and purple needle grass) looking for prey. White kites and swallows swoop along the canyon's dramatic walls.

Dripping Springs Grotto is a lovely place with water trickling down rock walls and a kind of hanging garden of flowering plants and the protruding roots of shrubs and trees. Water springs out of fissures in the cliff year-around; its rainwater that's accumulated in a fault. Tangles of wild blackberry, maidenhair fern, scarlet monkeyflower and stream orchid thrive around the grotto.

A hundred years ago, ranchers pumped water from Dripping Springs for their cattle to drink. You can see the remains of rusty pipe sticking out of the ground and oriented to the springs.

There aren't any cows around anymore. Or any cowboys. Close your eyes and listen to the dripping springs

DIRECTIONS TO TRAILHEAD: From its intersection with Jamboree Road, head east on Santiago Canyon Road for 5 miles. (If you spot Silverado Canyon Road, you've overshot the turnoff.). Turn right (south) onto Hicks Canyon Haul Road. The hiking begins inside the vehicle gate across the road.

O'NEILL PARK

LIVE OAK TRAIL
From Trabuco Canyon to Ocean Vista Point is 3 miles round trip with 600-foot elevation gain

The soldier who lost his firearm when marching with Captain Gaspar de Portolá in the 1769 expedition in this hilly region would no doubt be astonished at the number of Orange County placenames inspired by his mistake. Trabuco, which means "blunderbuss" in Spanish, now names a canyon, a creek, a plain, a trail, a road and even a ranger district of the Cleveland National Forest.

If the unknown soldier who lost his blunderbuss trekked this way again he would be amazed at the names on the land, and even more amazed at the land itself, so drastically has it changed. Maybe though, he would recognize Trabuco Canyon, at least that part of it saved from suburbanization by O'Neill Regional Park. Here the modern trekker can explore a small slice of the pastoral Southern California of two centuries ago.

This land of grassy meadows, rolling hills and oak woodland was originally part of Rancho Trabuco, two leagues granted to Santiago Arguello in 1841 by Mexican Governor Alvarado. The rancho had various lessees and owners until it was purchased by James Flood, a wealthy businessman and his partner Richard O'Neill, a packing house owner. O'Neill built up quite a ranching empire here and elsewhere in California. O'Neill's Orange County property passed to various heirs who, in turn, gave 278 acres of Trabuco Canyon to Orange County for a park in 1948. Today, after various gifts and purchases, the park encompasses 3,000 acres of woodland and brushy hills, taking in Trabuco Canyon and neighboring Live Oak Canyon.

This hike leaves the wooded canyon behind and ascends to Ocean Vista Point. The vistas include nearby peaks, canyons and the promised Pacific.

DIRECTIONS TO TRAILHEAD: From the San Diego Freeway (5) in Lake Forest, exit on El Toro Road and head 7.5 miles east to the junction known as Cook's Corner. Santiago Canyon Road angles left (north) but you veer right on Live Oak Canyon Road (S19) and follow Live Oak Canyon Road east then south 3 miles to the O'Neill Regional Park entrance on the right. Past the park entry station, make a right to reach the parking area and signed Live Oak and Spaulding Nature Trail trailhead in a quarter-mile.

THE HIKE: Continue past the junction with Edna Spaulding Trail on your left and head north. When you reach some hillside water tanks, the trail very briefly joins the water tank road, and then you'll resume with Live Oak Trail on the climb up the west wall of the canyon.

You'll pass junctions with Pawfoot Trail, Homestead Trail and Coyote Canyon Trail as you ascend along a ridge. The views begin before the vista point and what you see are two scenes typical of this side of Orange County: red-tailed hawks circling over classic Southland ranching country and suburbs, as well as suburbs-in-the-making. From the 1,492-foot summit, enjoy clear-day coastal views from Santa Monica Bay to San Clemente, with Catalina Island floating on the horizon.

After enjoying the views, choose between two or more return routes. One way back is by retracing your steps on Live Oak Trail, then joining Coyote Trail to Homestead Trail and back to Live Oak Trail. Another way to go is by way of Valley Vista Trail which drops steeply into Live Oak Canyon. An old park service road paralleling the highway returns you to the heart of the park.

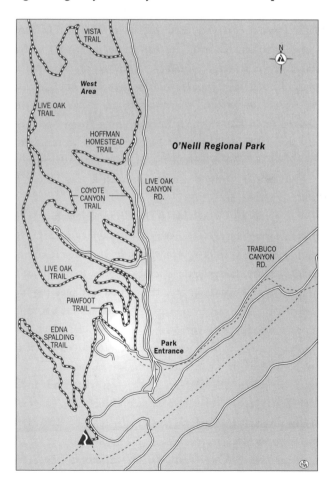

CASPERS WILDERNESS PARK

NATURE, OAK, BELL CANYON TRAILS
2 to 4 mile loops

Crisscrossing Caspers Wilderness Park are thirty miles of trail that explore grassy valleys, chaparral-cloaked ridges and native groves of coastal live oak and sycamore. Visitors have a good chance of sighting wildlife: Deer, rabbits and coyote, as well as more furtive animals such as foxes and bobcats. Bird-watchers will want to consult the park's bird list and test their skill by identifying the many species found in the park.

Centerpiece of the park is oak-lined Bell Canyon. Acorns from the oaks were an important food source for the Juaneno Indians who lived in the canyon. As the legend goes, the Indians would strike a large granite boulder with a small rock to make it ring. The sound could be heard for a mile through what is now known as Bell Canyon. "Bell Rock" is now housed in Bowers Museum in Santa Ana.

Bell Canyon, San Juan Canyon, and surrounding ridges were once part of Starr-Viejo Ranch, which was purchased by Orange County in the early 1970s. The park honors Ronald W. Caspers, chairman of the Orange County Board of Supervisors, who was instrumental in preserving the old ranch as a park.

To learn more about the region's human and natural history, drop by the park's visitor center. Exhibits interpret Native American life, birds, mammals, geology, and much more. The mostly level, Nature Trail-Oak Trail-Bell Canyon Trail-loop described below is only one of many possible day hikes you can fashion from the park's extensive trail network.

DIRECTIONS TO TRAILHEAD: From Interstate 5 in San Juan Capistrano, take the Highway 74 (Ortega Highway) exit. Drive 8 miles inland to the entrance to Caspers Wilderness Park. There is a vehicle entrance fee.

From the entry kiosk, take the park road 1.5 miles to its end at the corral and windmill. There's plenty of parking near the signed trailhead for Nature Trail.

THE HIKE: Nature Trail loops through a handsome grove of antiquarian oak. You might see woodpeckers checking their store of acorns, which the birds have stuffed in hidey-holes in the nearby sycamores. Beneath the oaks are some huge patches of poison oak, but the trail steers clear of them.

You'll pass a junction with a left-branching trail that leads to Gunsight Pass and West Ridge Trail, and soon arrive at a second junction. (If you want a really short hike, keep right at this junction and you'll loop back to the trailhead via Nature Trail.)

Head north on signed Oak Trail, which meanders beneath the oak and sycamore that shade the west wall of Bell Canyon. The trail never strays far from Bell Creek, its streambed, or sandy washes. During drought years, it's difficult to imagine that in the 19th century, black bears used to catch spawning steelhead trout in Bell Creek. Fragrant sages perfume the trail, which is also lined with lemonade berry and prickly pear cactus.

Oak Trail reaches a junction at Post "12." You may take a short connector trail east to Bell Canyon or head north on another short trail, Star Rise, and join Bell Canyon Trail. A wide dirt road, Bell Canyon Trail travels the canyon floor.

To return to the trailhead, you'll head south on Bell Canyon Trail, which passes through open oak-dotted meadows. Red-tailed hawks roost atop spreading sycamores. The trail returns you to the parking area, within sight of the beginning of Nature Trail, where you began your walk.

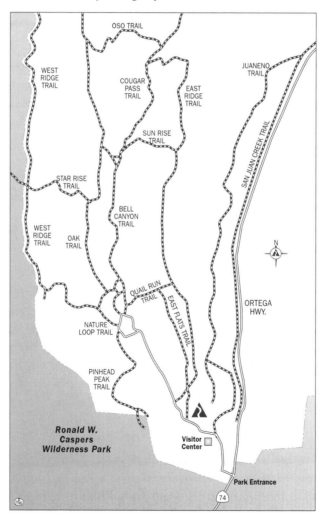

CRYSTAL COVE STATE PARK

MORO CANYON TRAIL

From Park Headquarters to the top of Moro Canyon is 7 miles round trip with 700-foot elevation gain

Extending three miles along the coast between Laguna Beach and Corona del Mar, and inland over the San Joaquin Hills, 3,000-acre Crystal Cove State Park attracts bird-watchers, beachcombers and hikers.

The backcountry of Crystal Cove State Park is part of the San Joaquin Hills, first used by Mission San Juan Capistrano for grazing land. Cattle raising continued under José Sepúlveda when the area became part of his land grant, Rancho San Joaquín, in 1837. In 1864, Sepúlveda sold the land to James Irvine and his partners and it became part of his Irvine Ranch. Grazing continued until shortly after the state purchased the property as parkland in 1979.

Former Irvine Ranch roads now form a network of hiking trails that loop through the state park. An especially nice trail travels the length of Moro Canyon, the main watershed of the park. An oak woodland, a seasonal stream and sandstone caves are some of the attractions of a walk through this canyon.

After exploring inland portions of the state park, allow some time to visit the park's coastline, highlighted by grassy bluffs, sandy beaches, tidepools and coves.

DIRECTIONS TO TRAILHEAD: Crystal Cove State Park is located off Pacific Coast Highway, about two miles south of the town of Corona del Mar or one mile north of Laguna Beach. Turn inland on the short park road, signed "El Moro Canyon." Drinking water, restrooms, interpretive displays and plenty of parking is available at the ranger station.

THE HIKE: Below the ranger station, near the park entry kiosk pick up the unsigned Moro Canyon Trail, which crosses the grassy slopes behind a school and former trailer park down into Moro Canyon. At the canyon bottom, you meet a fire road and head left, up-canyon.

The hiker may observe such native plants as black sage, prickly pear cactus, monkeyflowers, golden bush, lemonade berry and deer weed. Long before Spanish missionaries and settlers arrived in Southern California, a Native American population flourished in the coastal canyons of Orange County. The abundance of edible plants in the area, combined with the mild climate and easy access to the bounty of the sea, contributed to the success of these people, whom anthropologists believe lived off this land for more than four thousand years.

The canyon narrows, and you ignore fire roads joining Moro Canyon from the right and left. Stay in the canyon bottom and proceed through an oak woodland, which shades a trickling stream. You'll pass a shallow sandstone cave just off the trail to the right.

About 2.5 miles from the trailhead, you'll reach the unsigned junction with a fire road. If you wish to make a loop trip out of this day hike, bear left on this road, which climbs steeply west, then northeast toward the ridgetop that forms a kind of inland wall for Muddy, Moro, Emerald and other coastal canyons.

When you reach the ridgetop, unpack your lunch and enjoy the far reaching views of the San Joaquin Hills and Orange County coast, Catalina and San Clemente Islands. You'll also have a raven's-eye view of Moro Canyon and the route back to the trailhead. After catching your breath, you'll bear right (east) along the ridgetop and quickly descend back into Moro Canyon. A 0.75-mile walk brings you back to the junction where you earlier ascended out of the canyon. This time you continue straight down-canyon, retracing your steps to the trailhead.

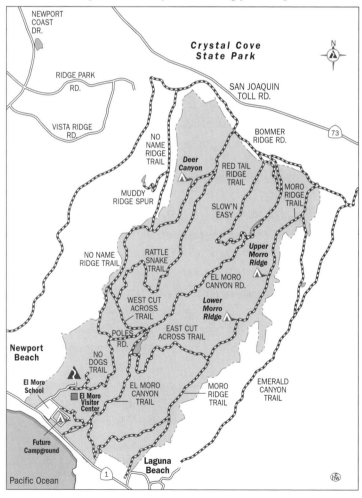

ALISO PEAK

OVERLOOK, ALISO PEAK TRAILS
From Seaview Park's Niguel Hill to Aliso Peak is 1.2 miles round trip with 300-foot elevation gain

Some hikers claim that the scenic overlook perched on a promontory in Seaview Park offers Orange County's best coastal view. Certainly the vistas from this obscure Laguna Niguel park are breathtaking, whether one is gazing down-slope to the hills back of Laguna Beach or down-coast all the way to San Clemente.

The park's overlook offers a particularly intriguing angle on Catalina Island, which appears so deceptively close on the horizon that you imagine you could hop in your kayak and in no time paddle right into Avalon Harbor. On clear nights, the isle's lights are quite distinct, too.

Along with the views, Seaview Park also boasts refreshing sea breezes and that Orange County rarity—secluded picnic tables—plus a sign-posted nature trail. With all these attractions, you'd think the park would be a more popular destination, but no, it seems to be completely off the radar of the throngs of beachgoers down at the coast, just a half-mile as the gull flies from Seaview Park.

DIRECTIONS TO TRAILHEAD: To reach Seaview Park, exit the San Diego Freeway (I-5) in Laguna Niguel on Crown Valley Parkway and head south 5 miles to Pacific Island Drive. Turn right (west) and ascend to the crest of the hill. Turn left on Talavera Street and follow it to the end of the cul de sac and the entrance to Seaview Park.

From Coast Highway (1) in Laguna Beach, you can head inland on Crown Valley Parkway to Pacific Island Drive, turn left and head up to Talavera Street and the park.

THE HIKE: A wide, gentle pathway of decomposed granite leads past interpretive panels and name-tagged plants that highlight the characteristic native flora communities in these parts—coastal sage scrub and chaparral. Most visitors are content with stopping at the overlook, watching the hawks soar over precipitous Aliso and Wood canyons, admiring the sea views, and returning the way they came.

The intrepid may continue beyond the overlook on a narrower, rougher path known as Aliso Peak Trail. You'll pass two left-branching side trails: the first, sometimes called Valido Trail, drops down to West Street in South Laguna Beach, while the second descends to Ceanothus Drive. Aliso Peak-bound hikers stay right and ascend the railroad tie-stabilized trail to another wonderful overlook and more stunning coastal views.

ALISO & WOOD CANYONS WILDERNESS PARK

ALISO CREEK, WOOD CANYON TRAILS

To Wood Canyon is 3 miles round trip; through Wood Canyon to Sycamore
Grove is 6 miles round trip; loop of Wood Canyon is 9 miles round trip

Aliso & Wood Canyons Wilderness Park, the largest park in the hills above
Laguna Beach, preserves 3,400 acres of pastoral Orange County.

Most locals and other hikers refer to the low hills that back the Orange
County coast from Corona del Mar to Dana Point as the Laguna Hills or "the
mountains behind Laguna Beach." Actually, the northerly hills are the San
Joaquin Hills—their cousins to the south are the Sheep Hills.

Here's how nature writer Joseph Smeaton Chase described an outing in the
Sheep Hills in his classic 1913 book, *California Coast Trails:* "A few miles along a
road that wound and dipped over the cliffs brought us by sundown to Aliso
Canyon. The walls of the canyon are high hills sprinkled with lichened rock,
sprinkled with brush whose prevailing gray is relieved here and there by bosses of
olive sumac. Our camp was so attractive that we remained for several days."

Aliso & Wood Canyons Wilderness Park is a great place to hike, but it does
present a minor access problem: From the parking area to the mouth of Wood
Canyon is a less-than-scintillating 1.5 mile walk alongside a road. Some hikers

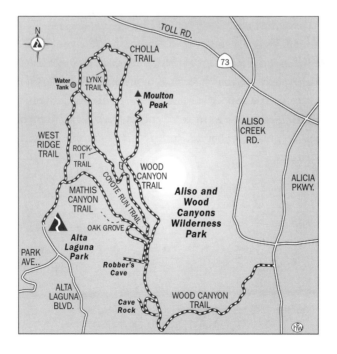

avoid this road walk by bringing their bikes—either mountain bike or standard bicycle will do—and cycling to the "true" trailhead. Cyclists can ride some of the park's trails (the wider dirt roads), then leave their bikes at conveniently placed racks and walk the narrower, hikers-only paths.

DIRECTIONS TO TRAILHEAD: From the San Diego Freeway (5) in Laguna Hills/ Mission Viejo, exit on Alicia Parkway and drive 4 miles south. Trailhead parking for Aliso & Wood Canyons Wilderness Park is located a quarter-mile south of Aliso Creek Road. Take a right into the parking lot, which is opposite Laguna Niguel Regional Park and near the Orange County Natural History Museum.

THE HIKE: From the parking area, hike along the paved road into Aliso Canyon. The road, and a parallel dirt path for hikers, heads southeast, and meanders just west of Aliso Creek.

After 1.5 miles of walking you'll arrive at the park's most significant signed junction (complete with restrooms no less). Join Wood Canyon Trail Trail (a dirt road) and begin a gentle ascent through Wood Canyon. Look left for the side trail leading to Cave Rock, where you'll find a number of caves, wind-sculpted into a substantial sandstone formation.

After rejoining Wood Canyon Trail, continue up-canyon to another left-branching side trail that leads to Dripping Cave a.k.a. Robbers Cave. The robbers who hid out here in the 19th century included cattle rustlers and highwaymen who held up stagecoaches. The "Dripping," much of the year anyway, refers to water seeping above the cave.

Wood Canyon Trail continues to meet Mathis Canyon Trail. A short distance up Wood Canyon Trail is an old sheep corral. You can turn around in this vicinity or choose to extend your hike in a couple of different ways.

If you want to leg it just a little more, head up Mathis Canyon, then north on Coyote Run Trail. Next, fork right to reconnect with Wood Canyon Trail. For a longer loop, bear left on northbound Rock-It Trail and connect with West Ridge Trail.

LAGUNA COAST WILDERNESS PARK

LAUREL CANYON, WILLOW CANYON TRAILS
Laurel-Willow canyons loop is 3.5 miles with 600-foot elevation gain; to
Bommer Ridge Overlook is 7 miles round trip

Laguna Coast Wilderness Park is the Orange County of the 19th century, a
lovely diversity of landscapes highlighted by woodlands, grasslands and scenic
ridgelines with handsome sandstone outcroppings. The 6,500-acre park also contains Orange County's only natural lakes, which provide habitat for fish as well as
for such waterfowl as geese, grebes, coots, cormorants and kingfishers.

James Irvine and his partners purchased the one-time Rancho San Joaquin in
1865 and the company grazed cattle on it for more than a century. Now, with the
Irvine Company's cooperation, substantial acreage in and around Laguna Canyon
is becoming parkland under the stewardship of Orange County Harbors, Beaches
and Parks.

That these hills and canyons don't resemble the developed Orange County of
the 21st century is a tribute to three decades of exemplary work by local conservationists, as well as state and local park agencies and municipalities.
Preservationists, with the support of then-California Senator Alan Cranston
attempted to create Orange Coast National Park in the late 1970s. In 1989, 8,000
people marched along Laguna Canyon Road to show their commitment to preserving the Laguna Hills. A year later the citizens of Laguna Beach voted over-
whelmingly to tax themselves $20 million in order to purchase land alongside
Laguna Canyon Road and far up into the hills. Lengthy negotiations among public entities and private parties, as well as increased preservation efforts spearheaded by the Laguna Canyon Foundation took place during the 1990s.

For more than a decade, access was restricted to an extent that only the most
connected local hikers were able to figure out when, where and how to hike this
park. Currently the park is open for hiking seven days a week.

Laurel Canyon is a hiking-only trail, in contrast to the park's many multi-use
trails, including Willow Canyon road, your return route on this hike. The canyon
has plenty of the laurel sumac that inspired its name, lots of old oaks, a wonderfully aromatic coastal sage community of flora, intriguing rock formations, and even
a seasonal waterfall. No wonder Laurel Canyon is one of the very best places to
take a guided nature hike.

DIRECTIONS TO TRAILHEAD: From the San Diego Freeway (405)
in Irvine, a few miles north of this freeway's junction with the Santa Ana
Freeway (5), exit on Laguna Canyon Road (133) and head south toward the coast

and Laguna Beach. Look for the main (Laurel Canyon) entrance to the park on the right (west) side of the road.

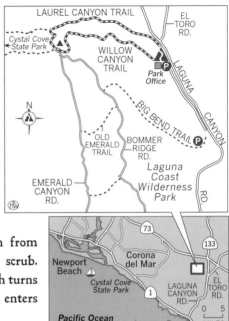

THE HIKE: Join the path leading north parallel to Laguna Canyon Road and soon pass a sandstone boulder sculpted by wind and water into a very small cave. Keep an eye out for more such caves and rock formations crowning the park's ridges.

The trail traverses an open slope that, with an end to cattle grazing, is making the environmental transition from annual grassland to coastal sage scrub. Buckwheat and sage line the path which turns away from Laguna Canyon Road and enters the quiet of Laurel Canyon.

Begin a westward ascent among live oaks and sycamores. The oaks appear to have recovered far better than the sycamores from the terrible 1993 Laguna Fire that blackened Laurel Canyon and thousands of acres around it. Certainly the vegetation in the canyon bottom regenerated quickly: what is now a brush-crowded narrow footpath up Laurel Canyon was actually a fairly wide ranch road before the fire.

The path leads by a seasonal creek (look for an ephemeral waterfall during the rainy season) and ascends to meet a dirt road. Turn left on this road and begin an ascent to a saddle on Willow Ridge and another junction. Go left again and descend Willow Canyon Road.

Most of the view on your descent east is of parkland, with the major exception of the San Joaquin Hills Toll Road which, alas, bisects Laguna Coast Wilderness Park. Your journey ends at the park office, a short walk from the trailhead and parking area.

JAMES DILLEY PRESERVE

CANYON, EDISON, TO THE LAKE TRAILS
From Laguna Canyon Road to Barbara's Lake is 3.5-mile loop with 300-foot elevation gain

Lakes are few and far between in Orange County, and for the most part are decorative contrivances created for city parks, golf courses and suburban neighborhoods.

Orange County's only natural lakes are the Laguna Lakes in Laguna Canyon. The largest of the three lakes is delightful to visit, particularly for the hiker, because it's accessible only by a trail through the engaging James Dilley Preserve.

Early maps referred to the lakes as *laguna*, Spanish for pond, while modern maps generally opt for the rather redundant Laguna Lakes. The lakes are replenished by rainfall and possibly some water from underground springs.

Barbara's Lake, largest of the lakes, honors conservation activist Barbara Stuart. Fringed by bulrush, cattail and willows, the lake offers habitat for coots, grebes and mallards.

From the preserve's high points, hikers get good views of Bubbles Lake, named for the hippopotamus named Bubbles who escaped from Lion Country Safari in the mid-1970s and took up residence in the little lake located on the west side of Laguna Canyon Road. For a time, the wayward hippo eluded capture, staying underwater by day and emerging only at night. Alas for Bubbles, she was shot with tranquilizers and died while attempting to elude her captors.

In the 1960s, James Dilley, a Laguna Beach bookseller, began promoting his vision: the creation of a band of parks and preserves surrounding Laguna Beach. Dilley's notion of a greenbelt ringing the coastal town was enthusiastically supported by local conservationists, and a broad cross-section of the community.

Thanks to "The Father of the Greenbelt," plus four decades of cooperative efforts among conservation groups, park agencies and the area's major landowner, the Irvine Company, Laguna Beach is green on three sides and Pacific blue on the fourth. All Southland communities should be so fortunate!

The preserve, owned by the city and managed by the county's parks department was established in 1978 and is the oldest portion of Laguna Coast Wilderness Park. Spearheaded by the nonprofit Laguna Canyon Foundation, conservation efforts continue in order to expand the park, preserve other hills and canyons, and open up the greenbelt to increased public use.

The preserve is something of an island on the land. It's bordered by Laguna Canyon Road on the west, El Toro Road and Leisure World on the east and the

San Joaquin Hills Trans- portation Corridor (toll road) on the south. The Laguna Lakes form the preserve's north bound- ary. James Dilley Pre- serve's "islandness" is apparent from looking at the map and even more obvious when contem-

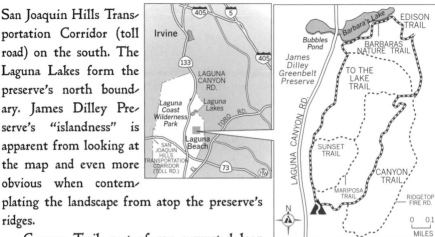

plating the landscape from atop the preserve's ridges.

Canyon Trail, part of my suggested loop around the preserve, is the first leg of a nature trail with numbered wooden mark- ers keyed to an interpretive pamphlet (sometimes available at the trailhead). The pamphlet is by no means necessary to enjoy the hike.

DIRECTIONS TO TRAILHEAD: From the San Diego Freeway (405) in Irvine, exit onto the Laguna Freeway (133), which soon becomes Laguna Canyon Road. Drive south miles to the signed entrance for James Dilley Preserve on the left (east) side of the road and park in the dirt lot. The preserve entrance is just north of San Joaquin Hills Transportation Corridor (toll road).

THE HIKE: From the parking area, take the dirt road east and soon join Canyon Trail. The path swings north up the canyon, which is lined with coastal live oak and sycamore, white sage, black sage and buckwheat.

Leaving the moist canyon bottom, the path climbs higher slopes with a change in elevation to prickly pear cactus, lemonadeberry and monkeyflower. Near a ridgeline the path forks. The left branch, sometimes called the Eagle Scout Trail, descends south toward the trailhead.

Continue up the remains of a dirt road to the top of the hill and you'll see a gravel road leading downhill west toward Laguna Canyon Road and a steep Edison fire road (Edison Trail) heading north. I prefer taking the Edison Trail for the views, which can include the San Gabriel Mountains on a clear winter day.

The more immediate view from the trail is of Orange County's largest natu- ral lake, with a surface area of about 12 acres. Cattle grazed the slopes back of the lake for more than 150 years.

Barbara's Nature Trail, another interpretive trail, leads along the lakeshore to an old pump house, and an intersection with To The Lake Trail, which heads south, parallel to Laguna Canyon Road back to the trailhead.

CHAPTER EIGHT

Chino Hills

Chino Hills State Park, located in Orange, San Bernardino and Riverside counties, preserves some much-needed "breathing room" in this fast-growing area. Considering that three million people live within sight of the Chino Hills and nine millions within a 40-mile radius, the park's trails offer surprisingly tranquil and away-from-it-all hiking. Perhaps because reaching the main trailheads requires driving on a dirt road, the park is lightly visited. The 13,000-acre park harbors an admirable biodiversity, including oak woodlands, stands of native California walnut and extensive grassland.

Stand on the summits of park high points such as San Juan Hill and you can see parts of four counties and a glorious amount of room to roam.

TELEGRAPH CANYON

HILLS-FOR-EVERYONE TRAIL
Along Ranch Road to McDermont Spring is 4 miles round trip with 400-foot gain; to Carbon Canyon Regional Park is 7.5 miles one way with 800-foot loss

Hills-for-Everyone Trail was named for the conservation group that was instrumental in establishing Chino Hills State Park. The trail follows a creek to the head of Telegraph Canyon. The creek is lined with oak, sycamore and the somewhat rare California walnut.

DIRECTIONS TO TRAILHEAD: Chino Hills State Park can be a bit tricky to find. The park is located west of Highway 71 between the Riverside Freeway (91) and the Pomona Freeway (60).

From Highway 71, exit on Soquel Canyon Parkway and travel one mile to a signed left turn at Elinvar Road, which bends sharply left. Look immediately right for a signed dirt road—Bane Canyon Road. Enter the park on this road (which returns to pavement in two miles) and follow signs to the park office and ranger station.

The road forks just before the ranger station. To the right is the ranger station and visitor center. Bear left one-half mile on the dirt road to a vehicle barrier and trailhead parking. The signed trailhead is located a short distance past the vehicle barrier on the right of the road.

THE HIKE: Hills-for-Everyone Trail descends to a small creek and follows the creek up canyon. Shading the trail—and shielding the hiker from a view of the many electrical transmission lines that cross the park—are oaks, sycamores and

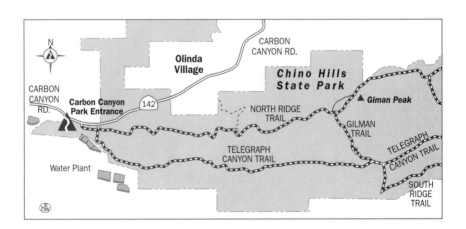

walnuts. Of particular interest is the walnut; often the 15- to 30-foot tall tree has several dark brown trunks, which gives it a brushy appearance.

The trail, which can be quite slippery and muddy after a rain, passes a small (seasonal) waterfall. The slopes above the creekbed are carpeted with lush grasses and miners lettuce.

Along the trail is found evidence of the park's ranching heritage, including lengths of barbed wire fence and old cattle troughs. For more than a century this land was used exclusively for cattle ranching.

Near its end, the trail ascends out of the creekbed to the head of Telegraph Canyon and intersects a dirt road. McDermont Spring is just down the road. Some of the livestock ponds, constructed during the area's ranching days, still exist, and hold water year-round. McDermont Spring—along with Windmill and Panorama ponds—provides water for wildlife.

To Carbon Canyon Regional Park: Telegraph Canyon Trail (a dirt road closed to public vehicular traffic) stays close to the canyon bottom and its creek. It's a gentle descent under the shade of oak and walnut trees. The walnuts are particularly numerous along the first mile of travel and the hiker not inclined to hike the length of Telegraph Canyon might consider exploring this stretch before returning to the trailhead.

The route passes an old windmill. Farther down the canyon, the walnuts thin out. A lemon grove, owned by the state park but leased to a farmer, is at a point where the dirt road intersects Carbon Canyon Road. Walk along the broad shoulder of the latter road 0.5 mile to Carbon Canyon Regional Park.

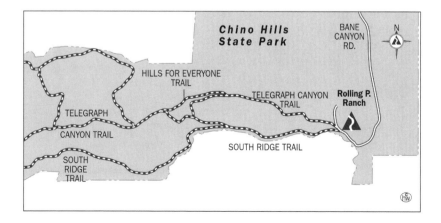

GILMAN PEAK

NORTH RIDGE AND GILMAN PEAK TRAILS
From Carbon Canyon Regional Park to Gilman Peak is 7 miles round trip with 1,200-foot elevation gain

Gilman Peak, a 1,685-foot Chino Hills promontory, is far from the top of the world but offers the hiker magnificent vistas—particularly on a clear winter's day. The San Gabriel Mountains, wearing a mantle of snow, rise to the north above the San Gabriel Valley. The Santa Ana Mountains border the southeastern vista while to the southwest the Orange County suburbanopolis spreads to the sea.

To the approaching hiker, Gilman Peak itself does not inspire great expectations. It appears as little more than just another bump on the ridgetop, a bald crown scarcely higher than neighboring peaklets. Ah, but the inspirational views from the summit more than make up for the dull appearance of the peak.

The three reasons for Gilman Peak's success at delivering views are location, location, and location. The peak is located at the far frontier of three counties: Los Angeles, Orange and San Bernardino. Parts of a fourth county—Riverside—can be viewed from the peak also.

Surrounded by all manner of residential, commercial and industrial developments, as well as four freeways, the wilder parts of the Chino Hills are indeed an island on the land. The range's "island" nature is apparent to the hiker on the trail to Gilman Peak.

DIRECTIONS TO TRAILHEAD: From the Orange Freeway (57) in Brea, exit on Lambert Road. Drive 4 miles east on Lambert (which changes to Carbon Canyon Road east of Valencia Avenue) to the entrance of Carbon Canyon Regional Park. There's a vehicle entry fee. Limited legal parking (free) also exists on the south shoulder of Carbon Canyon Road. From wherever you park, join the dirt road angling southeast just below the road.

THE HIKE: Walk up the dirt road past a citrus orchard to a state park bulletin board and a signed junction. Telegraph Canyon Trail (a dirt road) heads south, but you join North Ridge Trail (also a dirt road) on a climb past scattered California walnut.

A bit more than 2 miles from the trailhead, the path gains a sparsely vegetated ridgeline and travels across it. After dipping and rising to a couple "false" summits, you'll reach Gilman Peak. A wide summit trail takes you to the top.

SAN JUAN HILL

SOUTH RIDGE TRAIL
To the top of San Juan Hill is 6 miles round trip with 1,200-foot elevation gain

When the land for Chino Hills State Park was purchased in the mid 1980s, there was a lot of grumbling about the high cost—from the public, from politicians, and even from some conservationists who figured purchasing a redwood grove or two was a better use of hard-to-come-by funds.

Nowadays the large park seems like a bargain. And nowhere is this more apparent than on the trail to the park's high point, San Juan Hill.

The first glimpse of the park's great value is obvious when hiking the half mile of South Ridge Trail and looking at what you're leaving behind: all manner of brand-new suburbia pushing right up to the park's southern boundary. Without a park, every buildable slope would likely be smothered in subdivisions.

Farther up the trail, most traces of civilization vanish, and the hiker enters a wonderfully pastoral landscape of rolling grassland and drifts of oak. It would be difficult to place a dollar value on this wonderful experience.

Deer gambol through the high grasses, hawks circle overhead and a refreshing breeze (often) keeps the temperature down. Atop San Juan's slopes, hikers are often joined by kite-flyers, who take advantage of the robust gusts.

While that famed San Juan Hill in Cuba was a difficult charge for Theodore Roosevelt and his Rough Riders to make in an 1898 battle of the Spanish-

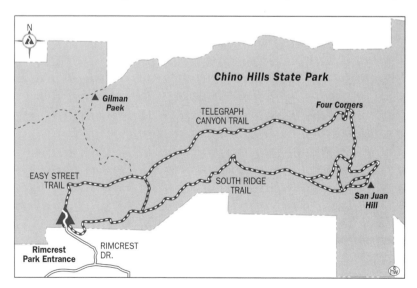

American War, you should have a rather mellow time conquering the San Juan Hill perched on the border of Orange and San Bernardino counties. The trail to 1,781-foot San Juan Hill is a well-graded fire road.

DIRECTIONS TO TRAILHEAD: From the Orange Freeway (57) in Brea, exit on Imperial Highway (90) and head southeast 4.5 miles to Yorba Linda Boulevard. Turn left (east) and drive 1.3 miles to Fairmont Boulevard. Turn left (east) and drive 1.5 miles to Rim Crest Drive. Turn left and proceed 0.3 mile to the signed trailhead on the right. Park alongside Rim Crest Drive. Heed the curbside parking signs because public parking is permitted only on some lengths of Rim Crest Drive; some parking is for residents (by permit) only.

THE HIKE: Walk 40 yards up the fire lane to the park information bulletin board and the signed beginning of South Ridge Trail. Begin your journey eastward with an ascent that soon removes you from virtually all of the sights and sounds of civilization.

The moderate climb leads over hills covered with wild oats, rye, mustard and wild radish. Trees are few and far between atop these hills, which means both little shade and unobstructed views of the surrounding countryside. Only the high-voltage powerlines bisecting the hills detract from the near-pastoral landscape.

Nearly three miles out, you'll reach a junction with the signed path to San Juan Hill. Walk 50 yards up a fire road toward a powerline tower, then join the narrow, unsigned footpath on the right leading 0.1 mile to the summit of San Juan Hill.

Crowning the hilltop is a concrete, hexagon-shaped column that reads: San Juan 1896. Puzzle over this number as you enjoy the billowing grass and the usually breezy summit, as well as commanding vistas of the Chino Hills.

CHAPTER NINE

Santa Ana Mountains

Extending the entire length of Orange County's eastern perimeter, the Santa Anas roughly parallel the coast, which has a cooling influence on what is often a very hot range of mountains. Except for the dog days of summer, most days offer pleasant hiking. While some local hikers know and appreciate the range's trails, visitation statistics indicate that in comparison to other Southland ranges, the Santa Ana Mountains may be one of the more overlooked and under-used recreation areas in Southern California.

If that's the case, get hiking on those great trails that explore the 136,500 acres of mountain range included in the Cleveland National Forest's Trabuco District.

SILVERADO CANYON

SILVERADO TRAIL
From Silverado Canyon Road to Bedford Peak is 7 miles round trip with 2,100-foot elevation gain

When experienced hikers refer to a trek as "a conditioning hike" you know you're in for a workout. The path to Bedford Peak most definitely fits into this category.

From the west (most populated) side of the Santa Ana mountains, Silverado Trail is the shortest and quickest way to Main Divide, the ridgecrest of the range. Of course, short and quick add up to steep as well, which is why this trail offers an aerobic workout.

Reward for the ascent to 3,800-foot high Bedford Peak is a great clear-day panorama of the Santa Ana, San Gabriel and San Bernardino ranges, along with the OC suburbanopolis and the Pacific Ocean.

The name Silverado comes from the high hopes of prospectors who swarmed into the canyon during the late 1870s. A few years later, the silver ore played out, and the boom went bust. These days the canyon is a surprisingly rural enclave of homes, general store and fire station.

On old maps, and on most new ones as well, Silverado Trail is labeled as Silverado Motorway. Originally constructed for fire patrol and control purposes, the fire road deteriorated over the years and de-evolved (evolved in the opinion of we hikers) into a footpath. Hikers might find it difficult to believe this now-vanished motorway was ever passable by vehicles.

DIRECTIONS TO TRAILHEAD: From the Newport Freeway (55) in Orange, exit on Chapman Avenue and drive east. About 6 miles out, Chapman becomes Santiago Canyon Road and, some 11 miles from the freeway, you'll intersect Silverado Canyon Road. Bear left and continue 5.5 miles to the parking area.

THE HIKE: Walk up the wide, shaded Maple Springs Road (a continuation of Santiago Canyon Road) for 0.1 mile. Just after crossing a seasonal creek, look and turn left (west) on unsigned Silverado Trail. At first it appears the path intends to return you to the trailhead, but it soon turns north and begins a steep, zigzagging ascent of the north wall of the canyon.

The trail is flanked by sage and exposed outcroppings of stratified sedimentary rock known as the Bedford Canyon Formation. Higher and higher you climb on switchbacks that offer ever-grander vistas of Silverado Canyon, until the entire canyon comes into view.

A bit more than 2 miles out, you'll reach a flat spot on the ridge between

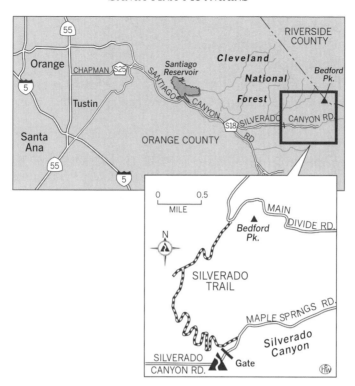

Silverado and Ladd canyons and a so-so view of the Santa Anas. If you feel sufficiently "conditioned", this is a good turnaround point.

Otherwise, continue along the ridgeline on a steep, but quite inspiring mile of trail to meet Main Divide Road. Turn right and walk 0.3 mile up the road to Bedford Peak.

Bedford is really more of a big bump in the road than a proper peak, but it does provide a modest platform from which to survey peaks near and far, as well as the advancing metropolis on both sides of the range.

MODJESKA CANYON

HARDING TRAIL
From Tucker Wildlife Sanctuary to Goat Shed Overlook is 3 miles round trip with 600-foot elevation gain; to Laurel Spring is 10 miles round trip with 2,300-foot gain

The story of Modjeska Peak and Modjeska Canyon in Orange County began in Warsaw, Poland in the 1870s. Count Karol Bozenta Chlapowski edited a fiercely nationalistic patriotic journal that protested the cultural and political imperialism of Czarist Russia and Germany. He and his wife, acclaimed actress Helena Modrzejewski, and other Polish writers and artists, yearned for the freedom of America and the climate of Southern California.

Helena mastered English, shortened her name to Modjeska, and under the Count's management, began her tremendously popular stage career. Madame Modjeska and the Count bought a ranch in Santiago Canyon and hired professionals to run it. Madame called her ranch "Arden" after the enchanted forest in Shakespeare's *As You Like It.* New York architect Stanford White was commissioned to design a dream home, which looked out over a little lake, across which glided swans.

For two decades the Chlapowski/Modjeska household was a center of artistic and literary life in Southern California. Today, a state historical marker on Modjeska Canyon Road commemorates their home.

The natural history of Modjeska Canyon is as intriguing as its human history. In 1939, Dorothy May Tucker, a canyon resident, willed her land to the Audubon Society and the Tucker Wildlife Sanctuary was created. California State University Fullerton took over its operation in 1969.

The sanctuary is best known for its hummingbirds, which may be viewed from an observation porch. Because the sanctuary includes a mixture of coastal

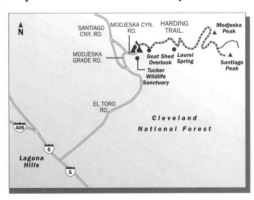

scrub, chaparral and oak woodland environments, it attracts a diversity of birdlife. Nearly 200 species have been spotted in the sanctuary.

Two short nature trails wind through the preserve. One trail interprets chaparral flora, and the other leads along the banks of Santiago Creek.

Tucker Wildlife Sanctuary is the trailhead for Harding Trail, a dirt road that ascends the western slopes of the Santa Ana Mountains. The trail, formerly known as Harding Truck Trail, is used by Cleveland National Forest fire crews and their trucks, but is closed to all other vehicles.

Old Saddleback, comprised of 5,687-foot Santiago Peak and 5,496-foot Modjeska Peak, forms the eastern boundary and highest portion of Orange County. You can reach the peaks via Harding Trail, but this would mean a 20-mile hike. A more reasonable destination, halfway up the mountain, is Laurel Spring, a tranquil rest stop tucked under the boughs of giant bay laurel. En route to the spring, you'll get great views of Madame Modjeska's peak and canyon, as well as much of rural Orange County.

DIRECTIONS TO TRAILHEAD: From the San Diego Freeway (5) in El Toro, exit on El Toro Road (S-18). Drive inland on the road, which after about 7 miles bends north and continues as Santiago Canyon Road. Eight and a half miles from the freeway, veer right onto Modjeska Grade Road, travel a bit more than a mile, then turn right and follow Modjeska Canyon Road a mile to its end at Tucker Wildlife Sanctuary. Park in the gravel lot by a tiny observatory. The trail begins at a locked gate on the north side of the road.

THE HIKE: Harding Trail immediately begins a no-nonsense ascent above Modjeska Canyon which, in all but its lower reaches, is officially known as Harding Canyon. To the northwest is Flores Peak, named for outlaw Juan Flores.

As you ascend, notice the lumpy, pudding-like clumps of conglomerate rock revealed by the road cuts. After a mile, the trail descends a short distance (the only elevation loss on the way to Laurel Spring), rounds the head of a canyon, and ascends to the remains of a funny-looking wood structure that locals call the Goat Shed. Enjoy the view of Modjeska Canyon. If you're feeling a bit leg weary, this is a good turnaround point.

Chaparral-lined Harding Trail continues climbing east along a sharp ridgeline. To your left, far below, is deep and precipitous Harding Canyon, and to your right— Santiago Canyon. Four and a half miles from the trailhead, Harding Trail offers clear-day views of the southern end of the Los Angeles Basin, the San Joaquin Hills and the central Orange County coastal plain, the Pacific and Catalina Island. The view serves notice that you're nearing Laurel Spring. A narrow trail descends 50 yards from the right side of the road to the spring. The spring (unsafe drinking water), waters an oasis of toyon, ferns and wonderfully aromatic bay laurel.

BEAR CANYON

BEAR CANYON, BEAR RIDGE, SITTON PEAK TRAILS
From Ortega Highway to Pigeon Springs is 5.5 miles round trip with 700-foot elevation gain; return via Bear Ridge Trail is a 6.5-mile loop; to Sitton Peak is 9.5 miles round trip with 1,300-foot gain

Bear Canyon Trail offers a pleasant introduction to the Santa Ana Mountains. The trail climbs through gentle brush and meadow country, visits Pigeon Springs, and arrives at Four Corners, the intersection of several major hiking trails through the southern Santa Anas.

One of these trails takes you to Sitton Peak for splendid, far-reaching views. Along the trail, refreshing Pigeon Springs welcomes hot and dusty hikers to a handsome glen. Bear Ridge Trail offers an alternate return route and a way to make a loop trip out of this jaunt around Bear Canyon.

DIRECTIONS TO TRAILHEAD: Take the Ortega Highway (California 74) turnoff from the San Diego Freeway (Interstate 5) at San Juan Capistrano. Drive east 20 miles to the paved parking area across from the Ortega Country Cottage Candy Store. Bear Canyon Trail starts just west of the store on Ortega Highway.

THE HIKE: From the signed trailhead, the broad, well-graded trail climbs slowly up brushy hillsides. The trail crosses a seasonal creek, which runs through a tiny oak woodland.

A half mile from the trailhead, the path enters San Mateo Canyon Wilderness and after a mile, a fork appears on the left (Morgan Trail). Bear

Check your bearings in Bear Canyon.

Canyon Trail climbs on, skirts the periphery of a meadow and crests a chaparral-covered slope.

Two miles of travel from the trailhead brings you to a signed intersection with Bear Ridge Trail (return route for this hike). Stick with Bear Canyon Trail, formerly known as the Verdugo Truck Trail, and head right (south) 0.75 to Pigeon Springs. The springs, including a horse trough, are located among oaks on the left of the trail.

From the springs, continue another half mile south, and past a gate to Four Corners and a meeting of five trails (fire roads), among them, Tenaja Trail, that descends to San Mateo Creek.

To proceed to Sitton Peak, bear right on Sitton Peak Trail, which begins to climb and contour around the peak. In a mile you'll be at the high point of Sitton Peak Trail, a saddle perched over San Juan Canyon. From this saddle, wend your way on a use trail past rocky outcroppings to the summit. On a clear day, there are superb views of the twin peaks of Old Saddleback (Mt. Modjeska and Mt. Santiago), Mt. San Gorgonio and Mt. San Jacinto, Catalina and the wide Pacific.

Meanwhile, back at Four Corners . . . head northeast on Bear Ridge Trail for an alternate return to the trailhead. The narrow pathway follows a ridge north, overlooking Bear Canyon. After bending west, the trail meets up again with Bear Canyon Trail.

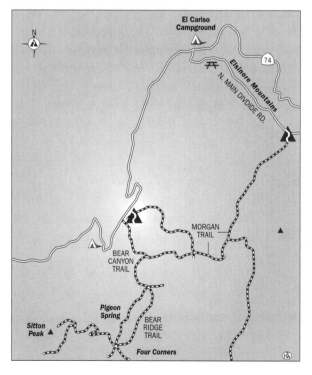

HOLY JIM WATERFALL

HOLY JIM TRAIL
From Holy Jim Creek to Falls is 2.5 miles round trip with 200-foot elevation gain

Holy Jim Trail, creek, waterfall and canyon take their names from "Cussin'" Jim Smith, an early Santa Ana Mountain settler who, when displeased, unleashed a string of unholy epithets. Early 20th-century mapmakers were unwilling to geographically honor such a blasphemer, so they changed his name to "Holy."

The trail is one of the most popular in the Santa Anas, though many hikers go only as far as the falls. Something of a Santa Ana Mountains sampler, the trail offers the hiker a creek, a lush canyon, a waterfall, a hike into history and, with the optional trek to Santiago Peak, a chance to conquer OC's highest summit.

Smith was a beekeeper by profession (perhaps explaining his proclivity toward profanity). His operation and those of neighboring beekeepers were targets of a grizzly bear dubbed "Honey Thief." Believed to be the last grizzly in the Santa Ana Mountains, the bear was shot near the mouth of Trabuco Canyon in 1907.

Evidence of Smith's life in the canyon remain behind in the form of a stone wall from his cabin, which burned in a severe 1908 fire. Fig trees gone wild are descendants from those that once grew in Smith's orchard.

Strictly by the tape measure, Holy Jim Falls at 20 feet high does not wow the hiker with its stature. Ah, but the "wow factor" is the waterfall's setting—a lovely grotto with ferns springing from the rock walls around it.

Some hikers think getting to the trailhead is half the fun. It's definitely a bumpy ride along Trabuco Canyon Road to the trailhead. Passenger cars with good ground clearance can make it over the wash-boarded, pot-holed road. The dirt road is no route for low-slung cars, though the drivers of such vehicles are usually not discouraged from coaxing them to the trailhead.

You'll spot a number of cabins, privately owned but on land leased from the Forest Service, in the Holy Jim-Trabuco Canyon area. During the 1930s, it was Forest Service policy to encourage city dwellers to experience the great outdoors and overnight in a vacation cabin.

DIRECTIONS TO TRAILHEAD: From the San Diego Freeway (5) in Lake Forest, exit on El Toro Road and drive east 7 miles. Turn right on Live Oak Canyon Road and proceed 4.2 miles (a mile past O'Neill Regional Park) to Trabuco Creek Road. Make a left and follow this rough dirt road 4.6 miles to the trailhead parking area just past the volunteer fire station.

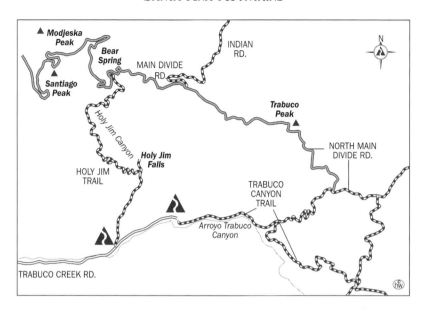

THE HIKE: From the trailhead parking lot, hike up the canyon road a half mile to the beginning of the trail. Head up the vine- and oak-filled canyon. The trail stays near Holy Jim Creek, crossing and re-crossing the bubbling waters several times.

You'll spot stone check dams, built in the 1950s by the California Department of Fish and Game in order to create deep pools for fish. A clearing allows a glimpse at Santiago Peak and, while tramping creekside, look for aptly named Picnic Rock.

The trail crosses the creek a final time and comes to a fork. Holy Jim Trail embarks on a climb up Holy Jim Canyon on the way to Santiago Peak, but you take the right fork and head up-creek. A quarter-mile of boulder-hopping and creek-crossing brings you face to face with Holy Jim Falls.

HOLY JIM CANYON & SANTIAGO PEAK

HOLY JIM TRAIL

From Trabuco Creek Road to Main Divide Road is 10 miles round trip with 2,200-foot gain; to Santiago Peak is 15 miles round trip with 4,000-foot gain

Looking up at Santiago Peak from various points near the trailhead has a way of prompting hikers to examine their plans: Do we really want to climb way up there?

Well, yes you do. Admit it, Orange County's 5,687-foot landmark peak calls to you. Although I was referring to a kind of spiritual beckoning to the hiker, but now that we're discussing calling, I should mention that Santiago Peak is topped with transmitting stations and thickets of antennae, so crucial these days to microwave relays and cell phone signals.

The northern Santa Anas were once known as Sierra de Santiago for this dominant peak. Santiago is the higher of the two neighboring summits (Modjeska Peak is the other) comprising Old Saddleback. You can get a 360-degree view from the top of Santiago Peak, but not from any one place, crowded as it is by one of the very densest clusters of telecommunications found on any peak in California. The view includes five counties worth of urban-suburban sprawl, as well as east to Mount San Jacinto and Mount San Gorgonio, south to Mount Palomar, and Catalina Island and San Clemente Island way out in the Pacific Ocean.

Trails and fire roads approach Orange County's highest peak from all directions, but Holy Jim Trail is the most scenic route to the summit of Santiago. Don't underestimate the challenge of this hike: It's pretty good trail, but the gain is substantial.

DIRECTIONS TO TRAILHEAD: See account of Holy Jim Falls Trail.

THE HIKE: After the last creek crossing, Holy Jim Tail begins a stiff climb up the west side of the canyon. The path presents some hearty switchbacks and begins a lengthy contour along the canyon wall.

About 3.5 miles into the hike, the trail gets less brushy, and there is some flora you can look up to: oaks, sycamores and an occasional big-cone Douglas fir. At the 4.5 mile-mark, the trail meets Main Divide Road by Bear Spring, a tank and water trough built by the Forest Service. The spring was named long ago for the grizzly bears sighted in the high country.

Hit the road for another three miles of hiking on the Main Divide (gaining 1,800 feet) to Santiago Peak. Enjoy the grand vista of most of the Southland's mountain ranges including the Palomars, the San Bernardinos, the San Gabriels and Santa Monicas.

LOS PIÑOS PEAK

NORTH MAIN DIVIDE, LOS PIÑOS TRAILS
From Main Divide Road to Los Piños Peak is 4.5 miles round trip with 900-foot elevation gain.

Trail Trivia Question: Name the four highest peaks in Orange County.

1. Santiago Peak (5,687 feet
2. Modjeska Peak (5,496 feet)
3. Trabuco Peak (4,604 feet)
4. Los Piños Peak (4,510 feet)

Experienced hikers—and others with more than a passing interest in the county's geography—may have guessed numbers one and two—the peaks comprising the landmark Old Saddleback. Orange County's number 3 and number 4 peaks are much more obscure.

Los Piños Peak, located about three miles as the hawk flies from the southeast corner of Orange County where it meets both San Diego and Riverside counties, offers terrific clear-day vistas and is well worth the moderate hike. From the summit, the hiker looks down to Lake Elsinore and up at snow-capped Mt. Baldy and the high peaks of the San Gabriel Mountains, as well as over to the San Bernardino Mountains and San Jacinto Mountains. Gaze west over miles of hills and valleys to the great blue Pacific.

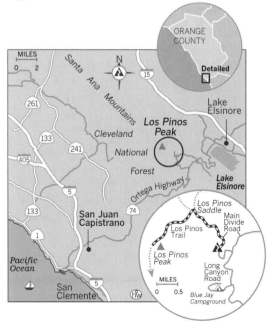

The wary trekker might suspect that such a view would come at enormous cost but in the case of Los Piños Peak, only a modest effort is required in order to earn this rewarding panorama.

Another positive aspect of this hike is that the trailhead is accesssible by paved roads. (Veteran travelers of the range's rough dirt roads can tell you what a pain in the axle some of them can be!) The trail itself presents a moderate (but not mountain goat-like) climb.

A great time to scale Los Piños is in the springtime when lupine, bush poppy and ceanothus splash color on the slopes of the mountain. Crisp, clear autumn days are good ones to head for the peak, too. Winter storms sometimes dust the crest of Los Piños with a bit of snow. Stay away from this summit and others in the Santa Anas in summer. It's way too hot for hiking.

DIRECTIONS TO TRAILHEAD: From Interstate 5 in San Juan Capistrano, exit on Highway 74 and follow it 22 miles northeast to Long Canyon Road. Turn left (northwest) and follow this paved road 2.5 miles to Blue Jay Campground, then another mile to a pullout on your left. The gated road is signed "North Main." Park in the pullout.

Another way to go: From Interstate 15 in Lake Elsinore, exit on Highway 74 and drive 11 miles southwest to Long Canyon Road, then follow the above directions.

From Highway 74 you can also turn west on Main Divide Road (signed "To Blue Jay Campground") and follow this paved road 4 miles to the trailhead.

THE HIKE: From the gate, follow the wide dirt road, which soon gains elevation and good views. A mile out, look for a particularly good vista of Lake Elsinore and out to high mountain peaks to the north and east.

About 1.25 mile from the start, the road brings you to Los Piños Saddle, where you'll spot guardrails and a convergence of trails. Leave Main Divide Road, which goes right, and step onto signed Trabuco Trail. Almost immediately look left and fork left onto signed Los Piños Trail. The path soon gains the top of the ridge and you quickly learn why Los Piños Trail is often called Los Piños Ridge Trail.

The steep path gains a high point that is only 20 feet lower in elevation than your goal, then dips, climbs again, dips some more, and finally climbs steeply to the top of Los Piños Peak. Savor the great views and retrace your steps back to the trailhead.

TENAJA FALLS

TENAJA FALLS TRAIL
1.5 miles round trip with 300-foot elevation gain.

When the Southland is blessed with a rainy, rainy season, Tenaja Falls spills over granite ramparts with great vigor. With five tiers and a drop of some 150 feet, it's a large waterfall, particularly in comparison to other falls in the Santa Ana Mountains.

Tenaja's size is all the more a delightful surprise considering its locale: a rather dry section of the Cleveland National Forest near the boundary of Orange and Riverside counties. Some hikers claim Tenaja Falls is the most intriguing natural highlight of the national forest, and even in that crown jewel of the mountains—the San Mateo Canyon Wilderness.

For Tenaja Falls-bound hikers, there's good news and bad news. Good news: the trail is a wide dirt road, easy enough for the whole family. Bad news: the drive to the trailhead is circuitous to say the least.

For nature photographers, there's one more minor bit of bad news: No viewpoint allows an angle of the whole of Tenaja Falls, that is to say, all five cascades at once.

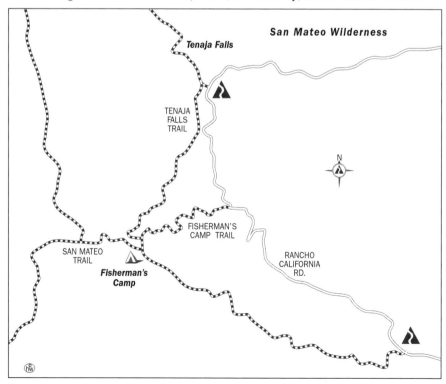

Two tiers at a time is the usual view from the trail.

DIRECTIONS TO TRAILHEAD: From I-15 (Temecula Valley Freeway) in Murietta, exit on Clinton Keith Road and drive 5 miles south into Santa Rosa Plateau Ecological Reserve. After a sharp right bend, continue on what is now Tenaja Road for 2 more miles and turn right again to stick with Tenaja Road. Proceed another 4.3 miles to Cleveland Forest Road, turn right and follow this narrow, one-lane pave road to the signed trailhead and parking area on the left.

THE HIKE: Meander over to the fence that bars motorized entry to the San Mateo Canyon Wilderness. Cross the creek on the concrete vehicle ford. If the creek is high, you'll have to wade carefully across, though skilled rock-hoppers can sometimes cross without getting their boots wet. Another creek-crossing option is to walk along the creek until you find a narrower place to cross.

The trail/road ascends northward over brush-clad slopes and before long serves up distant vistas of Tenaja Falls. Just keep walking toward the falls.

The trail leads right to Tenaja's top tier. Exploration of the lower cascades is tricky, and for experienced rock-climbers only. Those granite boulders are darn slippery.

If you're bound and determined to reach the lower falls, a somewhat safer and saner way to go is retrace your steps back down the trail, then bushwhack through the brush to the banks of the creek.

SAN MATEO CANYON WILDERNESS

FISHERMAN'S CAMP, SAN MATEO CANYON TRAILS
From Tenaja Road to Fisherman's Camp is 3 miles round trip with 300-foot loss; loop via Tenaja Road is 5 miles round trip with 400-foot elevation gain; to Lunch Rock is 8 miles round trip with 400-foot loss

Two-hundred-year-old oaks, tangles of ferns, nettles and wild grape, and the quiet pools of San Mateo Creek make the bottom of San Mateo Canyon a wild and delightful place. This section of the Santa Ana Mountains is steep canyon country, sculpted by seasonal, but vigorous streams. San Mateo Creek, a cascading waterway in winter, slows to a gurgle in summer and flows above ground only sporadically in the fall.

San Mateo Canyon Wilderness, set aside by Congress in 1984, protects 40,000 acres of the Cleveland National Forest, including the headwaters and watershed of San Mateo Creek. During the 1930s, anglers were attracted by superb fishing for steelhead and trout. San Mateo Canyon Trail was a favorite route to the fishing holes. Steelhead ran these waters then; current environmental efforts are being made to coax them back.

San Mateo Canyon takes its name from one of the padres' favorite evangelists and holy men. It's the crown jewel of the Santa Ana Mountains, a relatively untouched wilderness of oaks, potreros and cattail-lined ponds. It's a haven for turtles and rabbits. Spring brings prolific wildflower displays. The canyon drops from 3,500 feet to the coastal plain at Camp Pendleton.

This day hike plunges through the southern part of San Mateo Canyon, easily the wildest place in the Santa Ana Mountains. The San Mateo Canyon Trail and other riding and hiking trails in the wilderness have been in use for more than a century. Volunteers work on the trail, but it's often in rough shape. Creek crossings are sometimes difficult to spot.

You can travel almost as far down the canyon as you like in one day. It's nine miles from Fisherman's Camp to the Marine base, with a hundred ideal picnic spots along the way.

DIRECTIONS TO TRAILHEAD: From I-15 (Temecula Valley Freeway) in Murietta, exit on Clinton Keith Road and drive 5 miles south into Santa Rosa Plateau Ecological Reserve. After a sharp right bend, continue on what is now Tenaja Road for 2 more miles and turn right again to stick with Tenaja Road. Proceed another 4.3 miles to Cleveland Forest Road, turn right and follow this narrow, one-lane paved road for a mile to the signed Tenaja Trailhead. Proceed another 2.5 miles to the small parking area on the left side of the road.

THE HIKE: Walk down an old fire road, now a footpath, often lined with wildflowers in spring. About 1.5 miles of travel brings you to Fisherman's Camp, once a drive-in campground and now an oak-and sycamore-shaded trail camp.

From the camp, the path angles north toward San Mateo Canyon and a junction with San Mateo Canyon Trail on the west side of the creek.

Those hikers heading down San Mateo Canyon will follow the trail that climbs among ceanothus to a ridge that offer a view of the canyon. After 0.5 mile, the path switchbacks down to San Mateo Creek and follows it along the heavily vegetated canyon bottom.

Along the creek, the trail may be indistinct; simply continue down-creek. About a mile after reaching the creek, you'll come to a small potrero dotted with oaks and sycamore. Here Bluewater Creek flows into San Mateo Creek and the Bluewater Trail leads off three miles to the Clark Trail and Oak Flat. Picnic under the oaks near the trail junction and return, or continue down the canyon.

Resume your down-creek passage on the San Mateo Canyon Trail, which follows the right side of the canyon, now and then dropping to wide sandy beaches along bends in the creek. The boulders get bigger, the swimming holes and sunning spots nicer. One flat rock, popular with hikers, has been nicknamed "Lunch Rock." A cluster of massive boulders form pools and cascades in the creek. It's a nice place to linger.

San Mateo Canyon Wilderness offers plenty of solitude.

CHAPTER TEN

Riverside County Parks & Preserves

Crossing Riverside County is a little like crossing the continent: you journey from suburbia to desert spas, from rich agricultural lands to pine forest, from snow-capped mountains to mega-suburbs and exurbs. I have a number of favorite county hikes, beginning with the ascent of Mt. Rubidoux for a superb 360-degree panorama of the county. Ancient and rare Engelmann oaks, as well as vernal pools and thousands of acres of rolling grassland are preserved in Santa Rosa Plateau Ecological Reserve.

BOX SPRINGS MOUNTAIN

SKYLINE TRAIL
4 to 6-mile loop with 500-foot elevation gain

Far too steep for suburban housing developments, the Box Springs Mountains in Riverside County remain a place to get away from it all. "It" in this instance is the hustle and bustle of the Inland Empire which surrounds this little-known mountain range.

Little-known the mountains may be, but remote they are not. Four freeways—the San Bernardino, Riverside, Pomona and Escondido—surround the Box Springs Mountains. Their location might remind football fans of a quarterback barking signals: "10-91-60-215-Hike!"

The peaks of the range rise sharply from the floor of the Moreno Valley to 3,000 feet and offer commanding clear-day views of the city of Riverside, the San Bernardino and San Jacinto Mountains, as well as a great portion of the Inland Empire.

The mountain's namesake peak, as well as 2,389 acres of native Southern California coastal sage terrain is preserved in Box Springs Mountain Park under the jurisdiction of Riverside County. The park is a natural island amidst one of the fastest growing urban and suburban areas in California.

Vegetation includes members of the coastal sage scrub community: chamise, lemonade berry, brittlebush, white sage, black sage and buckwheat. More than 30 types of wildflowers brighten the park's slopes in the spring.

Wildlife—coyotes, jackrabbits, skunks and kangaroo rats—is attracted by the tiny springs that trickle from the mountain. Wildlife biologists call Box Springs Mountain a "habitat island" because it provides a home for animals while being surrounded by development.

The mountains, along with "The Badlands" to the east of the range, were shaped in part by the San Jacinto Fault, a major branch of the San Andreas system. Some geologists believe that the granites of Box Springs were once attached to the granites of the San Jacinto Mountains but were moved to their present location, some 20 miles, by lateral displacement along the fault.

Perhaps the most eccentric resident of Box Springs Mountain was Helene Troy Arlington, who moved to the mountain in 1945. The self-styled hermit secluded herself in a mountain retreat she called Noli Me Tangere, a Latin phrase meaning "Do Not Touch Me."

Arlington was devoted to dogs, particularly Dalmatians, and kept many of them in her home. She wrote canine poems and magazine articles under the pen name "Dear Dog Lady." On a plot of land next to her home she established "Arlington Cemetery," a final resting place for her four-legged friends.

Dogs, in fact, were her only friends. She sold her land to the Riverside County Parks Department in 1974 and moved to Arlington, Virginia to be near the grave of her long-dead husband Masefield. She wrote the parks department: "There was no reason to remain there any longer, as I still do not have one friend in California."

Park trails include 3-mile long Pigeon Pass Trail, which offers great views, and 1.5 mile long Ridge Trail which travels over Box Spring Mountain. (Avoid Two Trees Trail, which climbs from Two Trees Road in Riverside to meet Box Springs Mountain Road inside the park. Trailhead access is poor, as is the trail itself.)

The park's premiere path is Skyline Trail, which loops around Box Springs Mountain. If Riverside can be said to have a skyline, this is it; not tall office buildings but skyscraping granite and a top-of-the-world view.

DIRECTIONS TO TRAILHEAD: From the Pomona Freeway (60) in Moreno Valley, exit on Pigeon Pass Road. Proceed some 4.5 miles north, then a short distance west. Pigeon Pass Road turns north again, but you continue west, joining a dirt road and following the signs into Box Springs Mountain Park. Signed Skyline Trail is on your right.

THE HIKE: From Box Springs Mountain Road, Skyline Trail heads west, soon serving up views of the city of Riverside. Next the trail contours north, passing rock outcroppings that are geologically and aesthetically similar to those found atop Mt. Rubidoux, Riverside landmark and site of a long-popular Easter service.

The path comes to an unsigned junction. Skyline Trail angles east and begins contouring around a hill back to the trailhead. Hardier hikers will join an extension of the trail known as "Second Loop" and make an even larger circle back to the trailhead.

Commanding views of the wild side of the Inland Empire.

MT. RUBIDOUX

MT. RUBIDOUX TRAIL
3 mile loop with 500-foot elevation gain

The isolated, 1,337-foot high granite hill towering above the Riverside's western edge has long been a landmark to travelers and residents alike, ever since the 1880s when Riverside emerged as the quintessential Southern California citrus town. The mountain was named for one of its 19th-century owners, wealthy ranchero Louis Robidoux.

Frank Miller, owner of the lavish pride-of-Riverside, Mission Inn, purchased the mountain in 1906 with the intention of using the mountain as an attraction to sell residential lots at its base. Mt. Rubidoux was landscaped and a road constructed to the summit, where a cross was planted. Some historians believe America's first Easter sunrise service took place atop Rubidoux in 1909 and inspired similar observances around the continent.

Credit the developers for going all out on the road; they hired the engineer who designed Yellowstone National Park's road system. While the developers originally viewed Rubidoux strictly as a way to boost lot sales, their vision (particularly Miller's) soon expanded dramatically.

The road to Rubidoux was designed to be more than a mere recreational walk or drive; it was a pilgrimage to a cross and to monuments of famous men of the time. This "trail of shrines" ascended to a long white cross honoring missionary Father Junípero Serra credited, by early developers anyway, for "the beginning of civilization in California." Thus today's pilgrim views an assortment of plaques, monuments and memorials on Rubidoux that is eclectic and eccentric.

Rubidoux's most significant sights-to-see are the Peace Tower and Friendship Bridge. Frank Miller was a lifelong advocate for world peace and his friends constructed the distinct tower to honor him in 1925.

For many, many years, Mt. Rubidoux was a drive, not a hike. Arrows painted on rocks indicated an "up" route and "down" route for autos. The mountain has been closed to vehicles since 1992.

Autumn sunsets, when nearby mountains glow red, purple and blue, are particularly memorable. Winter brings vistas of snow-capped summits.

Locals access the mountain from several trailheads, but the best route for first-time Rubidoux ramblers is by way of the Ninth Street gate, an inspired beginning for what can be an inspiring jaunt.

DIRECTIONS TO TRAILHEAD: From the Pomona Freeway (60) in Riverside, exit on Market Street and proceed east into downtown. Turn west

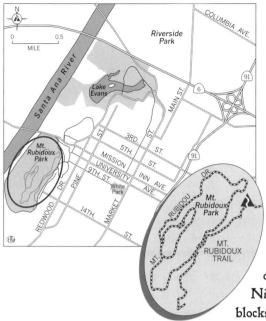

(right) on Mission Inn Avenue and drive 7 blocks to Redwood Drive. Turn left and head 2 blocks to Ninth Street, turn right and continue 2 more blocks to the distinct trailhead (gated Mt. Rubidoux Drive) on the left. Park safely and courteously on adjacent residential streets.

From the Riverside Freeway (91) in Riverside, exit on University Avenue and head west through downtown to Redwood Drive. Turn left, travel one block, then turn right on Ninth Street. Proceed two more blocks to this hike's start on the left.

THE HIKE: Pass through the entry gate and walk along and landscaped lane past pepper trees, eucalyptus and huge beavertail cactus. After 0.3 mile of south-bound travel, the road makes a very tight hairpin turn north and nearly—but not quite—intersects the downward leg of Mt. Rubidoux Road, which makes a similar hairpin turn from north to south. Note this junction because on your return jour-ney you'll need to cross from one leg of the road to the other to close the loop.

The road ascends rather bare slopes, dotted with brittlebush, mustard and century plant. Lupine and California poppies brighten the way in spring.

After passing a memorial to Henry E. Huntington, "man of affairs, large in his bounty, yet wise," the road bends west, then south. City views are exchanged for more rural ones, including the Santa Ana River that gave Riverside its name.

The main Mt. Rubidoux road junctions a circular summit road, which you'll join to see the sights—the Peace Tower, Friendship Bridge and plenty of plaques. From the Father Junipero Serra Cross at the summit or from one of the peak's other fine vista points, partake of the 360-degree panorama of great mountains and metro-Riverside.

Return to the main Mt. Rubidoux Road for a short (0.75 mile) descent that loops south, east, then back north. Just as this downward leg bends sharply south, leave the road and step over to the other road leg that you used to ascend the mountain. Retrace your steps a final 0.3 mile back to Ninth Street.

LAKE PERRIS

TERRI PEAK TRAIL

From Campfire Center to Terri Peak is 3.5 miles round trip with 800-foot elevation gain; to Indian Museum, return via lakeshore, is 6 miles round trip

Perris in the Spring. No need to battle the hordes of tourists flocking to that other similar-sounding place of romance across the Atlantic. No need to travel 6,000 miles and spend lots of money to have a good time.

For just a few euros you can visit a manmade wonder, Lac de Paris, otherwise known as Lake Perris State Recreation Area. So pack du pain et du vin and head for the most romantic Pomona Freeway offramp in all of Southern California.

Few nature-lovers—or lovers of any kind—have discovered the romance of Perris. True, a million and a half visitors come to the lake each year, but the only nature most are interested in is that found wriggling on the end of a hook.

While the parc is oriented to les autos et les bateaux, there is a network of trails for those visitors who wish to explore Perris à pied. Perris pace-setters will enjoy the trek to Terri Peak, easily the most romantic spot in all of the Bernasconi Hills.

Springtime colors the hills with a host of wild fleurs, including goldfields, California poppy, fiddleneck, baby blue eyes and blue dicks. The view from Terri Peak on smog-free days is très fantastique.

DIRECTIONS TO TRAILHEAD: From the Pomona Freeway (60), a few miles east of its intersection with I-215, exit on Moreno Beach Drive and proceed 4 miles to the park. Immediately after paying your state park day use fee at the entry kiosk, turn right on Lake Perris Drive. Look sharply right for the strange-looking international symbol indicating a campfire and an amphitheater. Park in the campfire/interpretive center lot. The unsigned trail begins to the left of the campfire area.

THE HIKE: The trail ascends gradually west and occasionally intersects a horse trail. The unsigned path is tentative at first but an occasional wooden post helps keep you on the trail, which climbs boulder-strewn slopes.

The coastal scrub community—sage, buckwheat, chamise and toyon predominates. Also much in evidence are weedy-looking non-native species, as well as mustard, prickly pear cactus, morning glory and Russian thistle.

The trail climbs to a small flat meadow then turns southwest and climbs more earnestly to the peak. From atop Terri Peak, enjoy clear-day views of the San Bernardino Mountains to the northeast and the Santa Ana Mountains to the southwest. Below is fast-growing Moreno Valley, checkerboarded alternately with green fields and subdivisions. You can see all of Lake Perris, Alessandro Island, and hundreds of boaters, anglers and swimmers.

The trail from Terri Peak down to the Indian Museum is sometimes in poor condition. You may lose the trail a couple of times; however you won't get lost because it's easy to stay oriented with the lakeshore on your left and the Indian Museum ahead.

After a steep descent, the trail bends sharply east and deposits you at the Indian Museum's parking lot. The museum includes exhibits interpreting the Cahuilla, Chemehuevi, Serrano and other desert tribes and how they adapted to life in the Mojave Desert region.

From the museum, you follow the asphalt road down to Lake Perris Drive, cross this main park road and continue down to Perris Beach. Here, and at Moreno Beach one mile to the west, you may cool off with a swim.

Improvise a route along the lakeshore using the sidewalk and bicycle trail until you spot the main campground entrance on your left. Enter the camp-ground, pass the kiosk, then pick up the intermittent footpath that winds through the campground. This path and some improvisation will bring you to Lake Perris Drive and back to the trailhead.

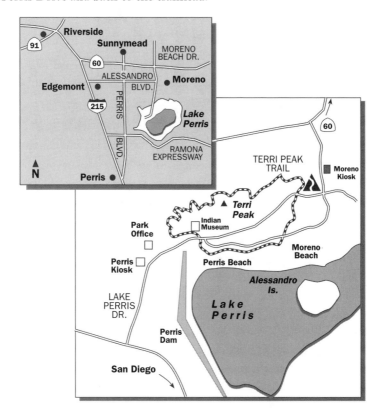

Santa Rosa Plateau Reserve

COYOTE, TRANS PRESERVE, VERNAL POOL TRAILS
From Hidden Valley Trailhead to Vernal Pools is 6 miles round trip

Use your imagination and step back a century and a half in time to an era when Santa Rosa Plateau was part of the 47,000-acre Rancho Santa Rosa granted to cattle rancher Juan Moreno by Governor Pio Pico. The adobes dating from 1845 that you'll visit on this hike will certainly help you imagine mid-19th century California.

Fortunately for those of us who would like a glimpse into that bygone era, the landowners following Juan Moreno did little to this early California landscape of oak woodlands, rolling grasslands and vernal pools but use it for grazing cattle. The relatively gentle use of the land is in part responsible for the remarkable bio-diversity flourishing on the Santa Rosa Plateau today. Known for its rare Engelmann oaks, the plateau also hosts about half of all the species of plants and animals considered to be rare in the Inland Empire.

Good thing a sizeable portion of Old SoCal was preserved because off the plateau it's very much the 21st century; that is to say, huge housing developments have pushed up Clinton Keith Road and left today's ecological reserve something of an island on the land.

Citizen activists, attempting to thwart a developers plans to con-struct 4,000 homes on the plateau, worked in concert with national, state and county government, as

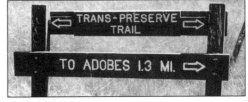

well as The Nature Conservancy, to come up with the money to purchase the property and make it a preserve, which now totals 8,300 acres. The Nature Conservancy handles resources management while Riverside County Regional Parks and Open Space District provides for visitors.

Trans Preserve and a supporting cast of trails offer and grand tour of the reserve. Depending on your time, inclination and energy level, you can hike for two hours, four hours or an entire day on the reserve's 18 named trails. The exten-sive trail network in the reserve's southeast section allows for plenty of options and seems to encourage a hiker's spontaneous decision-making.

This hike takes you to the vernal pools atop Mesa de Colorado and to the ver-nal pools. The mesa is capped with basalt, meaning it's an ideal rainwater collec-tor. Depressions in the rock collect water into seasonal ponds. One pool measures nearly 40 acres and is considered one of the largest in California.

The vernal pools offer habitat to the unusual fairy shrimp and some rare plants that ring the waterline. In winter, seasonal pools attract waterfowl, includ-ing grebes, Canada geese and green-winged teal. The pools are a colorful sight in spring when goldfields and other wildflowers surround them.

DIRECTIONS TO TRAILHEAD: Most Orange County and L.A. County residents bound for the reserve will opt for the Riverside Freeway and take it eastbound to the I-15 south. In the Wildomar area, between Lake Elsinore and Murrietta, exit I-15 on Clinton Keith Road. Drive 5 miles southwest to the Santa Rosa Plateau Ecological Reserve Visitor Center. Continue another mile as the road turns abruptly right (west) and assumes a new name—Tenaja Road.

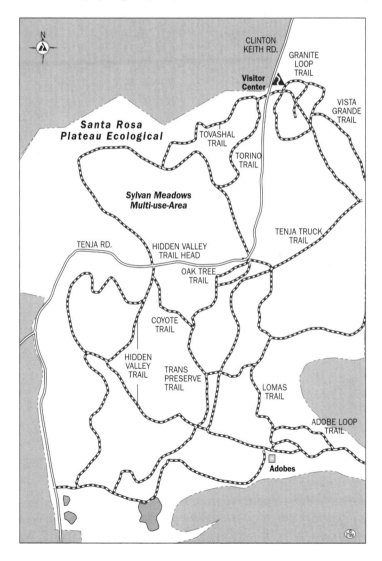

Englemann Oaks and rolling grassland are highlights along the reserve's 18 trails

Proceed another half mile farther to Hidden Valley Trailhead, where you'll find parking on both side of the road and the trailhead on the south side.

THE HIKE: Begin on Coyote Trail, named for one of the many animals that roam the reserve, though birders tend to watch for white-tailed kites when hiking along this path. A half-mile's travel brings you to a junction, where you gear right (south) on Trans Preserve Trail.

Across the reserve you go, hiking over the rolling hills and viewing both woodlands and native grasslands. Trail junctions for paths leading east and west may tempt you, but stick with Trans Preserve Trail all the way up to the top of Mesa de Colorado and a junction with Vernal Pool Trail.

Hike east and check out the vernal pools, then descend from the mesa to the historic adobes, located a bit more than three miles from the trailhead. After taking a break and inspecting the oldest structures in Riverside County, head north on Lomas Trail.

Bear right on Monument Road, and follow it only for a brief time, because Lomas Trail soon resumes and you'll follow it northbound. When you reach Tenaja Truck Trail, cross it to reach Oak Tree Trail (see Englemann Oaks Exploration in this guide). Take the left fork of this looping nature trail and hike in close company with the rare Englemann oaks to Trans Preserve Trail, which you follow southwest to the Coyote Trail.

Okay, after all those turns, trails and junctions, you know what to do now: retrace your steps a half-mile on Coyote Trail back to the trailhead.

CHAPTER ELEVEN

San Bernardino Mountains

Rim of the World Highway, leading from San Bernardino up
to Lake Arrowhead and Big Bear Lake offers a grand scenic
tour of the San Bernardino Mountains and access to terrific
low-, middle- and high-elevation trails. Many quiet places in the
mountains, under the protection of the 700,000-acre
San Bernardino National Forest, beckon the hiker to behold
waterfalls, stunning fields of wildflowers and golden eagles
soaring above lofty crags. The "wildest" area in the
Southland is the San Gorgonio Wilderness,
a magnificent high country of alpine meadows,
sparkling lakes and mighty Mt. San Gorgonio
(Old Grayback, 11,502 feet), highest peak
in Southern California.

THE ARROWHEAD

ARROWHEAD TRAIL

Rim of the World Highway (18) to The Arrowhead is 6 miles round trip with 1,400-foot elevation loss.

Branded into the San Bernardino Mountains by an unusual natural process, the Arrowhead is one of the Southland's most distinct landmarks. The close-to-perfect arrowhead, in downward trajectory, points directly to a hot springs, itself the center of many colorful stories.

The arrowhead can be viewed from afar by the visitor to San Bernardino's Wildwood Park or by the motorist on Rim of the World Highway. Hikers can view the Arrowhead up-close by trekking the Arrowhead Trail.

The Arrowhead can be environmentally explained thus: Just 18 inches under the arrowhead is solid granite; only the short-rooted mountain sage and a couple more light, gray-green brush species with shallow roots can survive here. Outside the outline of the Arrowhead, deeper and more fertile soil supports chamise and darker-complexioned plants. So the Arrowhead is really a kind of trompe l'oeil, caused by differing colors of vegetation.

A more mystical explanation for the Arrowhead comes from Cahuilla Indian lore. The Cahuillas, fleeing aggressor tribes, saw the arrowhead as a divine sign suggesting it was time to relocate.

Mid-19th century medical quack David Noble Smith put the Arrowhead on the map by opening his "Hot Springs Infirmary" nearby. One of his worst "cures" was advising patients to plunge from the hot baths into an ice-cold creek.

A new, grand Arrowhead Spring Hotel arose in 1905. After serving as a Veterans hospital after World War I for a couple years, the hotel received a deluxe remodel and was purchased by entertainment industry investors, and during its 1920s and 1930s heyday, the hotel was frequented by movie stars.

Meanwhile, water bottled from springs around Arrowhead Peak by the Arrowhead Puritas Water Company of Los Angeles proved to be extremely popular with health-conscious Angelenos.

A severe fire destroyed the hotel in 1938. It was rebuilt in even grander style, but by this time its up-scale customers were going elsewhere. Several owners struggled with the six-story white elephant until it was purchased by the Campus Crusade for Christ in 1962.

In the old days, one made the pilgrimage to the Arrowhead by hiking up to it from the hotel; however, Campus Crusade for Christ closed off the lower part of the trail long ago. The only way to visit The Arrowhead these days is to hike down to it from Rim of the World Highway.

A virtually shadeless trail leads through chaparral and is thus best done on a cool day; in fact, this is terrain thoroughly scorched by the 2003 Old Fire. In my experience, this path has never had much trail maintenance; expect it to be eroded and brush-crowded. On clear day views you'll enjoy fine Inland Empire views.

DIRECTIONS TO TRAILHEAD: From San Bernardino, drive 12.5 miles north then east up Highway 18 to a junction with Highway 138. Continue on Highway 18 (Rim of the World Highway) another 1.6 miles to a turnout on the right side of the highway.

Be sure and stop at Wildwood Park, located at Waterman Avenue (Highway 18) and 44th Street, where you'll spot an exhibit about The Arrowhead.

THE HIKE: From the gate at the west end of the turnout, follow the abandoned fire road on a switchbacking descent toward Arrowhead Peak. The path then climbs, drops, then climbs again to the summit of 4,237-foot Arrowhead Peak. Enjoy vistas of the San Bernardino Valley below and San Bernardino Peaks above.

Call it a day here or drop very steeply for a mile on the trail to the top of The Arrowhead. The trail is closed at its lower end, so you need to retrace your steps back to the trailhead.

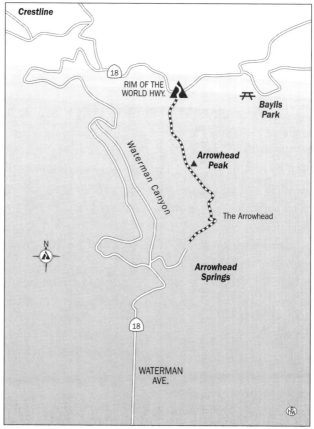

193

Deep Creek

BOWEN RANCH TRAIL
From Bowen Ranch to Deep Creek Hot Springs is 3 miles round trip with 700-foot elevation gain

Kick off your boots and slip into the relaxing waters of Deep Creek, site of one of SoCal's most popular (undeveloped) hot springs. Float awhile and gaze up at the sky. Feel your urban anxieties vaporize in one of nature's hot tubs.

Deep Creek is on the "must soak" list for scores of hot springs devotees throughout the Southwest. The hot springs can be crowded on the weekends. Weekdays, though, far fewer "take the cure."

Deep Creek is a study in contrasts. Upstream, it contains pools of great size, flanked by sheer masses of stone. The water has scoured great basins and the creek bounds down the water-worn rocks from one pool to the other. The pools are home to rainbow trout, which attract the angler. Downstream, Deep Creek is but a shadow of its former self. It ends ingloriously in the desert sands; only water-polished stones indicate its path among the dunes.

There are a couple of ways to reach the springs, including via a well-built stretch of Pacific Crest Trail. The Bowen Ranch route begins at a private ranch and drops rather steeply down to Deep Creek. Plan for an all uphill hike back to the trailhead.

DIRECTIONS TO TRAILHEAD: From I-15 in Hesperia, 6 miles north of Cajon Pass, take the Hesperia exit and follow Main Street through town. As Main Street curves south at a Y, veer left (east) onto Rock Springs Road. After driving 10 miles from the interstate, and reaching the end of Rock Springs Road, turn left (north) on Roundup Way and, after 0.5 mile, go right (east)another 4.5 miles to Bowen Ranch Road. Turn right (south) and travel 6 miles to the Bowen Ranch.

Stop a the ranch house, register, and pay the entrance fee. The trailhead is a bit father at road's end atop a hill.

THE HIKE: Descend to a gate and Forest Service land. The path angles along a ridge then drops to Deep Creek. The hot springs are located just down-creek along the south bank.

HEAPS PEAK ARBORETUM

SEQUOIA TRAIL
0.75-mile loop through Arboretum.

San Bernardino National Forest is not only huge, it's botanically diverse; the forest hosts ecological communities ranging from sagebrush to subalpine, from Joshua tree to limber pine. One of the best places to learn about national forest flora is at Heaps Peak Arboretum, located near the tiny San Bernardino Mountains community of Running Springs. Most of the arboreteum is filled with mixed stands of pine and fir—the typical forest community of these parts. In addition, the arboretum grows trees and shrubs that are representative of other parts of the forest.

A walk through the arboretum is a relaxing—and quite educational—experience. Numbered stops along the trail are keyed to a pamphlet which can be picked up at the trailhead. The entertaining pamphlet, published by the Rim-of-the-World Interpretive Association, is a mini-botany course.

Nature lovers of all hiking abilities will learn something from the interpretive displays along Heaps Peak Trail. Did you know that the willow contains salicylic acid, the active ingredient in asprin? Did you know that the Coulter pine's 8-pound pine cones are the world's largest?

It's hard not to like a nature trail that begins with the forest philosophy of Buddha and ends with the natural history of the gooseberry.

DIRECTIONS TO TRAILHEAD: From Interstate 10 in Redlands, exit on Highway 30 and doggedly follow the highway signs through minor detours and suburbs-in-the-making. As Highway 30 begins to climb into the San Bernardino Mountains, it becomes Highway 330. Eighteen miles from Redlands, you'll reach a highway junction on the outskirts of Running Springs. You'll bear northwest on Highway 18 (following signs toward Lake Arrowhead). Four miles of driving along this winding mountain road brings you to Heaps Peak Arboretum. There's plenty of parking just off the road.

CHAMPION LODGEPOLE PINE & SIBERIA CREEK

LODGEPOLE PINE & SIBERIA CREEK TRAIL

From Forest Road 2N11 to Champion Lodgepole Pine is 1 mile round trip with 100-foot loss to Siberia Creek Trail Camp is 12 miles round trip with 2,500-foot loss

California nurtures some superlative trees. The tallest tree on Earth is a coast redwood, the oldest tree a bristlecone pine. And in the San Bernardino Mountains gows the world champion lodgepole pine.

It's a pleasant stroll, suitable for the whole family, to the world champion. More ambitious hikers will enjoy tramping down Siberia Creek Trail to the appropriately named rock formation "The Gunsight," and on to Siberia Creek Trail Camp for a picnic.

Siberia Creek, born atop the high mountains near Big Bear Lake, is a delightful watercourse. It flows southwest through a deep coniferous forest and lush meadowlands, then cascades down a steep rocky gorge and adds it waters to Bear Creek.

From Forest Road 2N11, Siberia Creek Trail passes the Champion Lodgepole, the largest known lodgepole pine in the world. It then travels alongside Siberia Creek through a wet tableland, detours around a ridge while Siberia Creek crashes down a precipitous gorge, then rejoins the creek at Siberia Creek Trail Camp.

This is an "upside-down" hike; the tough part is the trek uphill back to the trailhead. Pace yourself accordingly.

DIRECTIONS TO TRAILHEAD: From Highway 18 at the west end of Big Bear Lake Village, turn south on Tulip Lane. A half mile from the highway, turn right on Mill Creek, which after 0.75 mile continues as Forest

Service Road 2N10. Proceed four more miles, then make a right on Forest Service Road 2N11. Drive one more mile to parking and the signed trailhead.

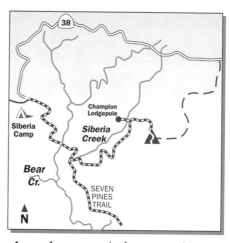

THE HIKE: The trail follows a fern-lined little brook. You'll notice some tall cornstalk-like plants—corn lilies—and a generous number of red flowers—Indian paintbrush.

A half-mile's travel brings you to a signed junction. Go right 75 yards to the Champion Lodgepole, which towers above the east end of an emerald green meadow. You can't miss it. It's the only 110-foot tree around.

Lodgepole—also called tamarack—pines are usually found at higher elevations, but here at 7,500 feet, nurtured by the rich, well-watered soil, they not only thrive, but achieve mammoth proportions. The World Champion is 75 inches in diameter (the species usually measures 12 to 24 inches), and is estimated to be more than 400 years old. Lodgepoles are easily identified by their yellow-green paired needles.

While hiking in Southern California, these pines are probably the only ones you'll come across that have two needles per bundle. By way of comparison, you might notice that the pinyon pine has one needle, the ponderosa three, and the limber pine five.

Return to the main trail and continue through open forest, skirting the meadowland. You cross and recross Siberia Creek. After the second crossing, the meadowland ends and the creek crashes down the gorge. The trail avoids the gorge and swings down and around the steep slopes of Lookout Mountain. About one mile from the Champion Lodgepole, an interesting rock formation called "The Gunsight" appears. Squint through "The Gunsight" at the metropolis trapped in the haze below.

From The Gunsight, the trail descends the slopes of Lookout Mountain. A series of switchbacks brings you to a junction with Seven Pines Trail, 5 miles from the trailhead. Bear right (north) on the Seven Pines Trail and proceed a mile to Siberia Creek Trail Camp. For the day hiker, this oak- and alder-shaded camp makes a nice picnic spot or rest stop.

Return the way you came—all uphill.

FAWNSKIN

GROUT BAY, GRAYS PEAK TRAILS
From Grout Bay Picnic Area to Grays Peak is 6 miles round trip with 1,000-foot elevation gain

Even today, Grout Bay doesn't sound like a place to play. The name suggests mortar, not lakeshore, and offers no clue to the considerable attractions offered by the bay and the woodsy hiking trail that offers vistas of Big Bear Lake.

Back in 1919, Los Angeles businessmen William Cline and Clinton Miller ran into serious consumer resistance when they tried to lure vacationers to the upscale summer resort they were developing on the north shore of Big Bear Lake. Marketing a community called Grout was difficult to say the least; they decided the name Grout had to go.

The developers changed the name to Fawnskin, appropriating the name from a nearby meadow. While the name evokes images of Bambi, Fawnskin's origin is one guaranteed to upset an animal rights activist. Back in 1891, hunters shot many deer fawns, stretched their hides on trees, and promptly disappeared. As the story goes, subsequent travelers observed the fawn skins and began referring to the meadow and surrounding area as Fawnskin.

During the 1920s, Fawnskin expanded to include the Swiss chalet-style Fawn Lodge, complete with tea room, a general store, post office, more than 100 fairly pricey homes along the lakeshore and in the surrounding woods, as well as the Theatre of the Stars, a stage for musicals and dramas.

A bit west of Fawnskin proper stood Gray's Lodge, a pier, store and rental cabins owned by Alex Gray. Gray's name now graces a boat landing and a 7,880-foot peak.

As for the name Grout, it didn't entirely slip between the cracks: Grout Bay and Grout Bay Trail remain on the map, perhaps a reminder that a name isn't everything.

Grout Bay Trail begins in the piney woods above the lake and climbs to the summit of Grays Peak. The trail begins at the outskirts of the drowsy hamlet of Fawnskin, where a couple of eateries offer the hiker pre-hike sustenance or post-hike refreshment.

DIRECTIONS TO TRAILHEAD: From the far west end of Big Bear Lake at the junction of Highway 18 (Big Bear Boulevard) and Highway 38 (North Shore Drive), take the latter highway northeast 2.5 miles to the outer fringe of Fawnskin. Turn west into the trail parking lot of the Grout Bay Picnic Area.

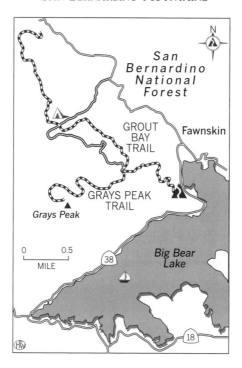

THE HIKE: The well-graded, signed path begins a moderate ascent over wooded slopes and soon offers views of Fawnskin, Grout Bay and Windy Point. Vistas soon close up as the trail traverses more heavily timbered terrain.

A bit less than a mile out, Grout Bay Trail meets and joins dirt Forest Service Road 2N68E. Assisted by a couple of "Trail" signs, follow the road west about 0.4 mile. (Grout Bay Trail resumes as a footpath and heads north toward Fawnskin Valley.)

This hike leaves the road and follows the signed trail west toward Grays Peak. Long, finely engineered switchbacks aid the ascent past conifers, jumbo boulders and impressive specimens of manzanita.

The trail ends just short of the peak at a rock outcropping, which provides a superb overlook of the lake, valley and surrounding San Bernardino Mountains, as well as fine picnic spot.

GRAND VIEW POINT

PINE KNOT TRAIL
From Aspen Glen Picnic Area to Grand View Point is 6.5 miles round trip with 1,200-foot elevation gain

Rim of the World Highway offers the traveler a fine view of Big Bear Lake. A better view, a hiker's view, is available from Pine Knot Trail, which climbs the handsome, pine-studded slopes above the lake and offers far-reaching panoramas of the San Bernardino Mountains.

Big Bear Lake is a great place to escape the crowded metropolis, and Pine Knot Trail is a great way to escape sometimes-crowded Big Bear Lake.

The idea for Big Bear Lake came from Redlands citrus growers, who wanted to impound a dependable water source for their crops. Farmers and city founders formed Bear Valley Land and Water Co. and in 1884, at a cost of $75,000, built a stone-and-cement dam, thus forming Big Bear Lake. In 1910 a second, larger dam was built near the first one. This second dam is the one you see today.

Pine Knot Trail takes its name from the little community of cabins, stores and saloons that sprang up when Rim of the World Highway was completed. After World War II the town of Pine Knot changed its name to Big Bear Lake Village.

While Pine Knot Trail offers grand views of the lake, this hike's destination—Grand View Point—does not overlook the lake. The grand view is a breathtaking panorama of the San Gorgonio Wilderness and the deep canyon cut by the Santa Ana River.

DIRECTIONS TO TRAILHEAD: From California 18 in Big Bear Lake Village, turn southwest on Tulip Lane (Mill Creek Road) and proceed about a half-mile to Aspen Glen Picnic Area on your left. The signed trail departs from the east end of the picnic area.

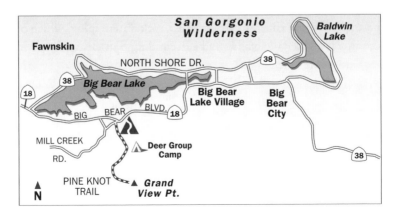

Grand views of Big Bear Lake from Pine Knot Trail

THE HIKE: From Aspen Glen Picnic Area, Pine Knot Trail climbs a low, lupine-sprinkled ridge. The path follows a fence line for a short distance, then dips into and out of a willow-lined creek bed. You will get great over-the-shoulder views of the south shore of Big Bear Lake.

Ascending through Jeffrey pine and ponderosa pine forests, the trail meets and joins a fire road; after a short distance, it again becomes a footpath. Now your over-the-shoulder view is of the north shore of Big Bear Lake.

Pine Knot Trail passes near one of the runs of the Snow Forest Ski Area, then meanders through an enchanted area of castellated rocks. About 2 miles from the trailhead the trail intersects a dirt Forest Service Road. Before you is a mead-ow, a rather amusing-looking landscape decorated with boulders, ponderosa pine, Indian paintbrush and skunk cabbage. Bear left on the dirt road for a short time, then pick up the signed footpath again.

Passing black oak and willow, Pine Knot Trail skirts a moist meadow and crosses and then parallels another dirt Forest Service road. Ahead of you are tanta-lizing views of San Gorgonio Wilderness peaks-just a hint of things to come when you reach trail's end.

Nearing the top of the ridge, the trail intersects dirt Forest Service Road 2N10. Cross the road and follow the signed trail on a 0.25-mile ascent to the sum-mit of Grand View Point.

Enjoy views of the San Gorgonio Wilderness, a panorama of Southern California's highest peaks.

COUGAR CREST

COUGAR CREST TRAIL
From Highway 38 to Bertha Peak is 6.5 miles round trip with 1,100-foot elevation gain; Season: April-November

Cougar Crest, the forested ridge between Big Bear Lake and Holcomb Valley is a treat for hikers. From the ridge, as well as from the ridge's two prominent peaks—Bertha and Delamar—enjoy great views of the lake, towering Mt. San Gorgonio and tranquil Holcomb Valley.

Holcomb Valley wasn't always so tranquil. In 1860, Billy Holcomb was out bear hunting and wandered over the ridge of hills that separates Bear Valley from the smaller, parallel valley to the north. He found gold. Prospectors swarmed into the valley from all over the West.

This day hike climbs the forested slopes above Big Bear Lake to a junction with the Pacific Crest Trail. From the PCT, you can ascend to Bertha Peak or to more distant Delamar Mountain for grand views of the middle of the San Bernadino Mountains.

DIRECTIONS TO TRAILHEAD: From Highway 18 in the town of Big Bear Lake, turn north on Stanfield cut off, crossing to the north shore of the lake and a junction with Highway 38. Turn left, drive a mile to the Big Bear Ranger Station, then a short distance beyond to the signed Cougar Crest trailhead and parking area off the north side of the highway.

THE HIKE: From the signed trailhead, join wide Cougar Crest Trail, a retiring dirt road. You climb through a pine and juniper woodland and pass a couple of old mining roads. After a mile, the trail narrows and begins ascending forested Cougar Crest via a series of well-constructed switchbacks. Soon you'll begin enjoying over-the-shoulder views of Big Bear Lake and its dramatic backdrop-the high peaks of the San Gorgonio Wilderness.

A bit more than two miles from the trailhead, Cougar Crest Trail reaches a

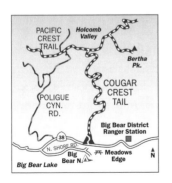

signed junction with the Pacific Crest Trail. To reach Bertha Peak you'll bear right (east) and continue along the ridge crest for 0.5 mile to an intersection with an old dirt road. PCT continues straight at this junction, but you bear right on the dirt road and ascend 0.5-mile through pinyon pine and juniper woodland to the small relay station atop Bertha Peak. Best views are a bit below the peak.

MILL CREEK, ALGER CREEK

MOMYER CREEK TRAIL

From Forest Falls to Alger Camp is 7.5 miles round trip with 1,600-foot elevation gain; to Dobbs Camp is 11 miles round trip with 1,700-foot gain; to Saxton Camp is 14.5 miles round trip with 2,900-foot gain; to Dollar Lake Saddle is 20 miles round trip with 4,500-foot gain

Thanks to the urging of retired San Bernardino postal superintendent Joe Momyer and Harry James, co-founders of the conservation group Defenders of the San Gorgonio Wilderness, Congress set aside the San Gorgonio Wilderness in 1965. Momyer Trail is a pleasant day hike in itself, or you can extend your trip deep into the wilderness by joining other paths. Hikers will enjoy the forested hollows en route, as well as the superb wilderness views.

DIRECTIONS TO TRAILHEAD: From Interstate 10 in Redlands, exit on Orange Avenue/State 38. Follow State 38 some eight miles east to Mill Creek Ranger Station. Pick up the required wilderness permit. Continue east on the state highway to the Forest Home turnoff and drive to the signed Momyer trail-head and parking area on the left side of the road.

THE HIKE: Momyer Trail drops into Mill Creek Canyon. Cross Mill Creek. The signed trail resumes on the other side of the creek. The well-constructed trail switch-backs up the brushy divide between Momyer Creek to the west and Alger Creek to the east. Several pockets of oak and Jeffrey pine offer shade and a chance to catch your breath.

After an ascent of nearly three miles, you'll arrive at a signed junction. (Continuing north is a rather rough and tough path climbing four steep miles toward San Bernardino Peak.) You angle east a short mile to Alger Creek Camp. Relax a while in the shade of pine, alder and incense cedar.

The trail ascends again, then contours around pine- and fir-dotted slopes before reaching a junction. To reach Dobbs Cabin Camp, head right and drop down a steep quarter-mile to Falls Creek and the shady camp.

Most day hikers will call it a day at Dobbs. However, the intrepid will return to the above-mentioned junction and tackle Falls Creek Trail for the stiff climb over forested slopes to Saxton Camp, on the fringe of damp Plummer Meadows.

Truly heroic day hikers will continue up manzanita-covered slopes to Dollar Lake Saddle and an intersection with three more wilderness trails. Dollar Lake Trail drops to Dollar Lake and lush South Fork Meadows. The western stretch of San Bernardino Peak Divide Trail climbs to San Bernardino Peak; the eastern length travels toward San Gorgonio Mountain.

San Bernardino Peak

SAN BERNARDINO PEAK TRAIL

From Angelus Oaks Trailhead to Columbine Spring Camp is 9 miles round trip with 2,000-foot elevation gain; to Limber Pine Bench Camp is 12 miles round trip with 3,200-foot gain; to San Bernardino Peak is 16 miles round trip with 4,700-foot gain; Season: May-November

Mt. San Bernardino, together with its twin peak, Mt. San Gorgonio, just five miles away and 900 feet higher, anchors the eastern end of the San Bernardino Mountains. At 11,499 feet, Mt. San Gorgonio is the peak by which all other Southern California peaks are measured. Mt. San Bernardino, too, is quite a landmark.

In 1852, Colonel Henry Washington and his Army survey party were directed to erect a monument atop Mt. San Bernardino. The monument was to be an east-west reference point from which all future surveys of Southern California would be taken.

The colonel's crew took many readings, but heat waves from the San Bernardino Valley below befuddled their triangulations. The surveying party ingeniously solved this dilemma by lighting bonfires atop the peak in order to make their calculations at night.

This trail takes you from deep pine forest to exposed manzanita slopes and visits the old survey monument. The higher slopes of Mt. San Bernardino are beautiful and rugged subalpine terrain. A number of trail camps along the way offer spring water and rest.

High elevation, coupled with a steep ascent, means this trail is best left to experienced hikers in top form. Beyond Columbine Spring the trail becomes very steep.

Camp Angelus trailhead is less visited than others at the edge of the San Gorgonio Wilderness, but it receives a lot of use, especially during summer weekends.

DIRECTIONS TO TRAILHEAD: From Interstate 10 in Redlands, exit on Highway 38 and drive 20 miles to Angelus Oaks. Turn right at a sometimes signed junction for San Bernardino Peak Trail. Make an immediate left and drive past a fire station. Turn right on a dirt road (1W07). Staying right at two forks, drive 0.3 mile to a large dirt parking lot and signed San Bernardino Peak Trail. (Access to this trailhead has been known to change; hopefully, directional signs will be posted to help you navigate those dirt roads.)

THE HIKE: The trail begins ascending through a mixed forest of pine, fir and oak, switchbacking up the beautifully wooded slope. You mount a ridge, walk

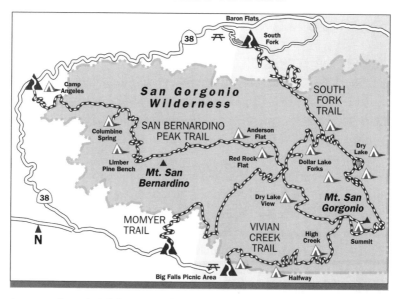

along its crest for a brief distance, then continue climbing. You're welcomed into the glories of the San Gorgonio Wilderness by a wooden sign, two miles from the trailhead. A little beyond the wilderness boundary, the grade grows less severe. As you climb above 8,000 feet, the Jeffrey pine become widely spaced. Shortly, the trail penetrates a manzanita-covered slope. You pass a side trail leading down to Manzanita Springs. Don't drink the water. The side trail continues on 0.25 mile to Columbine Springs Trail Camp, which usually has water later in the season than Manzanita.

To San Bernardino Peak: A short distance beyond Manzanita Springs Trail Junction, the trail begins climbing more earnestly. The trail ascends in fits and starts over slopes covered with manzanita and homely chinquapin; in 1.5 more miles, it reaches Limber Pine Springs Camp. (Actually, all the shade in the area is provided by lodgepole pines.) Another 0.25-mile up the trail is Limber Pine Springs, usually a dependable source of water.

The trail begins a long traverse south, switchbacking up to Camp Washington, a trail camp with plenty of view, but nothing to drink. One hundred yards from the trail is Colonel Washington's baseline monument, which looks like little more than a pile of stone rubble. The trail climbs another 0.5 mile, where it intersects a brief side trail that takes you to the summit of Mt. San Bernardino (10,624 feet).

Sign the summit register, enjoy the view, and return the way you came.

MT. SAN GORGONIO

SOUTH FORK TRAIL

From South Fork to South Fork Meadows is 9 miles round trip with 1,500-foot elevation gain; to Dollar Lake is 12 miles round trip with 2,500-foot gain; to Mt. San Gorgonio Summit is 21 miles round trip with 4,600-foot gain; Season: June-November

Most of us in the Southland have looked east and marveled at Mt. San Gorgonio, the highest peak in Southern California. The 11,499-foot mountain is most striking in winter when its snow-covered peak can be seen reaching far above the metropolis. In summer, the view from the basin is not so spectacular; the dull gray granite summit is hard to find among the hydrocarbons.

But summer and early autumn are the best seasons in the alpine high country, allowing you to look down at what you left behind. From the top, there's a 360-degree panoramic view from the Mexican border to the southern Sierra, from the Pacific Ocean to the far reaches of the Mojave Desert.

Native American legend has it that San Gorgonio and San Jacinto peaks were brothers and among the first born of Earth Mother, who made all things. It would be hard to improve on Earth Mother's handiwork here. Mt. San Gorgonio's alpine vegetation includes carpets of buttercups, and that venerable survivor of inclement weather, the limber pine. Mountain lions, mule deer and bighorn sheep roam the high slopes, and golden eagles soar over the summit.

The mountain got its name from an obscure fourth-century Christian martyr but irreverent Americans began calling the mountain "Grayback." Its bare, gravelly summit stretches laterally for some distance above the timberline, giving the appearance of a long, gray back.

Below the peak is some fine hiking on good trails that tour the heart of the San Gorgonio Wilderness. You'll pass through lovely meadows and visit two small lakes, Dry and Dollar. Ambitious hikers in top form will want to make the 21-mile round trip trek all the way to the top of Old Grayback for the best view of Southern California available to a hiker.

DIRECTIONS TO TRAILHEAD: From Interstate 10 in Redlands, exit on California 38. As you head up the highway into the San Bernardino National Forest, remember to stop at the Mill Creek Ranger Station just beyond the hamlet of Mentone and pick up your wilderness permit.

Follow the highway 19 miles past the ranger station to Jenks Lake Road. Turn right and proceed 2.5 miles to the South Fork trailhead, a fairly new and deluxe jump-off point as trailheads go.

Inviting lakeside campsites beckon weary Mt. San Gorgonio hikers.

THE HIKE: From the signed trailhead, the path ascends moderately through a mixed pine forest and across wide horse meadow. Enjoy the occasional views of Sugarloaf Peak behind you and San Gorgonio ahead.

Continue ascending through the woods. In a mile, South Fork Creek appears on your left, and you parallel it toward South Fork Meadows, also known as Slushy Meadows in days gone by.

Dozens of tiny streams, which form the headwaters of the Santa Ana River, roam through the ferns and wispy waist-high grasses. Lower South Fork Meadows Trail Camp and Middle South Fork Meadows Trail Camp offer places to picnic; the camps have been closed (probably permanently) due to overuse.

Locate an idyllic picnic spot beneath the ponderosa pine and white fir. If you're not feeling especially energetic, you could spend a day in South Fork Meadows and be quite happy.

The more energetic will continue on the trail as it skirts the west edge of the meadow and reaches a junction. The left fork, Whitewater Trail, heads toward Dry Lake (another fine day hike destination) and the summit of Mt. San Gorgonio. You take the right fork, South Fork Trail, and begin switchbacking up wooded slopes.

After a mile of climbing, first through ponderosa pine and then through lodgepole pine, you'll begin a long contour around the wall of the basin that holds Dollar Lake. The trail passes a manzanita-covered slope and reaches a junction 1.75 miles from South Fork Meadows. Go left.

In a few hundred yards you reach another junction and turn left again. Follow the easy 0.25-mile trail down the basin wall to the lake.

Dollar Lake, so named because it gleams like a silver dollar, is one of the most popular backcountry spots in the San Gorgonio Wilderness and is another ideal place to picnic or laze away a day. Return to the main trail the way you came.

If you're headed for the summit, resume climbing for another mile to Dollar Lake Saddle (approx. 10,000 feet) and a three-way junction. One half mile beyond the junction, you pass another junction with the rocky side-trail that ascends Charlton Peak. In another 0.5 mile you pass Dry Lake View Camp, a waterless trail camp amidst great boulders. From here, you can look down into Dry Lake Basin, where you'll pass if you return from the peak via Sky High Trail. Soon you'll pass junctions with the Vivian Creek Trail and the Sky High Trail. Keep to your left at both junctions. Cross a last rise and climb to the summit of San Gorgonio.

No other Southern California mountain commands such an uninterrupted panoramic view. To the north are the deep green meadowlands of the upper valley of the Santa Ana River. To the west is the murky megalopolis. To the east is the Mojave. South is San Gorgonio Pass and just across from it, nearly level with your feet, is Mt. San Jacinto.

After enjoying this 360-degree view from the top of the world, return the way you came or via the Sky High Trail, which descends the east slope of San Gorgonio to Mine Shaft Saddle and Dry Lake and deposits you in South Fork Meadows where you intersect the trail back to South Fork.

From the summit, retrace your steps on the main trail to its intersection with the Sky High Trail. Begin your descent from the clouds on the latter trail, circling first east, then north around the mountain's great shoulders. As you descend there are good views of the Whitewater drainage, gorges bearing snowmelt from San Gorgonio and carrying waters to the desert sands below. The awesome Whitewater country was in 1984 added to the San Gorgonio Wilderness.

Three and a half miles from the summit you reach Mine Shaft Saddle on the divide between Dry Lake Basin and the Whitewater River.

Continue your descent, and in two more miles you'll reach Dry Lake at 9,200 feet. Some years it is dry by midsummer, but in other years the lake is filled to the brim, its water lapping against the trail that surrounds the lake.

From the Dry Lake basin, you switchback down through pine and fir 1.75 miles to South Fork Meadows, where you intersect the trail back to South Fork trailhead.

VIVIAN CREEK

VIVIAN CREEK TRAIL

From Mill Creek Canyon to Vivian Creek Trail Camp is 3 miles round trip with 1,200-foot elevation gain; to Halfway Trail Camp is 6 miles round trip with 1,800-foot gain; to High Creek Trail Camp is 9.5 miles round trip with 3,400-foot gain; to Mt. San Gorgonio Peak is 16 miles round trip with 5,300-foot gain

"The mountains"–he continued, with his eyes upon the distant heights–"are not seen by those who would visit them with a rattle and clatter and rush and roar–as one would visit the cities of men. They are to be seen only by those who have the grace to go quietly; who have the understanding to go thoughtfully; the heart to go lovingly; and the spirit to go worshipfully."
                                   –Harold Bell Wright, *The Eyes of the World*, 1914

A half-dozen major trails lead through the San Gorgonio Wilderness to the top of Mt. San Gorgonio, Southern California's highest peak. Oldest, and often regarded as the best, is Vivian Creek Trail.

Not long after the formation of San Bernardino Forest Preserve in 1893, pioneer foresters built Government Trail to the top of San Gorgonio. This path was later renamed Vivian Creek Trail because it winds along for a few miles with its namesake watercourse before climbing the steep upper slopes of San Gorgonio.

Vivian Creek Trail begins in Mill Creek Canyon. The lower stretches of the canyon, traveled by Highway 38, displays many boulders, evidence of great floods in years past.

Upper Mill Creek Canyon

Big Falls lives up to its name.

is where Big Falls falls. Tumbling from the shoulder of San Bernardino Peak, snowmelt-swollen Falls Creek rushes headlong over a cliff near Mill Creek Road. (Unfortunately, too many foolish people were killed or injured by trying to climb Big Falls and the Forest Service has closed the 0.5-mile path leading to Big Falls Overlook.)

Mill Creek Canyon was the retreat for pastor-turned-novelist Harold Bell Wright (1872-1944). His wholesome, tremendously popular novels featured rugged individualists, as well as Southwest and Southland settings. One novel, *The Eyes of the World,* uses the San Bernardino Mountains as a setting and explores the question of an artist's responsibility to society and to himself.

Leaving the head of Mill Creek Canyon, Vivian Creek Trail climbs into the valley cut by Vivian Creek, visits three inviting trail camps—Vivian Creek, Halfway and High Creek—and ascends rocky, lodgepole pine-dotted slopes to the top of Old Grayback.

DIRECTIONS TO TRAILHEAD: From Interstate 10 in Redlands, exit on Highway 38 and proceed 14 miles east to a junction with Forest Home Road. (Halfway to this junction, on Highway 38, is Mill Creek Ranger Station, where you must stop and obtain a wilderness permit.) Follow Forest Home Road 4.5 miles to its end.

THE HIKE: The trail, an old dirt road, travels 0.75 mile through (closed) Falls Campground to another (the former) Vivian Creek trailhead. The trail, a dirt path from this point, crosses boulder-strewn Mill Creek wash, then begins a steep ascent over an exposed, oak-dotted slope. Soon you'll reach Vivian Creek Trail Camp, where pine- and fir-shaded sites dot the creek banks.

Past the camp, Vivian Creek Trail follows its namesake, crossing from one side to the other and passing little lush meadows and stands of pine and cedar.

Halfway, a relatively new trail camp, about halfway between Vivian Creek and High Creek Camps, is another welcome retreat. Another 1.5 miles of steep climbing up forested slopes brings you to High Creek Camp.

Above High Creek, located at 9,000-foot elevation, you leave behind the Ponderosa pine and cedar and encounter that hearty, high-altitude survivor, the lodgepole pine. Two miles high, you start getting some great views; at 11,000 feet, the trail ascends above the timberline.

When you reach a junction with the trail coming up from Dollar Lake you'll turn right. Soon you'll pass a junction with the Sky High Trail, cross a last rise and climb to the summit of San Gorgonio.

SANTA ANA RIVER

SANTA ANA RIVER TRAIL

From South Fork Campground to Heart Bar Campground is 9 miles round trip with 800-foot elevation gain; Season: March-November

For most of its length, Southern California's largest river is not a thing of beauty. Concrete-lined and channelized, the Santa Ana River that crosses Orange County is a thoroughly domesticated watercourse. Its riverbed has been covered with subdivisions, its natural course altered for human convenience. Glimpsing the river as it passes Costa Mesa backyards, Anaheim Stadium or the I-10/I-15 interchange does not inspire further exploration.

Fortunately for hikers and nature lovers, there's another Santa Ana River, unfettered and unchanneled. At its headwaters high in the San Bernardino Mountains, the river waters a beautiful meadow and cuts through a deep canyon that separates the high peaks of the San Gorgonio Wilderness from the mountains of the Big Bear Lake area. The river, born of natural springs and snowmelt, is an important wildlife habitat in its upper reaches.

The most intirguing segment of the Santa Ana River Trail begins at Heart Bar, first settled by Mormon pioneers in the 1850s. During the latter part of the 19th century and the first half of the 20th, cattle ranchers sent their herds to graze the lush Santa Ana River meadows. It was one rancher's brand—a heart with a bar beneath it—that gave the land its name.

Santa Ana River Trail parallels the river as it winds from South Fork Campground to Heart Bar Campground. The path stays in piney woods for most of its length. A few side trails allow passage to the river.

DIRECTIONS TO TRAILHEAD: From Interstate 10 in Redlands, take the Highway 38 exit and proceed north 32 miles to the turn-off for South Fork Campground. Almost opposite the entrance to the camp, on the north side of the highway, you'll find the Santa Ana River trailhead parking lot and the signed trail.

Santa Ana River Trail ends at Forest Road IN021, near Heart Bar Campground. If you want to make a one-way hike, you can arrange to have transportation waiting at the Forest Road IN021 trailhead. To reach this trailhead from the South Fork Campground trailhead, you would continue east on Highway 38 to the signed Heart Bar Campground turnoff, then drive a mile past the campground on the dirt Forest Road IN021 to the second signed Santa Ana River trailhead.

THE HIKE: From the parking area opposite South Fork Campground, Santa Ana River Trail meanders by its namesake, then veers under the Santa

Ana River Bridge. As you hike beneath the highway, notice the rugged construction of the bridge and the wide bed of the river, two indications of the Santa Ana's size and strength after a storm.

The trail makes a short circle, reaches a second signed trailhead at the entrance to South Fork Campground and heads west. Switchbacking up a slope, the trail soon turns east — your direction for the rest of this hike.

Most of the climb occurs in the first mile. The trail travels through a mixed forest of ponderosa and Jeffrey pine, white fir and black oak. Ground squirrels are abundant, and deer are seen occasionally.

Above you to the southwest is the San Gorgonio Wilderness, dominated by its 11,499-foot signature peak, highest point in Southern California. To the north, above the forested canyon of the Santa Ana River, is Sugarloaf Mountain (9,952 feet), highest peak in the San Bernardinos outside the wilderness.

About the trail's midpoint you'll spot Heart Bar Station, headquarters for a Forest Service fire crew. Continuing east, the trail offers great views of well-named Big Meadow. Watering the meadow are Heart Bar Creek, Coon Creek, Cienega Seca Creek and the headwaters of the Santa Ana. Big Meadow is especially pretty when a breeze sways the willows and tall grasses. During late spring and summer the meadow is splashed with colorful wildflowers. The meadows where cattle once grazed are now a valuable habitat for rabbits, foxes, skunks and raccoons. California golden beaver were brought into the area, and several pairs of them maintain dams on the Santa Ana River.

About a mile from trail's end you will intersect an unsigned side trail leading left down to Big Meadow and over to Heart Bar Campground. Continue straight at this junction to the end of this segment of Santa Ana River Trail at Forest Road 1No21.

ASPEN GROVE & FISH CREEK MEADOWS

ASPEN GROVE TRAIL

From Forest Road 1No5 to Fish Creek Meadows is 5 miles round trip with 600-foot elevation gain; Season: May-November

One of the prettiest sights of autumn is the fluttering of the aspen's golden-yellow leaves. From a distance, the trees stand apart from the surrounding dark forest. In the right light, the aspens seem to burn, like fire in the wind.

Botanists say the aspen is the most widely distributed tree on the North American continent. Even rough American fur trappers and mountain men of the 19th century were impressed by the tree's range and beauty.

The water-loving aspen is a rarity in Southern California, but there is a handsome little grove in the San Bernardino Mountains. Aspen Grove, reached by a trail with the same name, is an ideal autumn excursion.

The hike to Aspen Grove is particularly inviting after Jack Frost has touched the trees. After the first cold snap, the aspens display their fall finery, a display of color unrivaled in Southern California.

It's only a short 0.25-mile saunter to the aspens that line Fish Creek, but the trail continues beyond the grove, traveling through a pine and fir forest and a lovely meadow.

DIRECTIONS TO TRAILHEAD: From Interstate 10 in Redlands, exit on Highway 38 and proceed 32 miles east to the signed turnoff for Heart Bar Campground. (As you head up 38 into the San Bernardino National Forest, remember to stop at Mill Creek Ranger Station just beyond the hamlet of Mentone and pick up a wilderness permit.) Turn south (right) on dirt Forest Road 1No2, and drive 1.25 miles to a fork in the road. Stay right at the fork and follow it on a 1.5-mile climb to a small parking area and signed Aspen Grove Trail on your right.

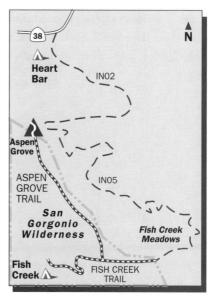

THE HIKE: The trail, for its first 0.25-mile an abandoned dirt road, descends toward Fish Creek. The very beginning of Aspen Grove Trail offers the best view of San Gorgonio Wilderness peaks—the highest in Southern California. To the west

stands mighty Grinnell Mountain, named for University of California zoologist Joseph Grinnell, who studied the animals of the San Bernardino Mountains. To the south is Ten Thousand Foot Ridge, headwaters for Fish Creek, which you soon see and hear meandering below.

At Fish Creek, a sign marks the boundary of the San Gorgonio Wilderness. Cross the creek and enjoy the aspen grove that lines Fish Creek. It's a small grove, but a pretty one. No one will blame you if you picnic among the whitewashed trunks and quaking leaves and hike no farther.

The aspens have been suffering of late at the hands of—or more accurately, the jaws of—a creature that loves the trees even more than humans. The aspen-chomping California golden beaver is not a native of the San Bernardino Mountains, but since its introduction it has found the area—and the aspens to its liking. Forest Service wildlife experts are working on a plan to manage both the native aspens and the beaver.

After admiring the aspens, continue on Aspen Grove Trail, which heads up-creek. The path soon wanders a bit away from Fish Creek and travels through a forest of ponderosa pine, Jeffrey pine and Douglas fir.

About a mile from Aspen Grove, the trail passes little Monkey Flower Flat. During late spring and early summer, columbine and lupine join the monkeyflowers in bedecking the flat.

Beyond Monkey Flower is a much larger flat—Fish Creek Meadow. Aspen Grove Trail skirts this meadow and ends at a signed junction with Fish Creek Trail. The left fork of Fish Creek Trails leads a bit more than 0.5 mile to Forest Road 1N05. Take the right fork of the trail, which angles toward Upper Fish Creek. The path ascends above the creek, passes through a pine and fir forest and, a bit more than a mile from the junction with Aspen Grove Trail, reaches Lower Fish Creek Camp. This fir-shaded camp is an ideal place to relax.

CHAPTER TWELVE

San Jacinto Mountains

Many hikers compare this range with the High Sierra.
The San Jacinto seem an island in the sky because of their
incredibly rapid rise from the desert floor. No other place in
California do alpine and desert vegetation thrive in such close
proximity. One of those magical places that lure hikers back
year after year, the range is a delight to hike whether you begin
in charming Idyllwild or get a lift from the Palm Springs
Aerial Tramway. The seasons are more distinct here than
anywhere else in Southern California and hikers love the
contrasts this range offers—the feeling of hiking
in Switzerland while gazing down on the Sahara.

SAUNDERS MEADOW

ERNIE MAXWELL SCENIC TRAIL
From Humber Park to Saunders Meadow 5 miles round trip with 300-foot elevation gain

The late founder of the *Idyllwild Town Crier* and longtime Idlyllwild conservationist is honored by the Ernie Maxwell Scenic Trail, a woodsy, 2.5-mile path through the San Jacinto Mountains. Maxwell hiked his namesake trail many times. (Seems like most pathways are named posthumously; how fortunate when one is named for a living person who so appreciates the honor.)

Maxwell explained that his trail came into being as a result of his horse's inability to get along with automobiles. After riding through the San Jacinto Wilderness, Maxwell and his fellow equestrians were forced to follow paved roads back through town to the stables.

Maxwell's barn-sour pack horses, so slow and sullen on the trail, would become suddenly frisky and unmanageable as they neared home. Equine-auto conflicts were frequent. Maxwell thought: Why not build a trail from Humber Park, at the edge of the San Jacinto Wilderness, through the forest to the stables, thus avoiding the horse-spooking congestion of downtown Idyllwild?

Maxwell got cooperation from the U.S. Forest Service and from Riverside County inmates, who provided the labor. Ernie Maxwell Trail was completed in 1959.

And a lovely trail it is. The path meanders through a mixed forest of pine and fir and offers fine views of the granite face of Marion Ridge.

Maxwell often wrote about what he wryly called "the urban-wildlands interface issue. That's the one that deals with more and more people moving into the hills."

People began moving into the hills with their axes and sheep more than a hundred years ago. Fortunately, the San Jacinto Mountains have had many conservation-minded friends, including Ernie Maxwell, who for many years served as president of the local chapter of the Izaak Walton League. The emphasis of the surrounding national forest has changed from com-

Ernie Maxwell and his Scenic Trail.

modity production to recreation; isolated Idyllwild has become a (sometimes too) popular weekend getaway. Local conservationists are aware that the future of the mountains depend to a large extent on the attitude of the millions of Southern Californians living 7,000 feet below and a 1.5-hour drive away from Idyllwild.

DIRECTIONS TO TRAILHEAD: From Interstate 10 in Banning, exit on California 243 (Banning-Idyllwild Highway) and proceed about 25 miles to Idyllwild County Park Visitor Center. A small museum interprets the history and natural history of the area.

From downtown Idyllwild, head up Fern Valley Road. Following the signs to Humber Park, drive two miles to the large parking area. Signed Ernie Maxwell Trail departs from the lower end of the parking lot.

THE HIKE: The trail begins at Humber Park, the main jumping-off point to the San Jacinto Wilderness for hikers and rock climbers. You'll get frequent over-the-shoulder views of the dramatic pinnacles popular with Southern California climbers.

The mostly level trail (the inmates did a great job!) contours gently around wooded slopes. Ponderosa, Jeffrey and Coulter pines, fir and incense cedar grace the mountainside and carpet the path with needles.

This hike's destination, Saunders Meadow, is named for Amasa Saunders, who in 1881 operated a huge sawmill not too far down slope in Strawberry Valley. Take a moment to be thankful that not all the pine and fir became grist for Saunders' mill, then scout the tree tops for the abundant birdlife. Look for Steller's jays, the white-headed woodpecker, and the colorful orange-headed, yellow-breasted Western tanager.

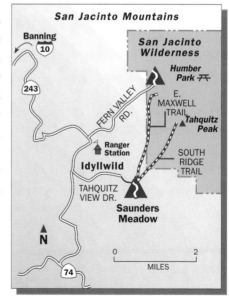

Ernie Maxwell Scenic Trail ends somewhat abruptly and ingloriously at dirt Tahquitz View Drive. Maxwell had envisioned that his trail would continue another few miles around Idyllwild and connect to the path leading to Suicide Rock, but this trail plan ended in a bureaucratic thicket.

Contemplating the notion that half a terrific trail is better than none, return the same way.

IDYLLWILD COUNTY PARK

YELLOW PINE FOREST, HILLSIDE & LOOP TRAILS
Nature trail is 0.5 mile loop; a longer loop is 2.5 miles round trip

With its towering pines and incense cedar, great boulders and lively creeks, Idyllwild County Park offers a family-friendly introduction to the pleasures of the San Jacinto Mountains. Such pleasures are visited by a couple of miles of trail that tour the forest and climb to viewpoints for far-reaching vistas of the stony ramparts of the range.

The adventure begins at the Idyllwild Nature Center, located just a mile north of the town of Idyllwild. Exhibits present the natural and cultural history of the mountains. Many of Idyllwild's slopes, including this parkland, were logged in the 19th century; thus, a majority of the forest is second-growth.

Still, there are some impressive trees in these parts, as you'll soon observe when you set out on Yellow Pine Forest Nature Trail, which departs from the nature center (where you can pick up an interpretive pamphlet for the path). The trail passes some impressive specimens of manzanita, and meanders past black oak

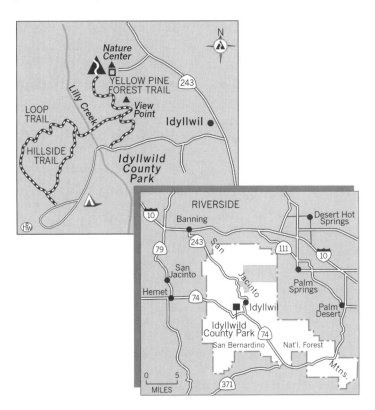

and boulders. With its soft reddish bark and stately stature, the incense cedars en route seem to personify tranquility.

About halfway along, the nature trail travels near Lily Creek and arrives at an impressive bit of bedrock where the native Cahuilla ground seeds and acorns. The resultant grinding holes (morteros) are evidence of exactly where the Cahuilla went to work—a scenic spot indeed for such labor!

The longer loop trail begins behind the visitor center and after a short, modest, ascent southward, reaches a turnoff for a Viewpoint. Enjoy grand mountain views, particularly of Lily Rock—or Tahquitz Peak if you prefer.

Continue south on the main trail on a switchbacking descent to a junction. The left fork heads down to the park campground, but you'll take the right and meander over a slope punctuated by some impressive boulders as well as a mixed forest of oak, pine and cedar.

Cross Lily Creek on a log bridge to a junction with the left-forking Hillside Trail and the straight-ahead bearing Loop Trail. (The two trails form a loop.) I like starting out with the more aggressive Loop Trail, which switchbacks steeply upward while offering great views.

After looping back toward the park campground, you'll close the loop, then retrace your steps. Re-cross the log bridge over Lily Creek and take the connector trail back to the nature center.

DIRECTIONS TO TRAILHEAD: From the town of Idyllwild, drive a mile north on Highway 243 to the signed turnoff for Idyllwild County Park. Proceed to the last parking lot and walk up the path to the Idyllwild Nature Center, where Yellow Pine Forest Trail begins. The longer trail loop begins behind the nature center.

There is a park entrance fee for both adults and children.

TAHQUITZ PEAK

SOUTH RIDGE TRAIL

From South Ridge Road to Tahquitz Peak is 6 miles round trip with 2,000-foot elevation gain; Season: May-October

Tahquitz Peak dominates the southern San Jacinto Mountains, lording over Strawberry Valley and Idyllwild on one side, and Tahquitz Valley on the other. A fire lookout tower is perched on the summit. The view from the peak is inspiring: clear-day vistas of the San Jacintos, the desert and the distant Santa Rosas.

You may notice what appear to be insect-like creatures high on the rock walls of the mountain. Southland rock climbers often come to practice their craft on the superb rock walls of Tahquitz.

Lily Rock, named for a surveyor's daughter, is the official name of the great rock, though most climbers prefer the more rugged-sounding Tahquitz. After taking one of the hundred routes (some quite hazardous) up the several faces of the rock, you can't blame the climbers for preferring something more dramatic than Lily.

South Ridge Trail, true to its name, ascends the steep south ridge of Tahquitz Peak. The trail climbs through stands of fine and fir and offers great views of Strawberry Valley and the storybook hamlet of Idyllwild.

If you want a longer hike than the six-mile round trip to Tahquitz Peak, there are a number of ways to extend your trek. By arranging a car shuttle, you could descend Tahquitz Peak to Humber Park at the outskirts of Idyllwild. For a very long loop hike, you could even follow the Ernie Maxwell Trail from Humber Park down to the foot of South Ridge Road, then up the road to the South Ridge trailhead.

DIRECTIONS TO TRAILHEAD: From Interstate 10 in Banning, exit on Highway 243 (Banning-Idyllwild Highway) and proceed about 25 miles to Idyllwild. After you've obtained your wilderness permit from the Forest Service Station in Idyllwild, you'll double back a wee bit to the south edge of town and make a left turn on Saunders Meadow Road. After 0.75 mile, turn left on Pine Avenue, drive 0.25 mile, then turn right on Tahquitz View Drive and proceed another 0.25 mile. Just prior to the road becoming dirt, turn right on South Ridge Road and travel a mile to parking and signed South Ridge Trail.

THE HIKE: From the trailhead at the top of South Ridge Road, the well-constructed path zigzags through a forest of Jeffrey pine and white fir. You'll get fine south views of Garner Valley and Lake Hemet, Thomas Mountain and Table Mountain. Far off to the west, on a clear day, you'll be able to pick out the Santa Ana and San Gabriel Mountains.

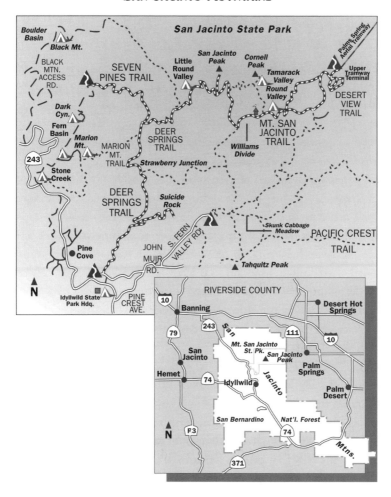

South Ridge Trail climbs to a boulder-strewn saddle, which marks the trail's halfway point. Here you'll find a rock window-on-the-world, a great place to rest or to frame a picture of your hiking mate.

From the saddle, the trail climbs in earnest past thickets of spiny chinquapin, and past scattered lodgepole pine. You'll sight the fire lookout tower atop Tahquitz Peak and many a switchback above you, but the last mile of trail goes by faster than you might expect with a slow, steady pace.

Enjoy the summit views, then either return the same way or follow your heart and forest service map through the San Jacinto Wilderness down to Humber Park and Idyllwild.

SUICIDE ROCK

DEER SPRINGS TRAIL
From Idyllwild to Suicide Rock is 7 miles round trip with 2,000 feet
elevation gain

Suicide Rock is a sheer granite outcropping that provides the romantic with a tale
of star-crossed lovers, and rewards the hiker with splendid views of Strawberry
Valley and a forest wonderland of pine and fir. Legend has it that the rock got its
tragic name from an Indian princess and her lover who leaped to their deaths over
the precipice rather than be separated, as their chief had commanded.

Suicide Rock is a splendid place to observe the ever-changing four seasons
(though you'll have a hard time climbing the rock in winter). The seasons fade in
and out with clarity and distinction in the San Jacintos. Fall colors tint the black
oak and azalea, winter brings a white blanket, spring is heralded by a profusion of
wildflowers, and the long, hot summers are tempered with thunder and lightning
displays. Views like this bring hikers back again and again to sample the beauty of
the San Jacinto Mountains.

DIRECTIONS TO TRAILHEAD: Deer Springs Trail begins across the
highway from the Idyllwild County Park Visitor Center parking area, one mile
west of town on the Banning-Idyllwild Highway 243. If you'd like to learn something about the history of the area, the nature museum at the county park is helpful.

The Forest Service's Idyllwild Ranger Station is on California 243 at Pine
Crest Avenue; the Mt. San Jacinto State Park Ranger Station in Idyllwild is at
25905 California 243.

THE HIKE: Signed Deer Springs Trail picks its way through an elfin manzanita forest, then ascends past spreading oaks and tall pines. You switchback up a
ridge to Suicide Junction, 2.3 miles from the trailhead. Here you leave the Deer
Springs Trail and bear east, contouring across Marion Ridge. You cross Marion
Creek, whose performance is seasonal, and on wet years, inspiring. A long mile
from Suicide Junction you reach the back side of Suicide Rock.

From the white granite rock you'll be able to look down and see tiny
Idyllwild and Strawberry Valley. On the far horizon are Tahquitz Peak and Lily
Rock.

DEER SPRINGS & LITTLE ROUND VALLEY

SEVEN PINES, MARION MOUNTAIN TRAILS

From Dark Canyon to Deer Springs is 7.5 miles round trip with 2,600-foot elevation gain; to Little Round Valley Camp is 10.5 miles round trip with 3,600-foot elevation gain; to San Jacinto Peak is 13.5 miles round trip with 4,400-foot gain

Seven Pines Trail ascends the cascading North Fork of San Jacinto River to its headwaters at Deep Springs. Energetic hikers will join the Deer Springs Trail for an ascent of Mt. San Jacinto.

DIRECTIONS TO TRAILHEAD: Take Highway 243 (Banning-Idyllwild Road) about 20 miles from Banning or 6 miles from Idyllwild. Just east of Alandale Ranger Station, take paved Marion Mountain Road (4S02) turnoff and drive one mile to Dark Canyon Campground. Take the one-way loop camp road through the campground and rejoin (dirt) Marion Mountain Road (4S02) at the top of the loop. Follow this road past Azalea Trails Girl Scout Camp to parking and the Seven Pines Trailhead, about 4.2 miles from the highway.

THE HIKE: Seven Pines Trail ascends the ridge between Dark Canyon and the canyon cut by the North Fork. You hike out of the San Bernardino National Forest into Mt. San Jacinto State Park. After a mile, the trails tops the ridge and descends eastward to the North Fork. In spring, when the river is swollen with snowmelt, the North Fork has quite a heady flow.

The trail climbs along a pine- and fir-covered slope, recrosses the river, and reaches a junction with Deer Springs Trail. (A right turn on the trail leads to Strawberry Junction, past Suicide Rock).

Follow Deer Springs Trail left (east) 0.25 mile to the former site of Deer Springs Trail Camp. The camp, overused in past years, has been abandoned by Mt. San Jacinto State Park. However, its all-year water supply and pleasant locale makes it an ideal lunch or rest stop.

To Little Round Valley Camp: A short walk up Deer Springs Trail from the former camp brings you to another junction. The leftward fork is Fuller Ridge Trail, which leads northwest 5 miles to Black Mountain Camp. Bear right at this junction. The trail passes through some meadowland on the way to Little Round Valley Trail Camp.

To Mt. San Jacinto: From Little Round Valley, the trail climbs through stands of lodgepole pine, and in a little more than a mile arrives at a junction with San Jacinto Peak Trail. A left turn on this trail takes you 0.25 mile past a stone shelter cabin to the top of the 10,084-foot peak.

MT. SAN JACINTO

MT. JACINTO TRAIL

From Mountain Station to Round Valley is 4 miles round trip with 600-foot elevation gain; to San Jacinto Peak is 11 miles round trip with 2,300-foot gain

Palm Springs Aerial Tramway makes it easy for hikers to enter Mt. San Jacinto State Wilderness. Starting in Chino Canyon near Palm Springs, a tram takes passengers from 2,643-foot Lower Tramway Terminal (Valley Station) to 8,516-foot Upper Tramway Terminal (Mountain Station) at the edge of the wilderness.

The day hiker accustomed to remote trailheads may find it a bit bizarre to enter Valley Station and find excited tourists sipping drinks and shopping for souvenirs. But the gondola rapidly leaves the station and carries you over one of the most abrupt mountain faces in the world. When you disembark at Mountain Station, your ears will pop and you'll have quite a head start up Mt. San Jacinto.

There's a strong geologic similarity between the High Sierra and the San Jacintos. While standing upon the summit of Mt. San Jacinto, the perceptive mountaineer may notice a subtle atmospheric similarity—both the San Jacintos

and Sierra Nevada can be called a "range of light." Powerful sunlight illuminates the San Jacintos, creating sharp contrasts between light and shadow, the kind of contrast found in an Ansel Adams photograph. There may be a six f-stop difference between the bright light shimmering on the rocky summit and the dark forest primeval below. The sun burns upon the lower slopes of Mt. San Jacinto like a fire in the wind, but the upper elevations receive a more gentle incandescent light and a fraction of the heat dispersed below. Our civilization measures time by the sun, yet as you watch sunlight and shadow play tag across the slopes, you are left with a feeling of timelessness.

DIRECTIONS TO TRAILHEAD: From Interstate 10, exit on California 111 (the road to Palm Springs). Proceed nine miles to Tramway Road, turn right, and follow the road four miles to its end at Mountain Station. Contact the Tramway office for information about prices and schedules.

THE HIKE: From Mountain Station, walk down the cement walkway through the Long Valley Picnic Area. Soon you will arrive at the state park ranger station. Obtain a wilderness permit here.

Continue west on the trail, following the signs to Round Valley. The trail parallels Long Valley Creek through a mixed forest of pine and white fir, then climbs into lodgepole pine country. Lupine, monkeyflower, scarlet bugler and Indian paintbrush are some of the wildflowers that add seasonal splashes of color.

After passing a junction with a trail leading toward Willow Creek, another 0.3 of a mile of hiking brings you to Round Valley. A trail camp and a backcountry ranger station are located in the valley, as well as splendid places to picnic in the meadow or among the lodgepole pines.

Palms to pines in twelve minutes

An alternative to returning the same way is to retrace your steps 0.3 of a mile back to the junction with the Willow Creek Trail, take this trail a mile through the pines to another signed trail north back to Long Valley Ranger Station. This alternative route adds only about a 0.25 mile to your day hike, and allows you to make a loop.

To Mt. San Jacinto Peak: From Round Valley, a sign indicates you may reach the peak by either Tamarack Valley or Wellman Divide Junction. Take the trail toward Wellman Divide Junction. From the Divide, a trail leads down to Humber Park. At the divide, you'll be treated to spectacular views of Tahquitz Peak and Red Tahquitz, as well as the more distant Toro Peak and Santa Rosa Mountain. You continue toward the peak on some vigorous switchbacks. The lodgepole pines grow sparse among the crumbly granite. At another junction, a half-mile from the top, the trail continues to Little Round Valley but you take the summit trail to the peak. Soon you arrive at a stone shelter—an example of Civilian Conservation Corps handiwork during the 1930s. From the stone hut, you boulder-hop to the top of the peak.

The view from the summit—San Gorgonio Pass, the shimmering Pacific, the Colorado Desert, distant Mexico—has struck some visitors speechless, while other have been unable to controle their superlatives. Helen Hunt Jackson's heroine Ramona found "a remoteness from earth which comes only on mountain heights," and John Muir found the view "the most sublime spectacle to be found anywhere on this earth!"

MARION MOUNTAIN

MARION MOUNTAIN, PACIFIC CREST TRAILS
From Fern Basin to San Jacinto Peak is 12 miles round trip with 4,400-foot elevation gain

It's the shortest, the steepest and, in the opinion of some hikers, the most scenic ascent of San Jacinto Peak. Marion Mountain Trail gains 2,400 feet in just 2.5 miles. The rest of the climb to the peak via Pacific Crest and Deer Springs trails is nearly as steep.

While reaching the summit of the great mountain is ample reward for most hikers, Marion Mountain Trail scatters additional rewards along the way. This is a hike for tree-lovers, a climb to remember through Conifer-Land.

Marion Mountain's lower elevations support stands of Jeffrey pine and even some oaks. Higher up the mountain grow ranks of sugar pine and white fir and higher still, some lofty lodgepole pine.

Marion Mountain Trail is a great conditioning hike for anyone planning a High Sierra adventure. The altitude and altitude gain of this hike approximates some Sierra sojourns.

Get an early start and allow plenty of time for this hike-six to nine hours, depending on your pace and how long you linger on the summit. Even if you're a well-conditioned hiker, don't be discouraged if it takes you four hours or more to make San Jacinto Peak. And don't rush the descent: the steep and rocky trail has a high ankle-turning and knee-wrenching potential.

The majority of Marion Mountain Trail traverses the Mt. San Jacinto State Park Wilderness; this means the hiker must obtain a wilderness permit, available from the state park headquarters at 29505 Highway 243 in Idyllwild.

DIRECTIONS TO TRAILHEAD: From Interstate 10 in Banning, exit on Highway 243 and ascend south some 19 winding miles. Just east of Alandale Ranger Station, take paved Marion Mountain Road (4S02) turnoff, fork left at a junction, and proceed a mile to a junction with Marion Mountain Campground Road. Bear right and drive a half-mile (passing the entrance to Fern Basin Campground) to a parking area and the Marion Mountain Trailhead located just below Marion Mountain Campground.

THE HIKE: Signed Marion Mountain Trail begins what is briefly (0.2 mile) a mellow ascent through the piney woods. You'll soon pass a spur trail leading down to Marion Mountain Campground and begin the vigorous ascent of the northwest flank of Marion Mountain.

A bit more than 1.25 miles up the trail, a sign informs hikers they've entered the

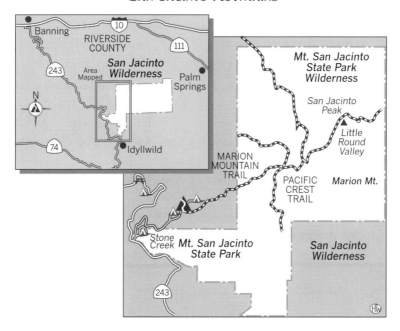

Mt. San Jacinto State Park Wilderness. Like a window on the world you left behind, the trailside view briefly opens up to reveal Highway 243 snaking through the mountains far below and the murky flatlands of the Inland Empire to the north.

Almost immediately, it's back to the trees, interspersed with ferns and big boulders. That hammering you hear could be from a high altitude headache but is more likely the rat-a-tat-tat of a woodpecker working away high atop one of the many snags near the trail.

After 2.5 miles of asent, you'll come to a junction. It's not quite the perfect four-way intersection pictured on trail maps, but it's well signed. You'll first encounter Pacific Crest Trail (Deer Springs Trail) coming in from the right (south). Turn left and walk 50 feet to a second junction. Seven Pines Trail descends to the north, but you continue your climb east on the signed PCT.

After a 0.3-mile ascent on the very well engineered and maintained PCT, you'll pass gurgling Deer Springs. The modest springs-spawned creek forms part of the headwaters of the North Fork of the San Jacinto River.

The ascent continues another 0.25 mile up the other side of the creek canyon and junctions Fuller Ridge Trail. Keep right, and keep switchbacking for another mile to Little Round Valley, where a small trail camp is located.

The trail curves east, still climbing, still switchbacking for another 1.3 miles and 800-foot elevation gain to San Jacinto Peak's summit ridge. A final 0.3-mile ascent via the summit trail leads past a stone mountaineers hut to the peak.

FULLER RIDGE

PACIFIC CREST TRAIL (FULLER RIDGE TRAIL)
From Fuller Ridge to San Jacinto Peak is 15 miles round trip with 3,200-foot elevation gain

True, you get a 7,700-foot head-start, but that doesn't make the ascent from Fuller Ridge the easiest route to the top of Mt. San Jacinto.

Do the math and the hike seems a moderate enough exercise: a climb that averages under 500 feet per mile.

Do the hike and the math seems fuzzy and downright irrelevant. Fuller Ridge presents the hiker with a much more difficult ascent than its numbers suggest.

Other paths to the peak lead through cool forest and, while by no means a walk in the park, seem to offer a kind of woodsy solace to the ascending hiker. The trail following Fuller Ridge is a challenging (the word "tortuous" comes to mind as well) series of tight switchbacks zigzagging amongst stone ramparts and wind-thrashed fir.

The attraction of ascending the mighty mountain by way of Fuller Ridge is more obvious to veteran hikers than novices. What you get is a trek on a grand, seldom-used stretch of Pacific Crest Trail, fabulous views of mountain ranges, the desert and the San Andreas Rift Zone, as well as the satisfaction of seeing the quizzical looks of the hikers who join you on the final mile of trail when you tell them you came by way of Fuller Ridge: "You came from where?" is the usual response from those taking shorter and easier ways to the top of San Jacinto.

Not to discourage you further, but Fuller Ridge is also the hardest of San Jacinto's trailheads to reach and requires a lengthy drive on dirt Black Mountain Road (closed from about late autumn to mid-spring depending on snow conditions). This is a good conditioning hike for, say, that trek to Nepal. If you're not in the mood for an all-day adventure, make the 4-mile round trip hike to the Fuller ridgeline and enjoy the far-reaching views.

Get an early start and allow plenty of time for this hike-seven to ten hours, depending on your pace and how long you linger on the summit. Even if you're a well-conditioned hiker, don't be discouraged if it takes you longer than you think to make San Jacinto Peak by this route. And don't rush the descent: the steep and rocky trail has a high ankle-turning and knee-wrenching potential.

DIRECTIONS TO TRAILHEAD: From Interstate 10 in Banning, exit on Highway 243 and ascend southeast some 15 winding miles to Black Mountain Road. (From the town of Idyllwild, drive about 8.5 miles north to Black Mountain Road.) Proceed 6 miles north to Black Mountain Campground and then another 1.5 miles to a brief, right-forking spur that leads to parking and Fuller Ridge Trailhead.

THE HIKE: The path ascends a mile (in a mellow manner at first) through open forest to a saddle. Another mile of ascent, passing the aptly named Castle Rocks, brings you to Fuller Ridge.

The path twists atop the ridgeline, dodging great boulders and contorted white fir. Savor eye-popping vistas of Mt. San Gorgonio, the Southland's 11,499-foot high point, as well as other tall peaks of the San Bernardino Mountains. Far, far below is San Gorgonio Pass, which separates the San Bernardino and San Jacinto ranges. You'll also get impressive views of the Coachella Valley.

After a bit more than a mile of squirming atop the ridgeline, PCT abandons it for the southern slopes of Mt. San Jacinto. PCT switchbacks and contours across the broad shoulders of the mountain past the headwaters of the north fork of the San Jacinto River and reaches a junction with Deer Spring Trail 5 miles from the start.

PCT continues south to soon meet up with Seven Pines and Marion Mountain trails, but you turn northeast and keep switchbacking for another mile to Little Round Valley, where a small trail camp is located.

The trail curves east, still climbing, still switchbacking for another 1.3 miles with a 800-foot elevation gain to San Jacinto Peak's summit ridge. A final 0.3-mile ascent via the summit trail leads past a stone mountaineers hut to the peak.

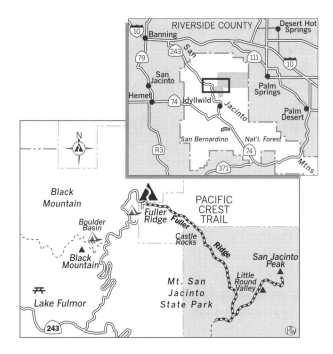

DESERT DIVIDE

SPITLER PEAK, PACIFIC CREST TRAILS
From Apple Canyon to Desert Divide is 10 miles roundtrip with 2,000-foot
gain; to Apache Peak is 12 miles round trip with 2,600-foot gain; to Antsell
Rock is 14 miles round trip with 2,600-foot gain

Riding the Palm Springs Aerial Tramway or driving the Palms to Pines Highway
are two ways to view the astonishing change in vegetation that occurs with a
change in elevation in the San Jacinto Mountains. A third way to observe the
startling contrast between desert and alpine environments is to hike up the back
side of the San Jacinto Mountains to aptly named Desert Divide. The imposing
granite divide, which reminds some mountaineers of the High Sierra, offers far-
reaching views of the canyons back of Palm Springs and of the Coachella Valley.

Most visitors to the San Jacinto Mountains begin their explorations in
Idyllwild or from the top of the tramway. Few hike—or even think about—Desert
Divide. Too bad, because this land of pine forest, wide meadows and soaring gran-
ite peaks has much to offer.

The trail begins in Garner Valley, a long meadowland bordered by tall pine.
Meandering across the valley floor is the South Fork of the San Jacinto River,
whose waters are impounded at the lower end of the valley by Lake Hemet.
Splashing spring color across the meadow are purple penstemon, golden yarrow,
owl's clover and tidy tips. Autumn brings a showy "river" of rust-colored buckwheat winding through the valley.

Spitler Peak Trail offers a moderate-to-strenuous route up to Desert Divide.
You can enjoy the great views from the divide and call it a day right there, or join
Pacific Crest Trail and continue to the top of Apache Peak or Antsell Rock.

DIRECTIONS TO TRAILHEAD: The hamlet of Mountain Center is
some 20 miles up Highway 74 from Hemet and a few miles up Highway 243
from Idyllwild. From the intersection of Highway 243 (Banning-Idyllwild
Highway) and Highway 74 in Mountain Center, proceed southeast on the latter
highway. After 3.5 miles, turn left on Apple Canyon Road and drive 2.7 miles to
signed Spitler Peak Trail. Park in the turnout at the trailhead.

THE HIKE: Spitler Peak Trail begins among oak woodland and chaparral.
The mellow, well-graded path contours quite some distance to the east before
beginning a more earnest northerly ascent. Enjoy over-the-shoulder views of Lake
Hemet and of Garner Valley. Actually, geologists say Garner Valley is not a valley
at all but a graben, a long narrow area that dropped between two bordering faults.
Garner Graben?

Nope, just doesn't have the right ring to it.

The trail climbs steadily into juniper-Jeffrey pine-Coulter pine forest. Most of the time your path is under conifers or the occasional oak. There always seem to be quite a number of deadfalls to climb over, climb under, or walk around along this stretch of trail.

About a mile from the divide the going gets steeper and you rapidly gain elevation. Finally you gain the windblown divide just northwest of Spitler Peak and intersect signed Pacific Crest Trail, five miles from the trailhead. Enjoy the vistas of forest and desert. Picnic atop one of the divide's many rock outcroppings.

PCT, sometimes known as Desert Divide Trail in these parts, offers the energetic a range of options. PCT heads north and soon passes through thick chaparral. After a half-mile you'll pass a side trail that descends steeply another 0.5-mile to Apache Springs. Another 0.5-mile along the PCT brings you to a side trail leading up to bare 7,567-foot Apache Peak.

Another mile brings you to a point just below 7,720-foot Antsell Rock. Unless you're a very good rock climber, stay off the unstable slopes and avoid the urge to ascend to the very top of the rock.

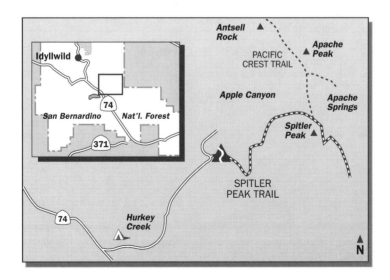

Mendenhall Valley from Mt. Palomar Observatory Trail.

CHAPTER THIRTEEN

Palomar Mountains

The Palomar Mountains, extending 25 miles along the
northern boundary of San Diego County, don't offer a huge
trail system but do offer a few fine day hikes in Palomar
Mountain State Park and the Cleveland National Forest near
Julian. After noticing large numbers of band-tailed pigeons in
the area, the Spanish named the mountains Palomar,
"pigeon roost." The mountains are certainly a diverse collection
of landscapes. Hike amidst blue lupine on sunny slopes, tiger
lilies in the shade, manzanita on dry slopes and azalea in damp
canyons. Visit the outwardly inhospitable, chaparral-blanketed
Agua Tibia Wilderness or the more welcoming oak valleys,
pine forests, spring-watered grasslands and
lush canyons of Palomar Mountain.

PALOMAR MOUNTAIN

OBSERVATORY NATIONAL RECREATION TRAIL
From Observatory Campground to Palomar Observatory is 4 miles round trip from 800-foot elevation gain

Astronomer George Hale will be remembered both for his scientific discoveries and his vision of constructing great observatories. His first vision materialized as the Yerkes Observatory with its 40-inch telescope, his second as Mt. Wilson Observatory with its 60- and 100-inch telescopes, and finally Palomar Observatory with its 200-inch telescope. The Great Glass at Palomar is the most powerful telescope in America and has done a great deal to increase our knowledge of the heavens.

Most visitors traveling to Palomar drive their cars all the way to the top, visit the Observatory and drive back down. Too bad! They miss a nice hike. Observatory Trail roughly parallels the road, but is hidden by a dense forest from the sights and sounds of traffic.

Palomar Mountain doesn't have the distinct cone shape of a stereotypical mountain top. It soars abruptly up from the San Luis River Valley to the south, but flattens out on top. Atop and just below the long crest, are oak valleys, pine forests, spring-watered grasslands and lush canyons.

All the great views from the top do not come from the Hale telescope. Palomar Mountain provides a bird's-eye view of much of Southern California. Miles and miles of mountains roll toward the north, dominated in the distance by peaks of the San Bernardino Mountains. Southward, Mt. Cuyamaca is visible, and even farther south, the mountains of Baja California. On the western horizon, orange sunset rays floodlight the Pacific.

Observatory National Recreation Trail is a delightful introduction to the geography of the Palomar Mountains. It leads from Observatory Campground to the peak, where you can learn about the geography of the heavens.

DIRECTIONS TO TRAILHEAD: From Interstate Highway 15, exit on Highway 76 east. Proceed to Rincon Springs. For a couple of miles, S6 joins with Highway 76. Continue on S6, forking to the left at South Grade Road (Highway to the Stars). South Grade winds steeply to Observatory Campground and up to the Observatory. Turn right into Observatory Campground. The Forest Service charges a day use fee. The campground closes for the winter in mid-December. Follow the campground road until you spot the signed trailhead between campsites 19 and 20. The Forest Service booklet "Guide to the Observatory Trail," which highlights flora and fauna found along the trail, is available at the trailhead.

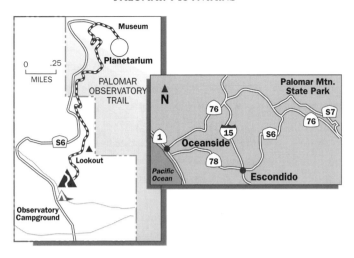

You could just as well hike the Observatory Trail from top to bottom and have a friend or family member pick you up at the bottom. To reach the upper trailhead, simply continue up the road to the Observatory parking area. The top of the trail is just outside the gates of the Observatory grounds.

THE HIKE: The signed trail begins at the edge of the campground. You begin climbing over wooded slopes and soon get a grand view of Mendenhall Valley. You continue ascending over slopes watered by the headwaters of the San Luis Rey River. As the Native American legend goes, young girls visited one of the trickling mountain springs whose waters rushed over beautiful slender stones. The maidens would reach into the water to gather these stones, the number found indicating the number of children she would bear.

The last part of the trail climbs more abruptly up manzanita-covered slopes. Soon you see the silvery dome of the 200-inch Hale telescope. This obelisk of symmetry and precision dwarfs nearby trees. Ever-changing patterns of sunlight and shade play upon the top of the dome.

Visit the Observatory gallery to see the great telescope. And take a look at the nearby museum whose exhibits explain some of the mysteries unraveled by the 200-inch lens.

PALOMAR MOUNTAIN STATE PARK

SCOTT'S CABIN TRAIL

From Silver Crest Picnic Area to Scott's Cabin; Cedar Grove Campground and Boucher Lookout is a 3.5-mile loop with 800-foot elevation gain

Palomar Mountain is a state park for all seasons. Fall offers dramatic color changes, and blustery winter winds ensure far-reaching views from the peaks. In spring, the dogwood blooms, and during summer, when temperatures soar, the park offers a cool, green retreat.

A mixed forest of cedar, silver fir, spruce and black oak invites a leisurely exploration. Tall trees and mountain meadows make the park especially attractive to the Southern California day hiker in search of a Sierra Nevada-like atmosphere.

The discovery of bedrock mortars and artifacts in Doane Valley indicate that native peoples lived in this area of the Palomars for many hundreds of years. The mountains' pine and fir trees were cut for the construction of Mission San Luis Rey. Remote Palomar Mountain meadows were a favorite hiding place for cattle and horse thieves, who pastured their stolen animals in the high country until it was safe to sneak them across the border.

This day hike is a grande randonnée of the park, a four-trail sampler that leads to a lookout atop 5,438-foot Boucher Hill.

DIRECTIONS TO TRAILHEAD: From Interstate 5 in Oceanside, drive northeast on State Highway 76 about 30 miles. Take County Road S6 north; at S7, head northwest to the park entrance. There is a day use fee. Park in the lot at Silver Crest Picnic Area just inside the park. Scott's Cabin Trail takes off from the right side of the road about 20 yards beyond the lot entrance.

THE HIKE: A trail sign points the way to Scott's Cabin, 0.5-mile away. Noisome Stellar's jays make their presence known along this stretch of trail. Scott's Cabin, built by a homesteader in the 1880s, is found on your left. The crumpled remains aren't much to view.

Descend steeply through a white fir forest and reach the signed jucntion with the Cedar-Doane Trail, which heads right (east). This steep trail, formerly known as the Slide Trail because of its abruptness, takes the hiker down oak-covered slopes to Doane Pond. The pond is stocked with trout, and fishing is permitted. A pond-side picnic area welcomes the hiker.

Continue past the Cedar-Doane Trail junction a short distance to Cedar Grove Campground. Follow the trail signs and turn left on the campground road, and then right into the group campground. Look leftward for the signed Adams

Trail, which cuts through a bracken fern-covered meadow. Once across the meadow, you'll encounter a small ravine where dogwood blooms during April and May. The trail winds uphill past some big cone spruce and reaches Nate Harrison Road.

The road is named in honor of Nathan Harrison, a Southern slave who followed his master to the California gold rush—and freedom—in 1849. Harrison laid claim to a homestead on the wild eastern edge of what is now state parkland, and had a successful hay-making and hog-raising operation, despite numerous run-ins with bears and mountain lions.

Across the road, your path becomes Boucher Trail, which ascends a north-facing slope through white fir, then through bracken ferns and black oaks, to the summit of Boucher Hill. Atop the hill is a fire lookout and microwave facility. From the summit, you get a view of the surrounding lowlands, including Pauma Valley to the west.

Return to the parking area via Oak Ridge Trail, which descends one mile between the two sides of the loop road that encircles Boucher Hill. The trail heads down an open ridgeline to a junction of five roads, where it's a mere hop, skip and a jump back to the Silver Crest Picnic Area.

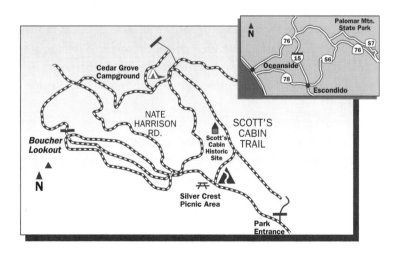

AGUA TIBIA WILDERNESS

DRIPPING SPRINGS TRAIL
From Dripping Springs Campground to Palomar-Magee Trail Junction is
13.4 miles round trip with 2,800-foot elevation gain (shorter hikes possible)

The rugged, 15,934-acre Agua Tibia Wilderness Area, located on the northwest
crest of the Palomar Mountains, seems outwardly inhospitable. Stream erosion
has carved deep and precipitous canyons in the slopes, which are blanketed in chaparral. Temperatures exceed 100 degrees in the summer and as much as two feet of
snow may fall on Agua Tibia Mountain in the winter.

The chaparral grows to gigantic proportions in this environment that
appears more desert than mountain. Much of what was known as the Giant
Chaparral (gargantuan 100-year old manzanita for example) burned in 1989 and
2000 wildfires, though the area remains attractive to the hiker seeking solitude in
the wilderness and spring wildflowers.

Dripping Springs Trail climbs Agua Tibia Mountain (4,799 feet) and offers
grand views of the mountains of Southern California, particularly panoramic
vistas of the San Bernardinos and San Jacintos. Ascend two to three miles and
you'll get some good views; continue to a junction with Palomar-Magee Trail and
even more terrific pine- and oak-framed views from the three-mile-long Agua
Tiba ridgeline.

DIRECTIONS TO TRAILHEAD: From I-15 near Temecula, take
Highway 79 southeast 11 miles to Dripping Springs Campground on your right.
Park in the trailhead parking lot.

THE HIKE: Stroll south through the campground, cross Arroyo Seco
Creek (the only water en route), and join Dripping Springs Trail. In a short distance, the path intersects the left-forking Wild Horse Trail. (Take this trail to the
top of Agua Tibia Mountain's crest for a 20-mile round trip hike to remember!)
Stick with Dripping Springs Trail, climbing south and southwest, switchbacking
forever and ever up one false summit after another on the north side of Agua
Tibia Mountain.

Arrive at what remains of the Giant Chaparral about 3.5 miles from the start.
A half-mile farther the trail descends and you get a view southeast over the
Palomars. Crowning a far-off ridge, the silver dome of Palomar Observatory
sparkles in the sun. This is a good turnaround point. Otherwise, resume switchbacking, rising above the chaparral to oak- and pine-dotted slopes. The trail ends at
an intersection with Palomar-Magee Trail, where you'll find a pleasant oak grove.

CHAPTER FOURTEEN

Cuyamaca Mountains

Plentiful rain and the Cuyamacas' geographical location between coast and desert make these mountains a unique ecosystem. The Cuyamacas offer four-season hiking at its colorful best: autumn with its brown, yellow and crimson leaves; winter snows on the higher peaks; spring with its wildflowers; and sudden summer thunderstorms.

More than 100 miles of hiking trails pass through Cuyamaca Rancho State Park, which protects a good portion of the mountains. In 2003, a severe wildfire scorched the mountains, with particularly devastating effects on the park's once rich forests of pine and fir. The park has reopened with new facilities and day-use areas and once again is becoming a pleasant place to hike.

Stonewall Peak

STONEWALL PEAK TRAIL
From Paso Picacho Campground to summit is 4 miles round trip with 900-foot elevation gain; Return via California Riding and Hiking Trail, Cold Stream Trail is 5.5 miles round trip.

Rounded Mount Cuyamaca (6,512 feet) is the highest peak in the range, but Stonewall Peak is more prominent. "Old Stony" is about 1,000 feet lower, but its huge walls of granite and crown of stone make it stand out among neighboring peaks.

In 2003, the Cedar Fire devastated the state park, burning black oak and pine forests, grassland and riparian corridors. It was the worst wildfire loss in state park history. However, nature's healing powers are truly miraculous. The park (except for its stands of pine) is recovering in extraordinary fashion.

Popular Stonewall Peak Trail leads to the top of the peak (5,730 feet) and offers grand views of the old Stonewall Mine Site, Cuyamaca Valley and desert slopes to the east. An optional route lets you descend to Paso Pichacho Campground via the California Riding and Hiking Trail and the Cold Stream Trail.

DIRECTIONS TO TRAILHEAD: From San Diego, drive east on Interste Highway 8. Exit on Highway 79 north. The highway enters Cuyamaca Rancho State Park and climbs to a saddle between Cuyamaca and Stonewall peaks. Park near the entrance of Paso Picacho Campground. The trail to Stonewall Peak begins just across the highway from the campground.

THE HIKE: From Paso Picacho Campground, the trail ascends moderately, then steeply through oak and boulder country. The black oaks display vivid colors in fall.

The trail switchbacks up the west side of the mountain. From the blackened forest, views from the north unfold. Cuyamaca Reservoir is the most obvious geographical feature. Before a dam was built to create the reservoir Cuyamaca Lake, as it was called, was a sometime affair. The Indians never trusted it as a dependable water source and the Spanish referred to it as *la laguna que de seco,* or "the lake that dries up." During dry years, the cows enjoy more meadow than reservoir and during wet years, have more reservoir than meadow.

Vegetation grows more sparse and granite outcroppings dominate the high slopes as the trail nears the top of Old Stony. A hundred feet from the summit, a guardrail with steps hacked into the granite helps you reach the top. Far-reaching views to the east and west are not possible because a number of close-in mountains block your view. You can, however, orient yourself to Cuyamaca geography from atop Stonewall Peak. Major Cuyamaca peaks, from north to south, are North Peak, Middle Peak and Cuyamaca Peak.

It's exciting to be atop Stonewall Peak when a storm is brewing over the Cuyamacas, but beware that the peak has been known to catch a strike or two. Black clouds hurtle at high speed toward the peak. Just as they are about to collide with the summit, an updraft catches them and they zoom up and over your head.

Return the way you came or via the California Riding and Hiking Trail by backtracking 100 yards on the Stonewall Peak Trail to an unsigned junction. From here, bear right (north). The trail descends steeply at first, then levels off near Little Stonewall Peak (5,250 feet). It then descends moderately to the California Riding and Hiking Trail, which traverses the west side of the park. You travel for one mile on the California Riding and Hiking Trail, which is actually part of the Stonewall Peak Trail. It forks to the right and crosses Highway 79. Don't take the fork, but continue a half-mile down the Cold Stream Trail, paralleling the highway, back to Paso Picacho Campground.

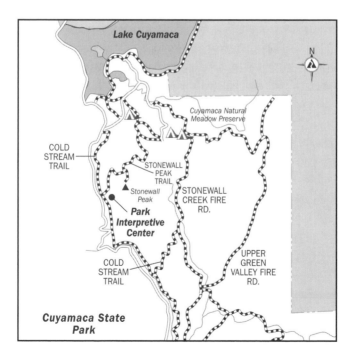

Cuyamaca Peak

CUYAMACA PEAK TRAIL
Paso Picacho Campground to Summit is 7 miles round trip with 1,600-foot elevation gain

Of the more than 100 miles of trails in Cuyamace Rancho State Park, the route offering the most spectacular views is surely the Cuyamaca Peak Trail, which climbs through a forest of oak, as well as charred pine and fir to the summit. From the 6,512-foot peak, the hiker has an open view from the Pacific to the Salton Sea.

Over the years, many day hikers have expressed their surprise to me about discovering such a densely forested mountain in Southern California. Encircling Mount Cuyamaca are silver fir and cedar, plus Coulter, sugar, ponderosa and Jeffrey pine. Or were. Many oaks survived the 2003 Cedar Fire, but the conifers were devastated in the conflagration.

Even before the 2003 fire, the road to Cuyamaca Peak passed through an area that was scorched by severe forest fires in 1950 and 1970. Quite a few tall trees were lost in those blazes, too.

The name Cuyamaca is believed to have been derived from the Native American word *ekui-amak*, variously meaning "rain from above," "rain from behind," and "place beyond rain." Mission padres called the mountain "Sierra de Cuyamat," and American mapmakers later recorded it as Kyamanc, Quiamac and even as Queermack.

Native legend has it that many more high peaks were once in the Cuyamaca Range, but the peaks took to quarreling amongst themselves. One troublemaking peak, Hilsh-ki-e (Pine Tree) battled the rest, who belched rocks upon his head. In the heat of battle, Hilsh-ki-e twisted the neck of Pook-k-sqwee, which acquired the name of Crooked Neck during this battle and is now known as Mount Cuyamaca. Hilsh-ki-e retreated and was exiled to lower elevation.

The trail, Cuyamaca Peak Fire Road, is a paved one-lane road (closed to public vehicle traffic) that winds slowly to the summit. While this guide and its author generally avoid pavement like the plague, an exception has been made for this road; it offers a most enjoyable hike and a memorable view. One view is of a park, of a mountain range, making an amazing recovery from the effects of wildfire.

DIRECTIONS TO TRAILHEAD: You may begin this hike from two places, neither of which has good parking. The Cuyamaca Peak Fire Road intersects Highway 79 just south of the park interpretive center. Look for a legal place to park along Highway 79. Or you can pick up the trail at the southernmost campsites in Paso Picacho Campground. There's a state park day use fee.

THE HIKE: The ascent, shaded by oaks, is moderate at first. Look over your shoulder for a fine view of Stonewall Peak. After passing the junction with the California Riding and Hiking Trail, the route grows steeper. Pine and fir predominate high on the mountain's shoulders.

Just about at the halfway point, the road levels out for a short distance and you'll spot Deer Spring on the left (south) side of the road. As you near the top, better and better views of Cuyamaca Reservoir and the desert are yours.

The road veers suddenly south, passes junctions with Conejos Trail and Burnt Pine Fire Road, and arrives at the summit.

The peak, located nearly in the exact center of San Diego County, provides quite a panorama. Some of the highlights include the Santa Rosa and Laguna mountains. You can look across the desert into Mexico and westward over to Point Loma, the Silver Strand and the wide Pacific. Atop Mount Palomar, the white observatory can be seen sparkling in the distance.

Return the same way, or perhaps improvise a return route back to Paso Picacho Campground via the California Riding and Hiking Trail and the Azalea Glen Trail.

CHAPTER FIFTEEN

Southern California Coast

The air and water temperatures are Mediterranean,
the place names Spanish, and the hiking, once you escape
the mass-use beaches, is surprisingly good.
For the day hiker, the Southern California coast offers
not only those white sand beaches depicted on postcards,
but a wide variety of shoreline features—the palms
of La Jolla and Santa Monica, the cliffs and bluffs
of Torrey Pines, San Clemente, Palos Verdes and Malibu.
Each of the Southland's five coastal counties—
San Diego, Orange, Los Angeles, Ventura and Santa Barbara—
has its own character. And each individual beach seems
to have its own personality: best surfing, clearest water,
grandest panoramic view or most birdlife.

CABRILLO NATIONAL MONUMENT

BAYSIDE TRAIL
From Old Point Loma Lighthouse to National Monument boundary is
2 miles round trip

Cabrillo National Monument, located on the tip of Point Loma, marks the point where Portuguese navigator Juan Rodríguez Cabrillo became the first European to set foot on California soil. He landed near Ballast Point in 1542 and claimed San Diego Bay for Spain. Cabrillo liked this "closed and very good port" and said so in his report to the King of Spain.

One highlight of a visit to the national monument is the Old Point Loma Lighthouse. This lighthouse, built by the federal government, first shined its beacon in 1855. Because fog often obscured the light, the station was abandoned in 1891 and a new one was built on lower ground at the tip of Point Loma. The 1891 lighthouse is still in service today, operated by the U.S. Coast Guard. The 1891 lighthouse has been wonderfully restored to the way it looked when Captain Israel and his family lived there in the 1880s.

Bayside Trail begins at the old lighthouse and winds past yucca and prickly pear, sage and buckwheat. The monument protects one of the last patches of native flora in southernmost California, a hint at how San Diego Bay may have looked when Cabrillo's two small ships anchored here.

DIRECTIONS TO TRAILHEAD: Exit Interstate 5 on Rosecrans Street (Highway 209 south) and follow the signs to Cabrillo National Monument. Obtain a trail guide at the visitor center.

THE HIKE: The first part of the Bayside Trail winding down from the old lighthouse is a paved road. At a barrier, you bear left on a gravel road, once a military patrol road. During World War II, the Navy hid bunkers and searchlights along these coastal bluffs.

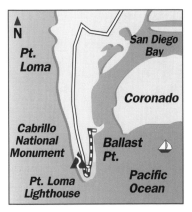

Bayside Trail provides fine views of the San Diego Harbor shipping lanes. Sometimes when ships pass, park rangers broadcast descriptions of the vessels. Also along the trail is one of Southern California's most popular panoramic views: miles of seashore, 6,000-foot mountains to the east and Mexico to the south. The trail dead-ends at the park boundary.

TORREY PINES STATE RESERVE

PARRY GROVE, GUY FLEMING TRAILS
From 0.4 to 1 mile nature trails

Atop the bluffs of Torrey Pines State Reserve lies a microcosm of old California, a garden of shrubs and succulents.

Most visitors come to view the 3,000 or so *Pinus torreyana,* which grow only here and on Santa Rosa Island, but the reserve also offers the walker a striking variety of native plants.

Be sure to check out the interpretive displays at the park museum and the native plant garden near the head of the Parry Grove Trail. Plant and bird lists, as well as wildflower maps (February through June) are available for a small fee.

Parry Grove Trail was named in honor of Dr. C.C. Parry, a botanist assigned to the boundary commission that surveyed the Mexican-American border in 1850. While waiting for the expedition to start, Parry explored the San Diego area. He investigated a tree called the Soledad (Spanish for "solitude") pine. Parry sent samples to his teacher and friend, Dr. John Torrey of Columbia, and asked that, if it proved to be a new species, it be named for Torrey. The Soledad pine became *Pinus torreyana,* or Torrey pine, in honor of the famous botanist and taxonomist.

Some 3,000 *Pinus torreyana* thrive in the state reserve.

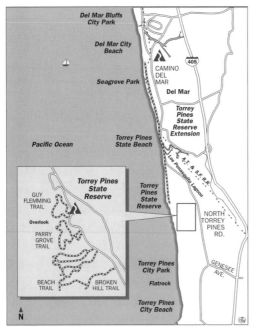

The 0.4 mile loop trail leads past toyon, yucca, and many other coastal shrubs. A five-year drought followed by an infestation of the Five Spined Engraver beetle devastated Parry Grove. Only a handful of mature Torrey pines remain, accompanied by saplings planted in 1998.

Broken Hill Trail visits a drier, chaparral-dominated, landscape, full of sage and buckwheat, ceanothus and manzanita. From Broken Hill Overlook, there's a view of a few Torrey pines clinging to life in an environment that resembles a desert badlands.

Beach Trail leads to Yucca Point and Razor Point and offers precipitous views of the beach below. The trail descends the bluffs to Flat Rock, a fine tidepool area.

Guy Fleming Trail is a 0.6 mile loop that travels through stands of Torrey pine and takes you to South Overlook, where you might glimpse a migrating California gray whale.

DIRECTIONS TO TRAILHEAD: From Interstate 5, exit on Carmel Valley Road and head west to North Torrey Pines Road (also known as old Highway 101). Carmel Valley Road dead-ends at a T; turn left (south) on North Torrey Pines Road. The main entrance to the reserve is at the base of the bluffs, where the park road climbs to a parking area near the reserve visitor center. You can also leave your car along the highway next to Torrey Pines State Beach and walk up the reserve road.

SAN ONOFRE STATE BEACH

BLUFFS BEACH TRAIL
From Beach Trail 1 to Beach Trail 6 is 5.6 miles round trip.

San Onofre is a place of steep bluffs overlooking a wide sandy beach. The beach, named for Egyptian Saint Onuphrius, is a joy to walk. But be aware that some sections are impassable at the highest tides. Check the tide table before you hike this beach!

Aptly named Bluffs Beach, part of San Onofre State Beach, is a three mile long sand strand with a backdrop of magnificent, 100-foot high bluffs. The dramatically eroded sandstone cliffs, a kind of Bryce Canyon by the sea, effectively shield the beach from sight and sound of two parallel transportation corridors—the railroad tracks and Interstate 5.

Unfortunately, something of the peaceful ambiance of the park's coastline is diminished by the giant twin spheres of the San Onofre Nuclear Power Plant located just north and Camp Pendleton Marine Base to the south. The nuke and the marines are still very much present, but public access to the splendid beach has loosened up some of late. It's possible to walk a considerable distance both north and south of the power plant.

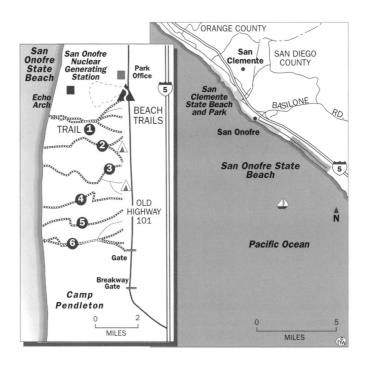

South of San Onofre State Beach is Camp Pendleton. The camp's beaches are officially off-limits, even if the no trespassing sign is removed, as it often is. However, the prevailing sentiment among beach goers is that the military is considerably less proprietary about its surf and turf these days.

San Onofre State Beach Campground is actually a length of old Coast Highway with some pull-outs. Charmless it is, but it's popular with surfers and other coastal recreationists who rate beach access over amenities.

And the beach access is first rate. A half-dozen signed trails (Beach Trail 1, Beach Trail 2 ...) descend from the bluffs to the beach. The paths vary in length from 0.1 to 0.3 mile.

DIRECTIONS TO TRAILHEAD: From Interstate 5, a few miles south of San Clemente, exit on Basilone Road. Head west, then south, following the signs to San Onofre State Beach. Park in the first day-use area near the signed trailhead for Beach Trail 1.

THE HIKE: I prefer starting with Beach Trail 1 and walking south along the state beach. From the beaches and bluffs, walkers sometimes spot dolphins, harbor seals and migrating California gray whales.

About three miles of beach-walking brings you to the end of state park property and onto Camp Pendleton's beach. The long sand strand south of the park is popular with nude sunbathers; while it's by no means a legally clothing-optional beach, be advised that some beach-goers opt for none.

Walk for miles along aptly named Bluffs Beach.

SAN CLEMENTE STATE BEACH

TRESTLES TRAIL
From State Beach to San Mateo Point is 3 miles round trip

"Our beach shall always be free from hurdy-gurdies and defilement. We believe beauty to be an asset as well as gold and silver, or cabbage and potatoes." This was the pledge of Norwegian immigrant Ole Hanson, who began the town of San Clemente in 1925. It was quite a promise from a real estate developer, quite a promise in those days of shameless boosterism a half-century before the California Coastal Commission was established.

Thanks in part to Hanson's vision, some of the peaceful ambiance of San Clemente, which he regarded as "a painting 5 miles long and a mile wide" has been preserved. And some of its isolation, too. Most everyone in the real estate community thought Hanson crazy for building in a locale 66 miles from San Diego, 66 miles from Los Angeles, but today this isolation attracts rather than repels. This isolation was one of the reasons President Richard Nixon (1969-74) established his Western White House on the bluffs above San Clemente Beach.

San Clemente State Beach is a great place for a walk. The beach is mercifully walled off from the din of the San Diego Freeway and the confusion of the modern world by a handsome line of tan-colored bluffs. Only the occasional train passing over Santa Fe Railroad tracks, located near the shore interrupt the cry of the gull, the roar of the breakers. The trestles located at the south end of the beach at San Mateo Point give Trestles Beach its name.

Trestles Beach is one of the finest surfing areas on the west coast. When the surf is up, the waves peel rapidly across San Mateo Point, creating a great ride. Before the area became part of the state beach, it was restricted government property belonging to Camp Pendleton Marine Base. During the 1960s and 1970s, surfers carried on guerrilla warfare with U.S. Marines. Trespassing surfers were chased, arrested and fined, and on many occasions had their boards confiscated.

This hike's destination, San Mateo Point, is the northernmost boundary of San Diego County, the beginning of Orange County. When the original counties of Los Angeles and San Diego were set up in 1850, the line that separated them began on the coast at San Mateo Point. When Orange County was formed from southern Los Angeles County in 1889, San Mateo Point was established as the southern point of the new county.

The enthusiastic, with the time and inclination, can easily extend this beach-hike several miles south to San Onofre State Beach. Another option worth considering is to take the train to San Clemente and walk south from the Amtrak station.

DIRECTIONS TO TRAILHEAD: From the San Diego Freeway (5) in San Clemente, exit on Avenida Calafia and head west very briefly to the entrance of San Clemente State Beach or a half-mile to Calafia Beach Park. Expect the usual entrance fee at the state beach, and metered parking at Calafia Beach Park.

North-bound motorists on I-5 will exit at Cristianitos Road, turn left and go over the freeway onto Ave. Del Presidente and drive north to the parks. Begin this hike from the state beach at the day-use area. Look for two signed beach trails.

THE HIKE: From Calafia Beach Park, cross the railroad tracks, make your way down an embankment and head south. As you'll soon see, San Clemente State Beach is frequented by plenty of shorebirds, as well as plenty of surfers, body surfers, and swimmers.

At distinct San Mateo Point, which marks the border of Orange and San Diego counties, you'll find San Mateo Creek. The headwaters of the creek rise way up in the Santa Ana Mountains above Camp Pendleton. A portion of the creek is protected by the Cleveland National Forest's San Mateo Canyon Wilderness. Rushes, saltgrass and cattails line the creek mouth, where sandpipers, herons and egrets gather.

You can ford the creek mouth (rarely a problem except after winter storms) and continue south toward San Onofre State Beach and the giant domes of San Onofre Nuclear Power Plant. Or you can return the same way.

Or here's a third alternative, an inland return route: Walk under the train trestles and join the park service road, which is usually filled with surfers carrying their boards. The service road takes you up the bluffs, where you'll join the San Clemente Coastal Bike Trail, then wind through a residential area to an entrance to San Clemente State Beach Campground. Improvise a route through the campground to the park's entry station and join the self-guiding nature trail (brochures available at the station). The path descends through a prickly pear- and lemonade berry-filled draw to Calafia Beach Park and the trailhead. The wind- and water-sculpted marine terraces just south of the trailhead resemble Bryce Canyon in miniature and are fun to photograph.

CORONA DEL MAR

CROWN OF THE SEA TRAIL
From Corona del Mar Beach to Arch Rock is 2 miles round trip; to Crystal Cove is 4 miles round trip; to Abalone Point is 7 miles round trip

In 1904, George Hart purchased 700 acres of land on the cliffs east of the entrance to Newport Bay and laid out a subdivision he called Corona del Mar ("Crown of the Sea"). The only way to reach the townsite was by way of a long muddy road that circled around the head of Upper Newport Bay. Later a ferry carried tourists and residents from Balboa to Corona del Mar. Little civic improvement occurred until Highway 101 bridged the bay and the community was annexed to Newport Beach.

This hike explores the beaches and marine refuges of "Big" and Little Corona del Mar beaches and continues to the beaches and headlands of Crystal Cove State Park. Snorkeling is good beneath the cliffs of "Big" and Little Corona beaches. Both areas are protected from boat traffic by kelp beds and marine refuge status.

Consult a tide table. Best beach-walking is at low tide.

DIRECTIONS TO TRAILHEAD: From Pacific Coast Highway in Corona del Mar, turn oceanward on Marguerite Avenue and travel a few blocks to Ocean Boulevard. Turn right and you'll soon spot the entrance to the Corona del Mar State Beach parking lot.

THE HIKE: Begin at the east jetty of Newport Beach, where you'll see sailboats tacking in and out of the harbor. Surfers tackle the waves near the jetty. Proceed down-coast along wide, sandy Corona del Mar State Beach.

At the south end of the beach, take the paved walkway and ascend to Inspiration Point, an overlook offering excellent views of the Orange County coast. Continue down-coast a few blocks on the sidewalk alongside Ocean Boulevard to the walkway leading down to Little Corona Beach. Highlight of this beach is well-named Arch Rock, which is just offshore and can be reached at very low tide.

The beach from Arch Rock to Irvine Cove, 2.5 miles to the south, is passable

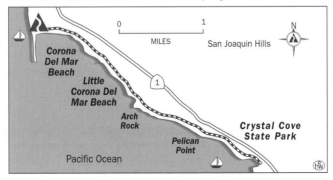

at low tide and is part of Crystal Cove State Park. Trails lead up the bluffs which, in winter, offer a good vantage point from which to observe the California gray whale migration.

Continuing your stroll down the undeveloped beach and past some tidepools brings you to the onetime resort community of Crystal Cove, site of a few dozen funky beach cottages. The wood frame cottages, little altered since their construction in the 1920s are on the National Register of Historic Places. Some of the cottages are restored and rented out by the night—by advance reservation only—as vacation getaways.

While "Cove" is something of a misnomer here because the beach here shows almost no coastal indentation, it sure is a pretty place. Rounding Reef Point, you'll continue along El Moro Beach, a sand strand that's sometimes beautifully cusped. The state park is transforming what was once a beach lined with private trailers into a day use area with beach access from a campground and the other side of Highway 1.

El Moro is a misspelling of the Spanish word *moro*, meaning round, and describes the round dome of Abalone Point, which lies dead ahead. The point, a rocky promontory located just outside Laguna Beach city limits, is made of eroded lava and other volcanic material distributed in the San Joaquin Hills. It's capped by a grass-covered dome rising two hundred feet above the water.

Return the same way or ascend one of the coastal accessways to the blufftops of Crystal Cove State Park. Blufftop trails offer a scenic alternative for a portion of your return route.

"Little Corona": Known for its gentle surf and excellent tidepools.

PALOS VERDES PENINSULA

PALOS VERDES PENINSULA TRAIL
From Malaga Cove to Rocky Point is 5 miles round trip; to Point Vincente
Lighthouse is 10 miles round trip

Palos Verdes Peninsula is famous for its rocky cliffs, which rise from 50 to 300 feet
above the ocean and for its thirteen wave-cut terraces. These terraces, or plat-
forms, resulted from a combination of uplift and sea-level fluctuations caused by
the formation and melting of glaciers. Today the waves, as they have for so many
thousands of years, are actively eroding the shoreline, cutting yet another terrace
onto the land.

While enjoying this walk, you'll pass many beautiful coves, where whaling
ships once anchored and delivered their cargo of whale oil. Large iron kettles, used
to boil whale blubber, have been found in sea cliff caves. Native Americans,
Spanish rancheros and Yankee smugglers have all added to the Peninsula's romantic history. Modern times have brought mansions to the Peninsula bluffs, but the
beach remains almost pristine. Offshore, divers explore the rocky bottoms for
abalone and shellfish. Onshore, hikers enjoy the wave-scalloped bluffs and splendid tidepools.

Hiking this beach is like walking over a surface of broken bowling balls. The
route is rocky and progress slow, but that gives you more time to look down at the
tidepools and up at the magnificent bluffs.

Check a tide table and hike only at low tide.

DIRECTIONS TO TRAILHEAD: Take Pacific Coast Highway to Palos
Verdes Boulevard. Bear right on Palos Verdes
Drive. As you near Malaga Cove Plaza, turn
right at the first stop sign (Via Corta). Make a
right on Via Arroyo, then another right into
the parking lot behind the Malaga Cove
School. The trailhead is on the ocean side of
the parking area where a wide path descends
the bluffs above the Flat Rock Point tidepools.
A footpath leaves from Paseo Del Mar, 0.1
mile past Via Horcada, where the street curves
east to join Palos Verdes Drive West.

THE HIKE: From the Malaga Cove
School parking lot, descend the wide path to
the beach. A sign indicates you're entering a

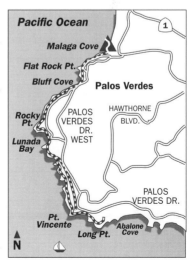

seashore reserve and asks you to treat tidepool residents with respect. To the north are sandy beaches for sedentary sun worshipers. Active rock-hoppers clamber to the south. At several places along this walk you'll notice that the great terraces are cut by steep-walled canyons. The first of these canyon incisions can be observed at Malaga Cove, where Malaga Canyon slices through the north slopes of Palos Verdes Hills, then cuts west to empty at the cove.

The coastline curves out to sea in a southwesterly direction and Flat Rock Point comes into view. The jade-colored waters swirl around this anvil-shaped point, creating the best tidepool area along this section of coast. Above the point, the cliffs soar to 300 feet. Cloaked in morning fog, the rocky seascape here is reminiscent of Big Sur.

Rounding Flat Rock Point, you pick your way among the rocks, seaweed and the flotsam and jetsam of civilization to Bluff Cove, where sparkling combers explode against the rocks and douse the unwary with their tangy spray. A glance over your right shoulder brings a view of Santa Moncia Bay, the Santa Monica Mountains in gray silhouette and on the far horizon, the Channel Islands.

A mile beyond Bluff Cove, Rocky (also called Palos Verdes) Point juts out like a ship's prow. Caught fast on the rocks at the base of the point is the rusting exoskeleton of the Greek freighter *Dominator,* a victim of the treacherous reef surrounding the peninsula.

Trek around Rocky Point to Lunada Bay, a good place to observe the terrace surfaces. From here you'll walk under almost perpendicular cliffs that follow horseshoe-shaped Lunada Bay. Shortly you'll round Resort Point, where fishermen try their luck. As the coastline turns south, Catalina can often be seen glowing on the horizon. Along this stretch of shoreline, numerous stacks, remnants of former cliffs not yet dissolved by the surf, can be seen.

The stretch of coast before the lighthouse has been vigorously scalloped by thousands of years of relentless surf. You'll have to boulder-hop the last mile to Point Vincente. The lighthouse has worked its beacon over the dark waters since 1926.

Passage is usually impossible around the lighthouse at high tide; if passable, another half-mile of walking brings you to an official beach access (or departure) route at Long Point.

Pt. Vicente Lighthouse warns mariners of the peninsula's rocky shores.

PT. DUME

ZUMA-DUME TRAIL
From Zuma Beach to Point Dume is 1 mile round trip;
to Paradise Cove is 3 miles round trip

Zuma Beach is one of Los Angeles County's largest sand beaches and one of the finest white sand strands in California. Zuma lies on the open coast beyond Santa Monica Bay and thus receives heavy breakers crashing in from the north. From sunrise to sunset, board and body surfers try to catch a big one. Every month the color of the ocean and the cliffs seem to take on different shades of green depending on the season and sunlight, providing the Zuma Beach hiker with yet another attraction.

During the whale-watching season (approximately mid-December through March), hikers ascending to the lookout atop Point Dume have a good chance of spotting a migrating California gray whale.

This walk travels along that part of Zuma Beach known as Westward Beach, climbs over the geologically fascinating Point Dume Headlands for sweeping views of the coast, then descends to Paradise Cove, site of a romantic little beach, a restaurant, and a fishing pier.

DIRECTIONS TO TRAILHEAD: From Pacific Coast Highway, about 25 miles up-coast from Santa Monica and just downcoast from Zuma Beach County Park, turn oceanward on Westward Beach Road and follow it to its end at a (fee) parking lot. Consult a tide table. Passage is easier at low tide.

THE HIKE: Proceed down-coast along sandy Westward Beach. You'll soon see a distinct path leading up the point. The trail ascends through a plant community of sea fig and sage, coreopsis and prickly pear cactus to a lookout point.

From atop Point Dume, you can look down at Pirate's Cove, two hundred yards of beach tucked away between two rocky outcroppings. In past years, this beach was the scene of much dispute between nude beach advocates, residents and the county sheriff.

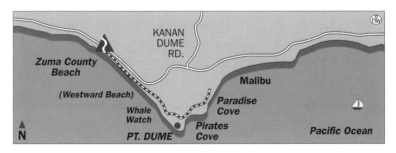

Zuma Beach

As you stand atop the rocky triangle projecting into the Pacific, observe the dense black Zuma volcanics and the much softer white sedimentary beds of the sea cliffs extending both east and west. The volcanics have resisted the crashing sea far better than the sedimentary rock and have protected the land behind from further erosion, thus forming the triangle shape of the point.

After enjoying the view and watching for whales, retrace your steps a short distance and continue on the main trail over the point, which has been set aside as a preserve under the protection of the California Department of Fish and Game. A staircase lets you descend to the beach. The tidepools are rich in marine life, especially starfish of several different colors.

A mile of beach-walking brings you to Paradise Cove, sometimes called Dume Cove. It's a secluded spot, and the scene of much television and motion picture filming. Paradise Cover Restaurant and a private pier are located at the cove. A $25 parking fee tends to restrict the number of beach-goers (who don't patronize the restaurant).

MCGRATH STATE BEACH

MCGRATH BEACH TRAIL

From State Beach to McGrath Lake is 4 miles round trip; to Oxnard Shores
is 8 miles round trip; to Channel Islands Harbor is 12 miles round trip

McGrath State Beach and McGrath Lake were named for the McGrath family
which had extensive land holdings in the Ventura coastal area dating from 1874.
Located on the western city limits of Oxnard, the two-mile long state beach
extends south from the Santa Clara River.

A small lake in the southern portion of the park helps to attract more than
two hundred species of birds, including black-shouldered kites, northern harriers,
owls and herons. Such rare birds as ospreys, white wagtails, black skimmers and
peregrine falcons have been sighted here. The lake, which is partially on private
property, was damaged by a 1993 oil spill caused by a ruptured pipeline.

The Santa Clara Estuary Natural Preserve on the northern boundary of the
park offers a haven for birds and habitat for weasels, skunks, jackrabbits, opossum,
squirrels and mice, plus tortoises and gopher snakes. Near the state beach entry
kiosk, a small visitor center features exhibits about the area's plants and wildlife.

This walk takes you on a nature trail through the Santa Clara River Estuary,
visits McGrath Lake and travels miles of sandy beach to Channel Islands Harbor.

DIRECTIONS TO TRAILHEAD: To reach McGrath State Beach, visitors southbound on Highway 101 take the Seaward Avenue offramp to Harbor
Boulevard, turn south on Harbor and travel 4 miles to the park. Northbound visitors exit Highway 101 on Victoria Avenue, turn left at the light to Olivas Park
Drive, then right to Harbor Boulevard. Turn left on Harbor and proceed 0.75
mile to the park. The signed nature trail leaves from the day use parking lot.
Signposts along the nature trail are keyed to a pamphlet, available at the entry
kiosk.

THE HIKE: From the parking lot, follow the nature trail through the estuary. The riverbank is a mass of lush vegetation: willow, silverweed and yerba
mansa. In 1980, the Santa Clara River area was declared a natural preserve, primarily to protect the habitat of two endangered birds—the California least tern
and Belding's Savannah Sparrow.

When you reach nature trail signpost 11, join a nearby trail that leads atop an
old levee, first along the river, then down-coast along the periphery of the state
beach campground. This trail joins a dirt road and continues down coast, but the
far more aesthetic route is along water's edge, so trudge over the low dunes and
walk along the shoreline.

Along the beach, visitors enjoy sunbathing or surf fishing for bass, corbina, or perch. In two miles, if you head inland a short ways, you'll spot McGrath Lake, tucked away behind some dunes.

As you continue south, more sandy beach and dunes follow. You pass a huge old Edison power plant, and arrive at Oxnard Shores, a development famous for getting clobbered by heavy surf at high tide. The beach is flat, and at one time it was eroding at the phenomenal rate of 10 feet a year. Homes were built right on the shoreline, and many have been heavily damaged. New homes are built on pilings, so the waves crash under rather than through them.

Past Oxnard Shores, a mile of beach walking brings you to historic Hollywood Beach. *The Sheik,* starring that great silent movie idol Rudolph Valentino, was filmed on the desert-like sands here. Real estate promoters of the time attempted to capitalize on Oxnard Beach's instant fame and re-named it Hollywood Beach. They laid out subdivisions called Hollywood-by-the-Sea and Silver Strand, suggesting to their customers that the area was really a movie colony and might become a future Hollywood, but it never became a mecca for the stars or their fans.

This walk ends another mile down-coast at the entrance to Channel Islands Harbor.

CARPINTERIA BEACH & BLUFFS

CARPINTERIA BEACH TRAIL
From Carpinteria State Beach to Harbor Seal Preserve is 2.5 miles round trip; to Carpinteria Bluffs is 4.5 miles round trip; to Rincon Beach County Park is 6 miles round trip

Carpinteria is one of the state park system's more popular beachfront campgrounds. A broad beach, gentle waves, fishing and clamming are among the reasons for this popularity. A tiny visitor center offers displays of marine life and Chumash history, as well as a children-friendly tidepool tank.

Carpinteria residents boast they have "The World's Safest Beach" because, although the surf can be large, it breaks far out, and there's no undertow. As early as 1920, visitors reported "the Hawaiian diversion of surfboard riding." Surfers, hikers and bird-watchers have long enjoyed the bluffs, which rise about 100 feet above the beach and offer great views of Anacapa, Santa Cruz and Santa Rosa islands.

For more than two decades a battle raged between development interests with plans to build huge housing and hotel projects and local conservationists who wanted to preserve the bluffs, one of the last stretches of privately-held, undeveloped coastline between Los Angeles and Santa Barbara.

Activists led by Citizens for the Carpinteria Bluffs and the Land Trust for Santa Barbara, along with local merchants, school children, hundreds of Santa Barbara county citizens and the California Coastal Conservancy raised money for the purchase of the property in 1998.

Although anti-drilling activitsts often blame this beach's asphalt and tar deposits on the offshore oil rigs, the truth is the seepage here is natural.

On August 17, 1769, the Captain Portolá's Spanish explorers observed the native Chumash building a canoe and dubbed the location *La Carpinteria*, the Spanish name for carpenter shop. The Chumash used the asphaltum to caulk their canoes and seal their cookware.

Around 1915, crews mined the tar, which was used to pave the coast highway in Santa Barbara County. In order to dig the tar, workmen had to heat their shovels in a furnace; the smoking tar would slice like butter with the hot blade. Long ago, the tar pits trapped mastodons, saber-toothed tigers and other prehistoric animals. Unfortunately, the pits, which may have yielded amazing fossils like those of the La Brea Tar Pits in Los Angeles, became a municipal dump.

The Carpinteria beach hike heads down-coast along the state beach to City Bluffs Park and the Chevron Oil Pier. A small pocket beach contains the Harbor

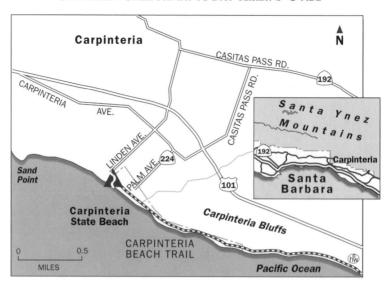

Seal Preserve. From December through May this beach is seals-only. Humans may watch the boisterous colony, sometimes numbering as many as 150 seals from a blufftop observation area above the beach.

After seal-watching, you can then sojourn over the Carpinteria bluffs or continue down the beach to Rincon Point on the Santa Barbara-Ventura county line.

DIRECTIONS TO TRAILHEAD: From Highway 101 in Carpinteria, exit on Linden Avenue and head south (oceanward) 0.6 mile through town to the avenue's end at the beach. Park along Linden Avenue (free, but time restricted) or in the Carpinteria State Beach parking lot (fee).

THE HIKE: Follow "The World's Safest Beach" down-coast. After a half-mile's travel over the wide sand strand you'll reach beach-bisecting Carpinteria Creek. During the summer, a sand bar creates a lagoon at the mouth of the creek. Continue over the sand bar or, if Carpinteria Creek is high, retreat inland through the campground and use the bridge over the creek.

Picnic at City Bluffs Park or keep walking a short distance farther along the bluffs past Chevron Oil Pier to an excellent vista point above the Harbor Seal Preserve.

From the seal preserve, you can walk another mile across the Carpinteria Bluffs. Time and tides permitting, you can continue still farther down-coast along the beach to Rincon Beach County Park, a popular surfing spot on the Santa Barbara-Ventura county line.

CHAPTER SIXTEEN

Channel Islands National Park

What you see on the islands is Southern California of a millennium ago; in fact, the islands have been dubbed "America's Galapagos." In 1980, five of the eight Channel Islands—Anacapa, Santa Cruz, Santa Rosa, San Miguel and Santa Barbara—became America's fortieth national park. Top park priorities include protecting sea lions and seals, endemic plants like the Santa Cruz pine, rich archeological digs, and the rich marine life around the isles. Thanks to newer, faster and smoother boats and more frequently scheduled voyages, visitors can reach the islands lots quicker (about an hour to Santa Cruz from Ventura Harbor) these days and have more time to hike.

Anacapa Island

ANACAPA ISLAND LOOP TRAIL
2 miles round trip

Anacapa, 12 miles southwest of Port Hueneme, is the most accessible Channel Island. It offers the hiker a sampling of the charms of the larger islands to the west. Below the tall wind-and-wave-cut cliffs, sea lions bark at the crashing breakers. Gulls, owls, and pelicans call the cliffs home.

Anacapa is really three islets chained together with reefs that rise above the surface during low tide. West Anacapa is the largest segment, featuring great caves where the Chumash Indians are said to have collected water dripping from the ceiling. The middle isle hosts a wind-battered eucalyptus grove.

The east isle, where the National Park has a visitor center, is the light of the Channel Islands; a Coast Guard lighthouse and foghorn warn ships of the dangerous channel. It's a romantic approach to East Anacapa as you sail past Arch Rock.

What you find on top depends on the time of year. In February and March, you may enjoy the sight of 30-ton gray whales passing south on their way to calving and mating waters off Baja California. In early spring, the giant coreopsis, one of the island's featured attractions, is something to behold. It is called the tree sunflower, an awkward thick-trunked perennial that grows as tall as 10 feet.

Anacapa is small (a mile long and a quarter of a mile wide), but perfect-sized for the usual visit (2 to 3 hours). By the time you tour the lighthouse and visitor center, hike the self-guided trail and have lunch, it's time to board the boat for home.

DIRECTIONS TO TRAILHEAD: For the most up-to-date information about boat departures to Anacapa and to the other islands, contact Channel Islands National Park at (805) 658-5730 or the park concessionaire, Island Packers in Ventura Harbor at (805) 642-1393.

THE HIKE: The nature trail leaves from the visitor center, where you can learn about island life, past and present.

Along the trail, a campground and several inspiring cliff-edge nooks invite you to picnic. The trail loops in a figure-eight through the coreopsis and returns to the visitor center.

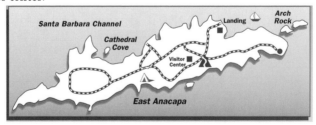

SANTA CRUZ ISLAND

CAVERN POINT, POTATO HARBOR, SMUGGLERS COVE TRAILS

From Scorpion Anchorage to Cavern Point is 1.2 miles round trip with 300-foot elevation gain; to Potato Harbor is 4.5 miles round trip with 300-foot elevation gain; to Smugglers Cove is 7 miles round trip with 500-foot elevation gain

When viewed from Ventura or Santa Barbara shores, Santa Cruz Island doesn't look that big. However, hike a trail up to one of the commanding east isle promontories and the island appears massive: row upon row of mountains alternating with deep canyons, as well as a seemingly endless series of stark bluffs extending to the horizon. The first time I took in this view I figured I was looking at a neighboring island but no, it was all Santa Cruz, all 96 square miles and 62,000 acres of it. For you city-slickers, the isle measures about four times the size of Manhattan.

Santa Cruz definitely offers hikers plenty of room to roam, as well as a far-reaching trail system composed mainly of old ranch roads. The only limitation on the hiker seems to be time: day-trippers are allowed about five hours on the island before it's necessary to catch to boat back to Ventura Harbor.

For more time on the island, consider camping near the anchorage in Scorpion Canyon. Many campers contend that the eucalyptus-shaded campground is the national park's best because it's the only one with shade, and because

Ranch house

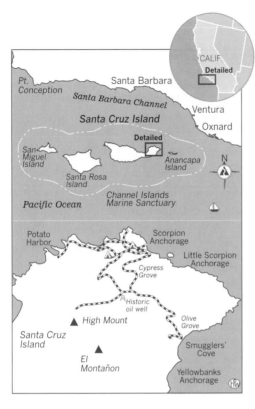

it's a convenient base for so many excellent hikes.

A short walk from the Scorpion Anchorage leads to picnic tables, restrooms and a historic two-story ranch house In the 1880s, a colony of French and Italian immigrants led by Justinian Caire began a Mediterranean-style ranch here, raising sheep and cattle, growing olives and almonds, and even making wine. The Gherini family, descendants of Caire, owned the east end of the isle until 1997, when the property was added to the national park. Rangers intend to create a visitor center at the old ranch house.

Thanks to a new higher-speed boat, the national park's primary concessionaire, Island Packers, now transports hikers from Ventura Harbor to Scorpion Anchorage on the eastern end of Santa Cruz Island in about half the time required by the company's earlier, slower craft. The ride takes about an hour non-stop, 15 minutes or so longer if the captain pauses for a bit of whale-watching or to observe the many dolphins, seals and other marine life. In the strictly subjective opinion of this seasickness-prone passenger, the new boat seemed rather smooth, too.

Island day-trippers have a choice of three trails.

Cavern Point: The short, but steep, climb on Cavern Point Trail leads the hiker to a stunning viewpoint. Look for seals and sea lions bobbing in the waters around the point, as well as cormorants, pigeon guillemots and black oyster-catchers swooping along the rugged volcanic cliffs.

Potato Harbor: The jaunt to Potato Harbor begins on a right-forking road just beyond the upper end of the campground. After a heart-stirring half-mile climb, the road levels and heads west.

This hike parallels the mainland coast so it's fun to look back at the cities and civilization you left behind-a unique perspective indeed. Two miles out a spur trail leads oceanward to an overlook of the distinctly tater-shaped cove backed by rugged cliffs.

Smugglers Cove: The signed dirt road to Smugglers Cove climbs east then west as it passes a cypress grove. At the two-mile mark, a spur trail leads to San Pedro Point, a worthy destination for the time-short hiker.

The road descends to an airstrip, then down to the beach. Note the century-old eucalyptus and olive trees in the vicinity of Smugglers Cove.

An optional return route is by way of Scorpion Canyon Trail, which travels through the habitat of the Santa Cruz scrub jay, a bird that's about 30 percent bigger and a much brighter blue than its mainland cousin, and found nowhere else in the world.

There are two more accessible landings (and good hikes accompanied by the Nature Conservancy) on the island known as The Main Ranch Trip, which emphasizes human history, and the Pelican Bay Trip, which stresses natural history.

Main Ranch Day Trip: From the landing at Prisoners Harbor, it's a three-mile hike under old oaks and through eucalyptus groves along an old fennel-lined ranch road. Your party will be accompanied by a Nature Conservancy employee who will point out some of the botanical and historical highlights encountered en route.

Upon arrival at the ranch, visitors eat lunch around a pool. After lunch you can take a tour of the ranch buildings, including a tiny cabin converted into an anthropology museum, the main ranch house and some dilapidated winery buildings. A restored stone Catholic church celebrated its 100th anniversary in 1991 with a visit by Archbishop (now Cardinal) Roger Mahony. Next to the old church is a cemetery where both humans and ranch dogs rest in peace.

Pelican Bay Day Trip: After arrival at Pelican Bay, landing is by a small skiff onto a rocky ledge. You'll have to climb up a somewhat precipitous cliff trail to reach the picnic spot overlooking the bay.

A Nature Conservancy naturalist leads your group on an educational hike (about 3 miles round trip) along the north shore. Two special botanical delights are a bishop pine forest and a grove of Santa Cruz Island ironwood.

SANTA ROSA ISLAND

LOBO CANYON, EAST POINT, CHERRY CANYON TRAILS
5 miles round trip around Lobo Canyon; 1 mile around East Point; 3 miles around Cherry Canyon.

Grasslands cover much of Santa Rosa Island, which is cut by rugged oak- and ironwood-filled canyons. Torrey pines are found at Beecher's Bay.

Santa Rosa had a considerable Chumash population when explorer Juan Rodríguez Cabrillo sailed by in 1542. Scientists who have examined the island's extensive archeological record believe the island was inhabited at least 10,000 years ago.

After the Chumash era, during Spain's rule over California, the island was land granted to Don Carlos and Don José Carrillo. For many years their families raised sheep on the island and were known on the mainland for hosting grand fiestas at shearing time.

In 1902, Walter Vail and J.W. Vickers bought the island and raised what many considered some of the finest cattle in California. The island became part of Channel Islands National Park in 1986.

The national park service offers a couple of ranger-guided walking tours of the island. Hikers are transported to the more remote trailheads by four-wheel drive vehicles. (See Anacapa Island hike for visitor information)

Lobo Canyon (5 miles round trip): Hikers descend the sandstone-walled

Santa Rosa's beaches and bluffs are a delight for hikers.

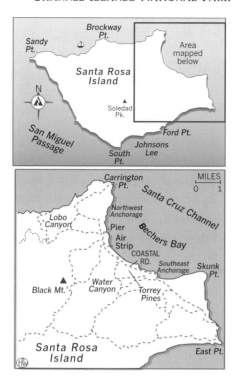

Canada Lobos, pausing to admire such native flora as island monkeyflower, dudleya and coreopsis. At the mouth of the canyon, near the ocean, is a Chumash village site. The hike continues, as the trail ascends the east wall of the canyon, then drops into Cow Canyon. At the mouth of Cow Canyon is an excellent tidepool area.

East Point Trail (1 mile round trip): Here's an opportunity for hikers to visit a rare stand of Torrey pines, and a large freshwater marsh where bird-watchers will enjoy viewing shorebirds and waterfowl. Trail's end is one of Santa Rosa's beautiful beaches.

The Torrey pines are an easy 3-mile round trip walk from the campground; the stand is located on a hillside. From the top of this hill are spectacular views of Beecher's Bay.

Cherry Canyon Trail (3 miles round trip): Walking Cherry Canyon offers the opportunity to see some plants and animals that are found nowhere else. The trailheads two miles up the canyon to an oak grove. On the return trip, the trail offers far-reaching views of the interior, roaming deer and Roosevelt elk, and the dramatic sweep of Beecher's Bay. Trail's end is the island's historic ranch complex.

SAN MIGUEL ISLAND

SAN MIGUEL ISLAND TRAIL
From Cuyler Harbor to Lester Ranch is 3 miles round trip with 700-foot elevation gain

San Miguel is the westernmost of the Channel Islands. Eight miles long, four miles wide, it rises as a plateau, 400 to 800 feet above the sea. Wind-driven sands cover many of the hills which were severely overgrazed by sheep during the island's ranching days. Owned by the U.S. Navy, which once used it as a bombing site and missile tracking station, San Miguel is now managed by the National Park Service.

Three species of cormorants, storm petrels, Cassin's auklets, and pigeon guillemot nest on the island. San Miguel is home to six pinniped species: California sea lion, northern elephant seal, steller sea lion, harbor seal, northern fur seal and Guadalupe fur seal. The island may host the largest elephant seal population on earth. As many as 15,000 seals and sea lions can be seen basking on the rocks during mating season.

A trail runs most of the way from Cuyler Harbor to the west end of the island at Point Bennett, where the pinniped population is centered. The trail passes two round peaks, San Miguel and Green Mountain, and drops in and out of steep canyons to view the lunar landscape of the caliche forest. You must hike with the resident ranger and stay on established trails because the island's vegetation is fragile.

DIRECTIONS TO TRAILHEAD: Plan a very long day-or better yet, an overnight trip to San Miguel. It's at least a five-hour boat trip from Ventura. (See Anacapa hike on page 266 for more visitor information).

THE HIKE: Follow the beach at Cuyler Harbor to the east. The harbor was named after the original government surveyor in the 1850s. The beach around the anchorage was formed by a bight of volcanic cliffs that extend to bold and precipitous Harris Point, the most prominent coastal landmark.

At the east end of the beach, about 0.75 mile from anchoring waters, a small

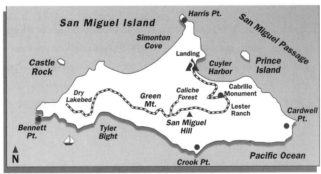

Snoozing elephant seal, one of thousands that bask on San Miguel's beaches.

footpath winds its way up the bluffs. It's a relatively steep trail following along the edge of a stream-cut canyon. At the top of the canyon, the trail veers east and forks. The left fork leads a short distance to Cabrillo Monument.

You can anchor and come ashore at "The Palm Trees" during rough weather or under heavy swell conditions. In calm weather, however, come ashore at Gull Rock right in front of Nidever Canyon. You will be able to see the trail above the east side of the canyon. When you get to the top of the canyon the ranger station and pit toilet are straight ahead. Instead of going straight you can turn east, The trail ascends a short distance to the Cabrillo Monument. The Lester Ranch is a short distance beyond that.

Juan Rodríguez Cabrillo, Portuguese explorer, visited and wrote about San Miguel in October 1542. While on the island he fell and broke either an arm or a leg (historians are unsure about this). As a result of this injury he contracted gangrene and died on the island in January 1543 and it's believed (historians disagree about this, too) he was buried here. In honor of Cabrillo, a monument was erected in 1937.

The right fork continues to the remains of a ranch house. Of the various ranchers and ranch managers to live on the island, the most well-known were the Lesters. They spent 12 years on the island and their adventures were occasionally chronicled by the local press. When the Navy evicted the Lesters from the island in 1942, Mr. Lester went to a hill overlooking Harris Point, in his view the prettiest part of the island, and shot himself. Within a month his family moved back to the mainland. Not much is left of the ranch now. The buildings burned down in the 1960s and only a rubble of brick and scattered household items remain.

For a longer 14-mile round trip the hiker can continue on the trail past the ranch to the top of San Miguel Hill (861 feet), down, and then up again to the top of Green Mountain (850 feet). Ask rangers to tell you about the caliche forest, composed of fossil sand casts of ancient plants. Calcium carbonate reacted with the plants' organic acid, creating a ghostly forest.

SANTA BARBARA ISLAND

SIGNAL PEAK LOOP TRAIL
Loop around isle is 2.5 miles round trip with 500-foot elevation gain.

Only one square mile in area, Santa Barbara is the smallest Channel Island. It's located some 38 miles west of San Pedro—or quite a bit south of the other islands in the national park.

Geologically speaking, Santa Barbara arose a bit differently from the other isles. The island is a volcano, leftover from Miocene times, some 25 million years ago, and shares characteristics with Mexico's Guadalupe Islands.

To bird-watchers, Santa Barbara means seabirds, lots of them—gulls, cormorants, pelicans and black-oyster catchers. And the island boasts some rare birds, too: the black storm-petrel and the Xantus murrelet.

Besides the birds, another reason to bring binoculars to the island is to view sea lions and elephant seals. Webster Point on the western end of the isle is a favorite haul-out area for the pinnipeds.

Early in this century, the isle's native flora was all-but destroyed by burning, clearing, and planting nonnative grasses, followed by sheep grazing. Besides the grasses, iceplant, a South African import, began to spread over the island. Even when the hardy iceplant dies, it hurts the native plant community because it releases its salt-laden tissues into the soil, thus worsening the odds for the natives. Park service policy is to re-introduce native plants and eliminate nonnatives.

Six miles of trail criss-cross the island. A good place to start your exploration is Canyon View Nature Trail. Request an interpretive brochure from the resident ranger and enjoy learning about island ecology.

DIRECTIONS TO TRAIL-HEAD: Santa Barbara Island is infrequently serviced by boat, but it is possible to join a trip. Contact park headquarters.

CHAPTER SEVENTEEN

Catalina Island

Catalina is located only 19 miles off the mainland (just an hour or so by the new fast ferry boats), but it's so quiet it seems a million miles from the L.A. megalopolis. Hikers can enjoy the isle's considerable romance while discovering secluded beaches, splendid backcountry and breathtaking Pacific vistas. Roaming the hills and savannas with visiting hikers are the island's resident buffalo (brought here by Hollywood moviemakers in the 1920s), deer, rabbits and wild boar. The hiker can take advantage of a shuttle bus system to create memorable one-way journeys across the island's interior, most of which is under the careful stewardship of Catalina Island Conservancy.

AVALON CANYON

AVALON CANYON ROAD, HERMIT GULCH TRAIL, DIVIDE ROAD, MEMORIAL ROAD

From Avalon to Hermit Gulch Campground is 3 miles round trip with 200-foot elevation gain; loop via Hermit Gulch Trail and Botanical Garden is 6.5 miles round trip with 1,000-foot gain

Botanical Garden is a showcase for plants native to Catalina, and to the Channel Islands. At the head of the canyon is the imposing Wrigley Memorial, a huge monument honoring chewing gum magnate William Wrigley, who purchased most of the island in 1919.

Families with children, and those visitors looking more for a walk than a hike, will enjoy a stroll through Botanical Garden. The garden (fee for entry) began in the 1920s, when Wrigley's wife Ada began planting native and exotic plants in Avalon Canyon. More recently, the garden has greatly expanded, emphasizing native Southern California flora. Particularly interesting are plants endemic to Catalina, including Catalina mahogany, Catalina manzanita, Catalina live-forever, and Catalina ironwood.

More adventurous hikers will undertake the second, more strenuous part of this loop trip; it utilizes Hermit Gulch Trail (one of the few genuine footpaths on the island) as well as fire roads, and offers a sampling of Catalina's rugged and bold terrain.

Don't miss The Nature Center, located just down Avalon Canyon Road from Hermit Gulch Campground. The center, operated by the very friendly and helpful staff of Catalina Island Conservancy, offers nature and history exhibits and is the place to go for the latest trail information. A (free) hiking permit is required for venturing into the Catalina backcountry.

DIRECTIONS TO TRAILHEAD: Several boat companies offer ferry service to Catalina, with departures from San Diego, Newport Beach, Long Beach and San Pedro. The modern fleet makes the 22-mile crossing to Catalina in a bit more than an hour from Long Beach.

If you want to skip the walk along island byways to the trailhead, the Avalon Trolley (modest fee) departs from the waterfront and downtown (3rd Street) locations and makes stops at Hermit Gulch Campground (where Hermit Gulch Trail begins)and Botanical Garden. The Trailmaster's suggestion: take the trolley up to the trailhead and walk back down to Avalon.

THE HIKE: Head uphill along Catalina Street past shops and residences, jog briefly right on Tremont Street, and join Avalon Canyon Road. You'll walk

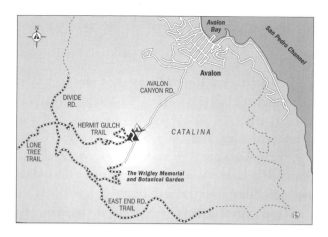

past the country club and golf course to one of William Wrigley's many contributions to the island, Bird Park, which once held thousands of unusual birds in the "largest bird cage in the world." On the left side of the road, bleacher bums will stop for a view of a baseball field and pay homage to the one-time spring training camp of Wrigley's beloved Chicago Cubs.

At Hermit Gulch Campground, located a few hundred yards below road's end and the Botanical Garden, join signed Hermit Gulch Trail and begin what at first is a vigorous ascent. The trail ascends 1.7 miles along the waterless canyon to the top of a divide and an intersection with aptly named Divide Road. From the 1,000-foot high divide, rest, read the poetry posted on a plaque, and partake of commanding views of both sides of the island and of the mainland.

Bear left on Divide Road. Walk along the divide, which bristles with prickly pear cactus. The slopes below are crisscrossed with trails made by the island's many wild goats. After about 0.75 mile of walking atop the divide, you'll join Memorial Road.

The descent on Memorial Road offers excellent views of Avalon Harbor. It's likely your approach will flush a covey or two of quail from the brush. Practiced birders might recognize the Catalina quail, a slightly larger and slightly darker subspecies than its mainland relatives.

Scrub oak, manzanita and lemonade berry—and many more of the native plants featured in the botanical garden—grow wild along the fire road, which leads to the back gate of Botanical Garden. Enter the garden and you'll soon come face-to-face with the Wrigley Memorial. At one time, Wrigley's body was entombed here. Climb up the many stairs to the 232-foot-wide, 130-foot-high monument, and enjoy the great view of Avalon Harbor.

Walk amongst the fascinating flora to the garden entrance and return to Avalon by foot or by trolley.

BLACK JACK

BLACK JACK TRAIL
From Black Jack Junction to Little Harbor is 8 miles one way with 1,500-foot elevation loss.

Catalina's terrain is rugged and bold, characterized by abrupt ridges and V-shaped canyons. Many of the mountaintops are rounded, however, and the western end of the island is grassland and brush, dotted with cactus and seasonal wildflowers. Bison, deer, boar and rabbits roam the savannas.

This walk is a good introduction to the island; it samples a variety of terrain on the island, inland and coastal. Transportation logistics are a bit complex, but the trail is easy to follow.

DIRECTIONS TO TRAILHEAD: From Avalon, travel to the trailhead via the Catalina Island Interior Shuttle Bus (fee), which departs from the information center in Island Plaza. Secure the necessary hiking permit (free) from the center.

THE HIKE: At signed Black Jack Junction, there's a fire phone and good views of the island's precipitous west ridges.

The trail, a rough fire road, ascends for one mile over brush- and cactus-covered slopes. You'll pass the fenced, but open shaft of the old Black Jack Mine (lead, zinc and silver). On your left a road appears that leads up to Black Jack Mountain, at 2,006 feet in elevation the island's second highest peak. Continue past this junction.

Ahead is a picnic ramada with a large sunshade and a nearby signed junction. You may descend to Black Jack Camp, which is operated by Los Angeles County.

Buffalo have a home and place to roam on Catalina.

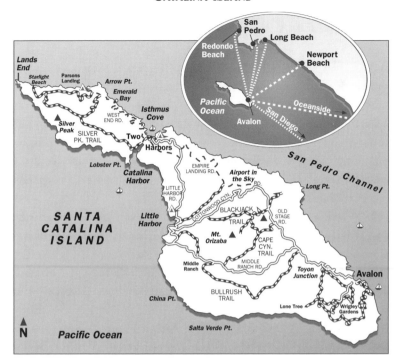

Here you'll find tables, shade, and water. Set in a stand of pine, the camp offers fine channel views.

Bear right on signed Cottonwood/Black Jack Trail. A second junction soon appears. Continue straight downhill. (The other trail ascends 2,097-foot Mt. Orizaba, Catalina's highest peak.)

The trail drops through a steep walled canyon, with vegetation—chaparral and grassland—is favored by a large herd of wild goats. At the bottom of the canyon, pass through three gates of a private ranch. (Close all gates behind you.)

The trail reaches the main road connecting Little Harbor with Airport-in-the-Sky. You may bear left at this junction and follow the winding road 3.5 miles to Little Harbor. For a more scenic route of about the same distance, turn right on the road. Hike about 200 yards to the end of the ranch fence line, then bear left, struggling cross-country briefly through spiny brush and intersect a ranch road. This dirt road follows the periphery of the fence line on the east side of the ranch to the top of a canyon. You bear left again, still along the fence line. Ascend and then descend, staying atop this sharp shadeless ridge above pretty Big Springs Canyon. When you begin descending toward the ocean, you'll spot Little Harbor.

Little Harbor is the primary campground and anchorage on the Pacific side of the island. It's a good place to relax while you're waiting for the shuttle bus, or to refresh yourself for the hike through buffalo country to Two Harbors.

LITTLE HARBOR

LITTLE HARBOR TRAIL
From Little Harbor to Two Harbors is 7 miles one way

From a distance, the mountainous land on Catalina's east end appears to be separated from a smaller portion on the west end; in fact, it's an optical illusion. The eye is tricked by a low-lying isthmus, the narrowest section of the island. Catalina Harbor lies on the ocean side of this isthmus, Isthmus Cove on the channel side, and together this area is called Two Harbors.

As the Wrigley family opened the island to tourism, Two Harbors pursued a destiny apart from Avalon. During the 1920s and 1930s, it was a peaceful sanctuary for Hollywood celebrities and the elite Southland yachting set.

This hike leads across the island from the Pacific side to the Channel side and offers fine views and a chance to observe buffalo. Your destination is Two Harbors, popular with campers and boaters.

DIRECTIONS TO TRAILHEAD: A shuttle bus transports you across the island from Avalon to Little Harbor and can pick you up in Two Harbors for the return to Avalon. If you purchased a ferry ticket from the mainland to Avalon, it's possible to leave the island from Two Harbors if you make arrangements with the ferry company.

THE HIKE: From Little Harbor, a onetime stagestop turned popular campground and anchorage, join Little Harbor Road and begin ascending higher and higher into Little Springs Canyon.

Buffalo graze both sides of the canyon and two reservoirs have been developed for the animals. In 1924, when Hollywood moviemakers were filming Zane Grey's classic Western, *The Vanishing American,* 14 buffalo were brought to the island. Recapturing them after filming proved impossible so the beasts were left to roam. The animals adapted well to life on Catalina and quickly multiplied. Today's population is held at 400 to 500, the ideal number for available pasturage.

At an unsigned junction a mile past Lower Buffalo Reservoir, bear left on Banning House Road, which leads 3.25 miles to Two Harbors. (Little Harbor Road continues north, then west, to Two Harbors if you prefer to stick to this road.) Rough Banning House Road ascends very steeply up a canyon roamed by wild boar. At the windswept head of the canyon, hikers are rewarded with superb views of the twin harbors of Catalina Harbor and Isthmus Cove, and can see both the eastern and western fringes of the island.

A steep northeasterly descent brings you to the outskirts of Two Harbors. Improvise a route past ranchettes and private clubs to the ferry building.

CHAPTER EIGHTEEN

West Mojave
(Antelope Valley)

Situated south of the Tehachapi Mountains and northwest of
the San Gabriel Mountains, the Antelope Valley makes up the
western frontier of the Mojave Desert. The West Mojave
presents great sandscapes, many flat areas and some isolated
ridges and buttes. The valley's natural attractions include a
reserve for the state's official flower—the California poppy.
Poppies bloom on many a grassy slope in the Southland but
only in the Antelope Valley does the showy flower blanket
whole hillsides in such brilliant orange sheets. Other parks
preserve a Joshua tree woodland (Saddleback Butte State Park)
and display the remarkable earthquake-fractured geology of this
desert (Devil's Punchbowl County Park).

VASQUEZ ROCKS

GEOLOGY, PACIFIC CREST TRAILS
From 1 to 3 miles round trip.

Chances are, you've seen the rocks on TV and the big screen many times—from old Westerns to modern sci-fi films. And you've probably seen Vasquez Rocks while motoring along the Antelope Valley Freeway; the famed formations are a short distance from California 14.

But the best place to see the Southland's most famous geological silhouette is Vasquez Rocks County Park Natural Area in Agua Dulce. Hiking trails circle the rocks, which are not only enjoyable to view, but fun to climb.

Through a camera lens, and from a distance, the rocks look insurmountable; actually, they're rather easy to climb. The rocks are only about 100 to 150 feet high, and you can find safe and mellow routes to the top of the sandstone outcrops.

The rocks themselves are tilted and worn sandstone, the result of years of earth-quake action and erosion by elements. The big beds of sedimentary rock known as the Mint Canyon Formation were laid down some eight to 15 million years ago. The Vasquez Rocks Formation is composed of coarser, redder layers underneath.

The Tataviam people occupied the area until the late 1700s, when their culture was overwhelmed and eventually extinguished by the soldiers, settlers and missionaries of the San Fernando Mission.

During the 1850s and 1860s, notorious highwayman Tiburcio Vasquéz used the rocks and canyons as a hide-out from the Los Angeles lawmen who were pursuing him. Even before he was hung for his crimes in 1875, the area was known as Vasquez Rocks.

The trail system at Vasquez Rock is a bit informal. Because of the open nature of the terrain, hikers can—and do—tend to wander where their rock fancy takes them. If you remember that the park entrance/office is more or less to the north and the Antelope Valley Freeway to the south, you'll stay fairly well oriented.

A favorite route of mine, a clockwise tour of three miles or so, is described below; however, part of the fun of Vasquez Rocks is going your own way.

DIRECTIONS TO TRAILHEAD: From the Antelope Valley Freeway (14), a few miles northeast of the outskirts of Canyon Country, exit on Agua Dulce Road. Head north 1.5 miles. Agua Dulce Canyon Road swings west and you join Escondido Canyon Road, proceeding 0.25 mile to the signed Vasquez Rocks County Park entrance on your right. You can park just inside the entrance at the small parking area near the park office, or continue to the main lot near the largest of the rock formations.

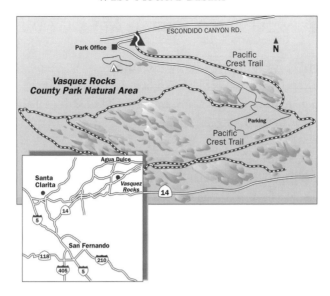

THE HIKE: Begin at the signed trailhead for Geology Trail just across the park road from the parking lot. (Pick up an interpretive brochure, as well as a trail map, from the office.) Soon after you begin your trail-side study of strata, Geology Trail intersects Pacific Crest Trail and you'll head right.

The mile-long stretch of PCT through the park is part of a segment that connects the San Gabriel Mountains to the south with the Sierra Pelona area of Angeles National Forest to the north. The path parallels the park road. To your left are some scattered residences and the open desert beyond; to your right are some of the most famous of the Vasquez Rocks.

Pacific Crest Trail joins a dirt road at the edge of the picnic area and continues west atop the north wall of Escondido Canyon. Very few park visitors, it seems, hike here, though the rock formations are stunning and a seasonal creek flows through the canyon. Only the annoying hum of the nearby Antelope Valley Freeway disturbs the natural beauty.

You can cross the creek with the PCT, double back along the other side of Escondido Canyon, and continue your exploration of the little-known southern part of the park. But to continue to the main rock formations, stay west with the dirt road and you'll soon reach a junction with the park's horse trail. You can take this trail if you wish, or continue a short distance farther and join the foot trail.

The Vasquez Rocks area is a transition zone between mountain and desert environments. Yucca, buckwheat, sage and California juniper are among the plants you'll pass en route.

The footpath drops northwestward then heads east to visit the most dramat-ic of the Vasquez Rocks.

DEVIL'S PUNCHBOWL NATURAL AREA COUNTY PARK

BURKHART, PUNCHBOWL TRAILS

From Visitor Center to Devil's Chair is miles round trip with 200-foot elevation gain; from South Fork Campground to Devil's Chair is 6 miles round trip with 500-foot gain

Southern California has many faults, and the mightiest of these is the San Andreas. Nowhere is the presence of this fault more obvious than in Devil's Punchbowl County Park. The dun-colored rocks have been tilted every which way and weathered by wind and rain. They are a bizarre sight to behold.

Punchbowl Trail takes you into the Devil's domain, a satanically landscaped rock garden on the desert side of the San Gabriel Mountains. The trip offers views of the Punchbowl Fault and the San Jacinto Fault—part of what seismologists call the San Andreas Rift Zone.

Winter is a fine time to visit the Punchbowl. Winds scour the desert clean and from the Devil's Chair, you can get superb views of this land, as well as the seemingly infinite sandscape of the Mojave.

Note that the six-mile-long Punchbowl Trail may be hiked from two directions or as a one-way with a car shuttle.

If you're looking for a much shorter hike check out the one-third mile-long nature trail, Pinyon Pathway, which introduces visitors to park geology and plant life, and a one-mile loop trail that offers grand views of the Punchbowl.

DIRECTIONS TO TRAILHEAD: From Highway 138 on the east edge of Pearblossom, exit on County Road N6 (Longview Road) and proceed south 7.5 miles to the entrance of Devil's Punchbowl Natural Area County Park.

To South Fork Campground: From Pearblossom Highway (Highway 138) in Pearblossom, turn south onto Longview Road, then briefly left on Fort Tejon Road and right on Valyermo Road. Continue three miles to Big Rock Creek Road. Two-and-a-half miles past this junction, turn right on a signed dirt road to South Fork Campground and proceed one mile to the special day use/hiker's parking lot below the campground. The road is suitable for passenger cars, but on occasion, Big Rock Creek may be too high for a low-slung car to ford; you may have to walk an extra mile to the trailhead. The signed trail departs from the parking area.

THE HIKE: At the south side of the parking lot, join signed Burkhart Trail, tracing the Punchbowl's northwest rim. A half-mile out, the path merges with a retiring road and reaches a trail junction amidst Coulter pine in another quarter-mile.

Join Punchbowl Trail, contouring around the heads of steep canyons that plunge into the Punchbowl. Descend steep switchbacks to a trail junction. A 0.1 mile connector trail leads across a narrow ridge (with some strategically placed protective fencing) to the Devil's Chair.

Take in the awesome panorama of the Punchbowl and its jumbled sedimentary strata. The somersaulted sandstone formation resembles pulled taffy. If you look west to the canyon wall, you can see the vertical crush zone of the fault, marked by white rocks.

From South Fork Campground: Join Punchbowl Trail and stay on it past the junction with South Fork Trail. Cross Big Rock Creek and begin a climb through manzanita and heat-stunted pinyon pine to a saddle where there's a view of the park and its faults. Descend from the saddle, down chaparral-covered slopes and over to Holcomb Canyon. Along the way, notice the strange dovetailing of three plant communities: yucca-covered hills, oak woodland, and juniper and piney woods.

From Holcomb Creek, the trail ascends steeply up another ridge through a pinyon pine forest to the Devil's Chair.

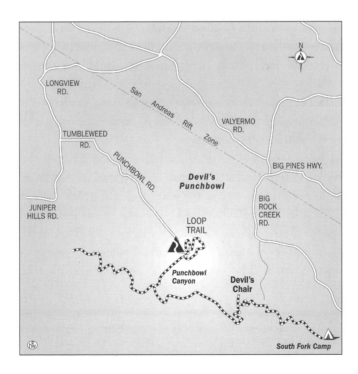

RED ROCK CANYON

HAGEN, RED CLIFFS TRAILS
1 to 2 miles round trip; Season: October–May

The view of Red Rock Canyon may very well seem like déjà vu. Cliffs and canyons in these parts have appeared in the background of many a Western movie.

A black-and-white movie of Red Rock Canyon would be dramatic: shadow and light playing over the canyon walls. Technicolor, however, might more vividly capture the aptly named red rock, along with the chocolate brown, black, white and pink hues of the pleated cliffs.

Gold fever in the 1890s prompted exploration of almost all the canyons in the El Paso Mountains. During this era, Rudolph Hagen acquired much land in the Red Rock area. He named the little mining community/stage stop Ricardo after his son Richard. The Ricardo Ranger Station is located at the site of the once-thriving hamlet.

Red Rock Canyon became a state recreation area in 1969; when it became obvious off-road vehicles were damaging the hills and canyons, Red Rock was upgraded to park status in 1982.

Best places to hike are in the park's two preserves. You'll find some trails to hike, but this park lends itself to improvisation.

Hagen Canyon Natural Preserve is a striking badlands, with dramatic cliffs capped by a layer of dark basalt. A primitive one-mile loop trail explores the canyon.

Red Cliffs Natural Preserve protects the 300-foot sandstone cliffs east of Highway 14. No developed trail exists; however hikers can enjoy a mile or so of cross-country travel through the preserve.

The park nature trail, a 0.75-mile path tells the geologic story of the area, and points out typical desert flora. It's keyed to an interpretive pamphlet available at the trailhead. Join the nature trail at the south end of the park campground.

DIRECTIONS TO TRAILHEAD: Red Rock Canyon State Park is located 25 miles north of the town of Mojave off Highway 14. Turn northwest off 14 onto the signed road for the park campground. Follow this road a short mile to Ricardo Ranger Station. The station has a small visitor center with nature exhibits.

SADDLEBACK BUTTE

SADDLEBACK BUTTE TRAIL

From Campground to Saddleback Peak is 4 miles round trip with 1,000-foot elevation gain; Season: October-May

Rarely visited Saddleback Butte State Park, located on the eastern fringe of Antelope Valley, is high-desert country, a land of creosote bush and Joshua trees. The park takes the name of its most prominent feature—3,651-foot Saddleback Butte, a granite mountaintop that stands head and shoulders above Antelope Valley.

Richard Dowen Nature Trail is a good introduction to the Joshua tree and other plant life found in this corner of the desert. The trail to the boulder-strewn summit of Saddleback Peak takes a straight-line course, with most of the elevation gain occurring in the last half-mile. From atop the peak, enjoy far-reaching desert views.

DIRECTIONS TO TRAILHEAD: From Highway 14 (Antelope Valley Freeway) in Lancaster, take the 20th Street exit. Head north on 20th and turn east (right) on Avenue J. Drive 18 miles to Saddleback Butte State Park. Follow the dirt park road to the campground, where the trail begins. Park (day use fee) near the trail sign.

THE HIKE: The signed trail heads straight for the saddle. The soft, sandy track, marked with yellow posts leads through an impressive Joshua tree wood-land. After 1.5 miles, the trail switchbacks steeply up the rocky slope of the butte. An invigorating climb brings you to the saddle of Saddleback Butte. To reach the peak, follow the steep leftward trail to the summit.

From the top, you can look south to the San Gabriel Mountains. At the base of the mountains, keen eyes will discern the California Aqueduct, which carries water to the Southland from the Sacramento Delta. To the east is the vast Mojave Desert, to the north is Edwards Air Force Base. To the west are the cities of Lancaster and Palmdale and farther west, the rugged Tehachapi Mountains.

ANTELOPE VALLEY, CALIFORNIA POPPY RESERVE

ANTELOPE LOOP TRAIL
From Visitors Center to Antelope Butte Vista Point is 2.5 miles round trip
with 300-foot elevation gain; Season: March-May

The California poppy blooms on many a grassy slope in the Southland, but only
in the Antelope Valley does the showy flower blanket whole hillsides in such brilliant orange sheets. Surely the finest concentration of California's state flower
(during a good wildflower year) is preserved at the Antelope Valley California
Poppy Reserve in the Mojave Desert west of Lancaster.

The poppy is the star of the flower show, which includes a supporting cast of
fiddlenecks, cream cups, tidy tips and goldfields. March through Memorial Day is
the time to saunter through this wondrous display of desert wildflowers.

The poppy has always been recognized as something special. Early Spanish
Californians called it *Dormidera*, "the drowsy one," because the petals curl up at
night. They fashioned a hair tonic/restorer by frying the blossoms in olive oil and
adding perfume.

At the reserve, you can pick up a map at the Jane S. Pineiro Interpretive
Center, named for the painter who was instrumental in setting aside an area
where California's state flower could be preserved for future generations to

California's state flower in its most magnificent display.

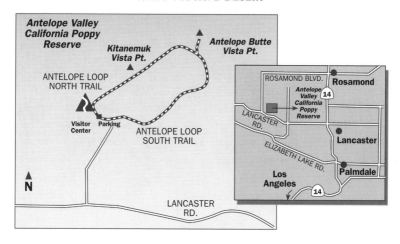

admire. Some of Pineiro's watercolors are on display in the center, which also has wildflower interpretive displays and a slide show.

Built into the side of a hill, the center boast an award-winning solar design, windmill power and "natural" air conditioning."

Antelope Loop Trail—and all trails in the reserve—are easy walking and suit-able for the whole family. Seven miles of gentle trails crisscross the 1,760-acre reserve; many hikers take every trail in the park without getting too tired.

DIRECTIONS TO TRAILHEAD: From the Antelope Valley Freeway (California 14) in Lancaster, exit on Avenue I and drive west 15 miles. Avenue I becomes Lancaster Road a few miles before the Poppy Reserve. The reserve (day use fee) is open 9 A.M. to 4 P.M. daily.

Spring wildflower displays are always unpredictable. To check on what's blooming where, call the park at (661) 942-0662 before making the trip.

THE HIKE: Begin on the signed Antelope Loop Trail to the left of the visitor center. The trail passes through an orange sea of poppies and fiddlenecks, then climbs briefly to Kitanemuk Vista Point, 0.75 mile from the visitor center. Atop Vista Point are those flowery symbols of faithfulness and friendship, forget-me-nots, and an unforgettable view of the Mojave Desert and the snow-covered Tehachapis.

After enjoying the view, continue on to Antelope Butte Vista Point, where another lookout offers fine desert panoramas. From here, join the south loop of the Antelope Loop Trail and return to the visitor center.

After you've circled the "upper west side" of the Poppy Reserve, you may wish to extend your hike by joining the Poppy Loop Trail and exploring the "lower east side."

CHAPTER NINETEEN

Palm Springs

Early 20th-century health-seekers and nature lovers
recognized Palm Springs for what is was—a true oasis.
Here was a palm-dotted retreat where an ancient hot springs
gushed forth. Here was nature, simple and unadorned.
While Palm Springs and satellite communities have achieved
international resort status, there yet remains a wild side ample
opportunities top experience the desert of old.
Especially compelling to the hiker are the so-called Indian
Canyons—Palm, Murray, Andreas and Tahquitz.
The Living Desert Preserve, Big Morongo Canyon and the
Coachella Valley Preserve are quiet places for the hiker
to commune with the desert nature writer Joseph Smeaton
Chase called "nature in her simplest expression."

BIG MORONGO CANYON

BIG MORONGO CANYON TRAIL
To waterfall is 2.5 miles round trip; to canyon mouth is 12 miles round trip
with 1,900-foot elevation loss

For many centuries native peoples used Big Morongo Canyon as a passageway
between the high and low deserts. The last of these nomads to inhabit the canyon
were a group of Serrano people known as the Morongo, for whom the canyon is
named. Today, Big Morongo Canyon is managed and protected by the Nature
Conservancy and the U.S. Bureau of Land Management.

The relative abundance of water is the key to both Big Morongo's long
human history and its botanical uniqueness. Several springs bubble up in the
reserve and one of the California desert's very few year-around creeks flows
through the canyon. Dense thickets of cottonwood and willow, as well as numerous water-loving shrubs line Big Morongo Creek. This lush, crowded riparian
vegetation sharply contrasts with the well-spaced creosote community typical of
the high and dry slopes of the reserve and of the open desert beyond.

The oasis at Big Morongo is a crucial water supply for the fox, bobcat, rac-
coon, coyote and bighorn sheep. Gopher snakes, rosy boas, chuckawallas and
California tree frogs are among the amphibians and reptiles in residence. The permanent water supply also makes it possible for the showy western tiger swallow-
tail and other butterflies to thrive, along with several species of dragon flies.

Big Morongo Canyon is best known for its wide variety of birds, which are
numerous because the canyon is not only at the intersection of two deserts, but
also at the merging of two climate zones—arid and coastal. These climates, coupled
with the wet world of the oasis, means the preserve is an attractive stopover for
birds on their spring and fall migrations.

More than two hundred bird species have been sighted, including the rare
vermilion flycatcher and the least Bell's vireo. Commonly seen all-year residents
include starlings, house finches and varieties of quail and hummingbirds.

The preserve offers several short loop trails ranging from a quarter to one
mile long. Some of the wetter canyon bottom sections of trail are crossed by
wooden boardwalks, which keep hikers dry and fragile creekside flora from being
trampled. Desert Wash, Cottonwood, Willow, Yucca Ridge and Mesquite Trails
explore the environments suggested by their names.

A longer path, Canyon Trail, travels the 6-mile length of Big Morongo
Canyon. Make this a one-way, all downhill journey by arranging a car shuttle or
by having someone pick you up on Indian Avenue. Families with small children

or the leg weary will enjoy a 2.5-mile round trip canyon walk to a small waterfall.

DIRECTIONS TO TRAILHEAD: From Interstate 10, 15 miles east of Banning and a bit past the Highway 111 turnoff to Palm Springs, exit on Highway 62. Drive 10 miles north to the signed turnoff on your right for Big Morongo Wildlife Preserve. Turn east and after 0.1 mile you'll see the preserve's service road leading to a parking area.

To reach the end of the trail at the mouth of Big

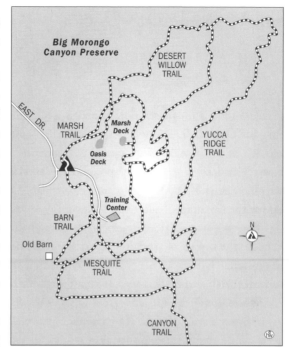

Morongo Canyon, you'll exit on Highway 62 on Indian Avenue and drive exactly a mile to a dirt road on your left. A dip sign precedes the turnoff and a pump enclosed by a chain link fence suggests your parking space.

THE HIKE: Pick up the trail by the Preserve's interpretive displays or join the dirt road that leads past the caretaker's residence.

To the right of the old ranch road is a pasture lined with cottonwood and a barn built in the 1880s. Often the road is muddy, so detour with the signed and aptly named Mesquite Trail which utilizes a wooden boardwalk to get over the wet spots. Pause on the boardwalk in the midst of Big Morongo Creek to listen to the sound of running water, the many chirping birds and croaking frogs.

Canyon Trail meanders with the creek for a gentle mile or so and arrives at a corrugated metal check dam that has created a small waterfall. For a family hike, this is a good turnaround point. The trail continues descending through the canyon with Big Morongo Creek until a bit over three miles from the trailhead, the creek suddenly disappears. Actually, the water continues flowing underground through layers of sand.

The canyon widens and so does the trail. About 5 miles from the trailhead is the south gate of the preserve. Compensating for Big Morongo's somewhat inglorious end is a stirring view of snow-capped Mt. San Jacinto, which lies straight ahead. Stick to your right at every opportunity as you exit the canyon and a dirt road will soon deliver you to Indian Avenue.

THOUSAND PALMS OASIS

MCCALLUM, SMOKE TREE RANCH, INDIAN PALMS TRAILS
1 to 5-mile loop

If it looks like a movie set, don't be surprised. Thousand Palms Oasis was the set-ting for Cecil B. DeMille's 1924 silent film epic, *King of Kings*, and the 1969 movie, *Tell Them Willie Boy is Here*, starring Robert Redford and Katherine Ross. The oasis is something special, and deserving of protection, but that's not why Coachella Valley Preserve was established. The reserve's raison d'être is habi-tat for the threatened Coachella Valley fringe-toed lizard.

For the most part, *Uma inornata* goes about the business of being a lizard beneath the surface of sand dunes, but scientists have been able to discover some of the peculiar habits of this creature, which manages to survive in places where a summer's day surface temperature may reach 160 degrees.

The eight-inch reptile is also known as the "sand swimmer" for its ability to dive through sand dunes. Its entrenching tool-shaped skull rams through the sand, while round scales on its skin reduce friction as it "swims." Fringes (large scales) on its toes give the lizard traction—as well as its name.

Alas, all is not fun in the sun for the fringe-toed lizard. The creature must avoid becoming dinner for such predators as roadrunners, snakes and loggerhead shrikes. But the biggest threat to the lizards continues to be real estate develop-ment and consequent loss of habitat.

Fortunately for the fringe-toed lizard, real estate developers, the U.S. Bureau of Land Management, Congress, the California Depart-ment of Fish and Game, the U.S. Wildlife Service and the Nature Conservancy were able to find a common ground and establish a 13,000-acre preserve in 1986. Some conservationists believe the $25 million price tag may be the most expensive single species preserva-tion effort of all time.

Still, the reserve would be something special even without its namesake lizard. It protects flora and fauna once common in the Coachella Valley before it grew grapefruit, golf courses and subdivisions.

Thousand Palms Oasis is California's second-largest collection of native California fan palms. Thousand Palms, along with Indian Palms, Horseshoe Palms and a couple of other oases in the reserve came into existence as the result of earthquake faults which brought water to the surface.

Before the reserve was set aside, the Thousand Palms area was purchased by turn of the century rancher Louis Wilhelm and his family. The Wilhelms built "Palm House" (now the reserve's visitor center)

and by the 1930s were using it as a commissary for campers, scientists, scout troops and anyone else who wanted to enjoy a weekend in one of their palm-shaded cottages.

Hikers can explore Coachella Valley Reserve on a half dozen trails. Three of these trails depart from Thousand Palms Oasis. Shortest (a 15-minute walk) is Smoke Tree Ranch Trail, which encircles the palms oasis. Good bird-watching is possible in the mesquite thickets and among the smoke trees. Watch for the smoke tree's bright blue/purple flowers in May or June.

Don't miss McCallum Trail, a 1.5-mile round trip nature trail. It meanders by a jungle of willows, palms, cottonwoods and mesquite. At the trailhead, pick up an interpretive pamphlet that's keyed to numbered posts along the path.

Indian Palms Trail leads 0.5 mile to small Indian Palm Oasis.

More ambitious hikers will head for Wash Trail which, true to its name, winds through washes in the northern portion of the reserve. You can also visit Bee Rock Mesa, where Malpais Indians camped 5,000 years ago, hike into adjoining Indio Hills County Park, and visit more oases—Horseshoe Palms and Pushawalla Palms.

DIRECTIONS TO TRAILHEAD: From Interstate 10, about ten miles east of where Highway 111 leads off to Palm Springs, exit on Washington Street/Ramon Road. Head north on Washington Street, which bends west and continues as Ramon Road. Soon after the bend, turn right (north again) onto Thousand Palms Canyon Road. Continue to the entrance to Coachella Valley Preserve and park in the dirt lot.

PALM SPRINGS DESERT MUSEUM

LYKKEN TRAIL
From Palm Springs Desert Museum to Desert Riders Overlook is 2 miles round trip with 800-foot elevation gain; to Ramon Drive is 4 miles round trip with 800-foot gain

Museum and Lykken Trails offer a good overview of the resort. This hike begins at Palm Springs Desert Museum, where natural science exhibits recreate the unique ecology of Palm Springs and the surrounding Colorado Desert.

Steep Museum Trail ascends the western base of Mt. San Jacinto and junctions with Lykken Trail, which winds through the Palm Springs hills north to Tramway Road and south to Ramon Road. Lykken Trail honors Carl Lykken, Palms Springs pioneer and the town's first postmaster. Lykken, who arrived in 1913, owned a general merchandise store, and later a department/hardware store.

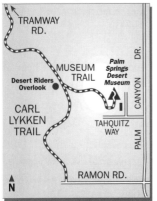

DIRECTIONS TO TRAILHEAD: From Highway 111 (Palm Canyon Drive) in the middle of downtown Palm Springs, turn west on Tahquitz Drive, then a right on Museum Drive. Park in Palm Springs Desert Museum's north lot.

The trail begins back of the museum, between the museum and an administration building, by a plaque honoring Carl Lykken. The trail is closed during the summer months for health and safety reasons (yours).

THE HIKE: The trail ascends the rocky slope above the museum. Soon you'll intersect a private road, jog left, then resume trail walking up the mountainside. As you rapidly gain elevation, the view widens from the Desert Fashion Plaza to the outskirts of Palm Springs to the wide-open spaces of the Coachella Valley.

A mile's ascent brings you to a picnic area, built by the Desert Riders, local equestrians whose membership included Carl Lykken. One Desert Rider, former Palm Springs Mayor Frank Bogart is a real trail enthusiast whose efforts have contributed much to the state's trail system. Bear left (south) on Lykken Trail, which travels the hills above town before descending to Ramon Road near the mouth of Tahquitz Canyon.

THE LIVING DESERT

JAEGER NATURE TRAIL

2-mile loop through Living Desert Reserve; return via Eisenhower Trail and
Eisenhower Mountain is 5 miles round trip with 500-foot elevation gain

A superb introduction to desert plant life and wildlife, The Living Desert is a
combination zoo, botanic garden and hiking area. The 1,200-acre, nonprofit facility is dedicated to conservation, education and research. Gardens represent major
desert regions including California's Mojave, Arizona's Sonoran and Mexico's
Chihuahuan. Wildlife-watchers will enjoy observing coyotes in their burrows and
bighorn sheep atop their mountain peak. The reserve also has a walk-through
aviary and a pond inhabited by the rare desert pupfish.

Nature and hiking trails provide an opportunity to form an even closer acquain-
tance with an uncrowded, undeveloped sandscape. Easy trails lead past the Arabian
Oryx and bighorn sheep, past desert flora with name tags and ecosystems with
interpretive displays, and over to areas that resemble the open desert of yesteryear.

Presidents Eisenhower, Nixon, Ford and Reagan relaxed in Palm Springs.
Eisenhower spent many winters at the El Dorado Country Club at the base of the
mountain that now bears his name. Palm Desert boosters petitioned the Federal
Board of Geographic Names to name the 1,952 (coincidentally, 1952 was the year of
his election)-foot peak for part-time Palm Springs resident Dwight D. Eisenhower.

The first part of the walk through The Living Desert uses a nature trail

Bighorn sheep roam the Living Desert.

295

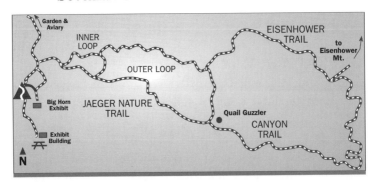

named after the great naturalist Edmund Jaeger. It's keyed to a booklet available from the entrance station. An inner loop of two-thirds of a mile and an outer loop of 1.5 miles lead past a wide array of desert flora and 60 interpretive stops. A longer loop can be made using Canyon Trail and Eisenhower Trail. The hike to Ike's peak ascends about halfway up the bald mountain and offers great views of the Coachella Valley.

DIRECTIONS TO TRAILHEAD: From Highway 111 in Palm Desert, turn south on Portola Avenue and drive 1.5 miles south to the park. Hours: 9 A.M. to 5 P.M.; closed mid-June to the end of August.

THE HIKE: The trail begins at the exhibit buildings. Follow either the numbered nature trail, beginning at number one, or make a short rightward detour to the bighorn sheep enclosure. The trail junctions once more and you begin heading up the alluvial plain of Deep Canyon. Walking up the wash, you'll observe the many moisture-loving plants that thrive in such environments, including smoke trees, desert willows and palo verde.

Stay right at the next junction and begin the outer loop of the Jaeger Nature Trail. You'll pass plenty of that common desert dweller, the creosote bush, and wind along the base of some sand dunes.

The trail climbs out of the wash and into a kind of plain that true desert rats call a "bajada." Here you'll find a quail guzzler which stores rainwater to aid California's state bird in the hot summer months. And here you'll find a junction with Canyon Trail (the south loop of the Eisenhower Trail).

Canyon Trail heads up the bajada. After climbing through a little canyon, the trail winds up the south slope of Eisenhower Mountain to a picnic area and a plaque describing the region's date industry.

From the picnic area, you'll descend Eisenhower Mountain, getting good views of the mountains and the Coachella Valley. After passing the signed Eisenhower trailhead, you'll reach the north loop of the Nature Trail and begin heading west down the brittlebush-dotted floodplain back to the exhibit buildings and the central part of the preserve.

MURRAY AND ANDREAS CANYONS

MURRAY CANYON TRAIL
From Andreas Canyon to Murray Canyon is 2 miles round trip with 200-foot elevation gain

In the foothills above Palm Springs are two lovely palm-lined canyons-Andreas and Murray. Both have hundreds of palms, crystalline streams and dramatic rock walls. Andreas, with about 700 native California fan palms and Murray with about 1,000 palms, are among the most populous palm groves in the state. The two canyons are tributaries of nearby Palm Canyon, undisputed king of California's palm oases.

Both canyons honor Palm Springs pioneers. Andreas is named after a Cahuilla chieftain of the late 1800s, while Murray honors botanist Dr. Welwood Murray, who built a hotel/health resort in the very early days of Palm Springs. Many of those making their way to the Murray Hotel came for the curative climate and the rejuvenation of their health, but a number of literary figures also visited and these scribes soon spread the word that Palm Springs was a very special place indeed.

Andreas Canyon was once a summer retreat for the Agua Caliente band of the Cahuilla; they spent the winter months in the warm Coachella Valley then sought the relative coolness of Andreas and other palm canyons during the warmer months.

Unlike most palm oases, which are fed by underground springs or sluggish seeps, Andreas is watered by a running stream. Fortunately for the palms and other canyon life, settlers were legally prevented from diverting this stream to the emerging village of Palm Springs. Ranchers and townspeople had to turn to the larger, but notoriously undependable Whitewater River.

Meandering through the tall palms, hikers can travel a ways upstream through Andreas Canyon. Adding to the lush scene are alders and willows, cottonwoods and sycamores.

The trail between Andreas Canyon

and Murray Canyon is only a mile long, but you can travel a few more miles up the canyons themselves.

DIRECTIONS TO TRAILHEAD: From the junction of State Highway 111 and South Palm Canyon Drive in Palm Springs, proceed south on the latter road for 1.5 miles, bearing right at a signed fork. After another mile you'll reach the Agua Caliente Indians Reservation tollgate.

Just after the tollgate, bear right at a signed fork and travel 0.75 mile to Andreas Canyon picnic ground. The trail begins at the east end of the splendid picnic area. A sign suggests that Murray Canyon is "20 min" away.

THE HIKE: Notice the soaring, reddish-brown rocks near the trailhead. At the base of these rocks are grinding holes once used by the Cahuilla.

The trail extends south along the base of the mountains. A dramatic backdrop to the path is the desert-facing side of the San Jacinto Mountains.

It's an easy walk, occasionally following a dry streambed. Here, away from water, you encounter more typical desert flora: cholla, hedgehog cacti, burrobush.

When you reach Murray Canyon, you can follow the palms and stream quite a ways up-canyon. Joining the palms are willows, cottonwoods, mesquite, arrowweed and desert lavender. Mistletoe is sometimes draped atop the mesquite and attracts lots of birds.

As you take the trail back to Andreas Canyon you can't help noticing the luxury housing and resort life reaching toward the palm canyons. And you can't help being thankful that these tranquil palm oases are still ours to enjoy.

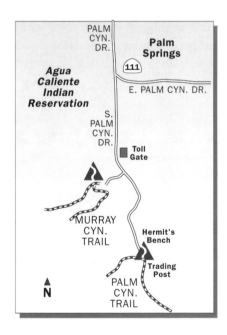

PALM CANYON

PALM CANYON TRAIL
From Hermit's Bench to turnaround is 4 miles round trip with 200-foot elevation gain

The hills and canyons bordering Palm Springs have the greatest concentration of palm trees in the U.S., and in number of trees, Palm Canyon is the uncrowned king of America's desert oases. A meandering stream and lush undergrowth complement over three thousand palms, creating a jungle-like atmosphere in some places.

Palm fans will enjoy viewing the largest concentration of California fan palms while visiting the Agua Caliente Indian Reservation.

DIRECTIONS TO TRAILHEAD: From Interstate 10, exit on Highway 111 (Palm Canyon Drive) and proceed to downtown Palm Springs. Continue through town on Palm Canyon Drive. At a fork, Highway 111 veers east and becomes known as East Palm Canyon Drive. You head straight ahead, on South Palm Canyon Drive, following the signs to "Indian Canyons." You reach the Agua Caliente Indians tollgate, where you must pay a fee to enter tribal lands. The reservation is open daily from 8:30 A.M. to 5 P.M. Parking is a short distance beyond the tollgate at the head of Palm Canyon at Hermit's Bench, where there is a trading post and a good view north into Palm Springs. Many signs remind visitors that they must be off the reservation before 5 P.M.

THE HIKE: From the trading post, the trail descends into the canyon. Some of the palms stand 60 feet tall, with three-foot trunk diameters. The trail follows the canyon for two miles to a tiny grotto that seems an ideal place to turn around.

Hearty adventurers will relish the challenge of proceeding up Palm Canyon seven more miles, gaining 3,000 feet in elevation, before reaching a junction with Highway 74, the Palms-to-Pines Highway. Note: This extremely strenuous hike is best done by beginning at the Highway 74 trailhead, hiking down Palm Canyon, and convincing a friend to pick you up at Hermit's Bench. Contact the BLM in Palm Springs for the latest trail advice.

Tahquitz Canyon

TAHQUITZ CANYON TRAIL
2 miles round trip with 350-foot elevation gain

After a 30-year closure, the lovely canyon named after the Cahuilla shaman Tahquitz was reopened to hikers in 2001. Storied Tahquitz Canyon, located just two miles as the phainopepla flies from downtown Palm Springs, was accessible by tribal ranger-led guided tours until 2005, and is now open for both escorted and independent hiking.

Hike highlights include ancient rock art, diverse desert flora, an early irrigation system and a 60-foot waterfall featured in Frank Capra's classic 1937 film, *Lost Horizon* starring Ronald Coleman and Jane Wyatt. Hikers can begin at the Tahquitz Canyon Visitor Center screening room and view "The Legend of Tahquitz Canyon" video, then step past bottled water and snack vending machines onto the trail.

As legend has it, Tahquitz, the Cahuilla's first shaman, at first practiced his art to good effect, but soon became increasingly mischievous, then downright dangerous. Such is his power that he can appear to people in downtown Palm Springs or manifest himself as an earthquake or as a fireball in the sky.

The Cahuilla closed the canyon to the public in 1969 when a rowdy crowd left a rock concert and descended into Tahquitz Canyon for several days of partying. In later years, "No Trespassing" signs, locked gates and fences slowed, but did not stop visitors. Most of the hikers and skinny-dippers enjoyed the picturesque falls and were respectful to the serene scene, but a number of vandals dumped garbage on the canyon floor and spray-painted graffiti on the rocks and boulders. Hippies, hermits, hobos and homeless folks took up residence in the canyon's caves.

With proceeds from the tribe's Spa Resort & Casino, the Agua Caliente band of the Cahuilla embarked on a three-year cleanup effort, and built a visitor center with educational and cultural exhibits.

The canyon is chock-full of native plants including brittle bush, creosote, cholla, hedgehog cactus, Mormon tea and desert lavender. Tour leaders detail the many ways the Cahuilla used the canyon's plants for food and medicine.

The hiker's view down-canyon over the sometimes smog-obscured Coachella Valley sprawl can be a bit discouraging; up-canyon vistas, however, are glorious. From Tahquitz Peak, a subsidiary summit of Mt. San Jacinto, a lively creek tumbles through an impressive gash in the towering rock walls.

I recommend getting an early start (Tahquitz Canyon Visitor Center opens at 7:30 A.M.) and arriving in time to watch the rising sun probe the dark recesses of the high walls of Tahquitz Canyon. If you take the first (8 A.M.) tour of the day, you'll beat the crowds, beat the heat, and have the best chance of spotting wildlife.

At just two-miles long, the hike is a family-friendly one; however, because it's an interpreted hike that proceeds at a very slow pace, it's not suitable for all ages, particularly for children under 6, who will not appreciate the tribal ranger's narrative, and may become a distraction to their parents and other hikers. Some restless older kids (and many adults, too) may prefer a self-guided hike through nearby Palm Canyon for a look at the largest collection of our native California fan palm.

Canyon hiking tours depart from the Tahquitz Canyon Visitor Center at 8 a.m., 10 A.M., 12 noon and 2 P.M. There is a cost for both adults and children, and reservations are strongly recommended.

DIRECTIONS TO TRAILHEAD: From Highway 111 in Palm Springs, head south on Palm Spring Drive through downtown to Mesquite Avenue. Turn right (west) and proceed 0.5 mile to the parking area below the Tahquitz Canyon Visitor Center.

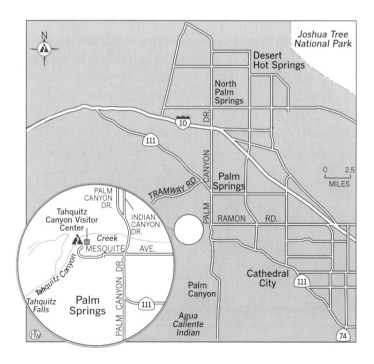

SANTA ROSA WILDERNESS

CACTUS SPRINGS TRAIL

From Pinyon Flat to Horsethief Creek is 5 miles round trip with a 900-foot loss; to Cactus Spring is 9 miles round trip with a 300-foot gain;

The Santa Rosas are primarily desert mountains and a unique blend of high and low desert environments. Desert-facing slopes of these mountains are treeless—scorched and sparse as the desert itself. Throughout the foothills and canyons, lower Sonoran vegetation—chamise, barrel cactus, ocotillo and waxy creosote—predominate. In some of the canyons with water on or near the surface, oases of native California fan palms form verdant islands on the sand. With an increase in elevation, the wrinkled canyons and dry arroyos give way to mountain crests bristling with pine and juniper.

The Santa Rosa Wilderness, set aside in 1984, lies within the boundaries of the San Bernardino National Forest. Trails are few in the Santa Rosas; most are faint traces of Cahuilla Indian pathways. The ancients climbed the mountains to hunt deer, gather pinyon pine nuts, and escape the desert heat. When the snows began, they descended from the high country to the gentle, wintering areas below.

Cactus Spring Trail, an old Indian path overhauled by the Forest Service, gives the hiker a wonderful introduction to the delights of the Santa Rosas.

The trail first takes you to Horsethief Creek, a perennial waterway that traverses high desert country. A hundred years ago, horse thieves pastured their stolen animals in this region before driving them to San Bernardino to sell. The cottonwood-shaded creek invites a picnic. Continuing on the Cactus Spring Trail, you'll arrive at Cactus Spring. Along the trail is some wild country, as undisturbed as it was in 1774 when early Spanish trailblazer Juan Bautista de Anza first saw it.

DIRECTIONS TO TRAILHEAD: From Highway 111 in Palm Desert, drive 16 miles up Highway 74 to the Pinyon Flat Campground. (From Hemet,

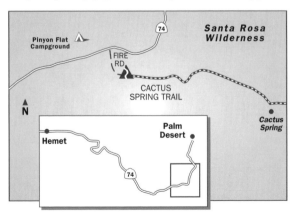

Horsethief Creek

it's a 40-mile drive along Highway 74 to Pinyon Flat Campground.) Opposite the campground is Pinyon Flat Transfer Station Road, also signed "Elks Mountain Retreat." You'll follow this road about 0.75 mile. Just before reaching the (trash) Transfer Station. A rough dirt road veers to the left. Follow this road 200 yards to road's end.

THE HIKE: Follow the dirt road east a short distance to Fire Road 7S01, then head south for 0.25 mile. You'll then take the first road on your left. A sign reassures you that you are indeed on the way to Cactus Spring, and you'll soon pass the abandoned Dolomite Mine, where limestone was once quarried. Approximately 0.25 mile past the mine site, the dirt road peters out and the trail begins. Here you'll find a sign and a trail register.

The trail bears east to the east and dips in and out of several (usually) dry gullies. A half-mile past the sign-in register, a sign welcomes you to the Santa Rosa Wilderness. Cactus Spring Trail does not contour over the hills, but zigs and zags, apparently without rhyme or reason. The bewitching, but easy-to-follow trail finally drops down to Horsethief Creek. At the creek crossing, Horsethief Camp welcomes the weary with flowing water and shade.

Return the same way, explore up and down the handsome canyon cut by Horsethief Creek, or continue to Cactus Spring.

To reach Cactus Spring, cross the creek, then climb east out of the canyon on a rough and steep trail past sentinel yuccas guarding the dry slopes. The trail stays with a wash for a spell (the route through the wash is unmarked except for occasional rock ducts), then gently ascends over pinyon pine-covered slopes. It's rolling wild country, a good place to hide out. Alas, Cactus Spring, located a few hundred yards north of the trail, is almost always dry.

CHAPTER TWENTY

Joshua Tree National Park

For some visitors, the Joshua trees are not only the essence but the whole of their park experience. Here in its namesake national park, it reaches the southernmost limit of its range. Joshua Tree National Park, however, is more than a tableau of twisted yucca and beckons the hiker with a diversity of desert environments, including sand dunes, native palm oases, cactus gardens and jumbles of jumbo granite. In JT, hikers get to roam two different deserts—the Mojave with its Joshua trees and mountains and the flatter, hotter Colorado with its cholla, ocotillo, smoketree and native California fan palms.

RYAN MOUNTAIN

RYAN MOUNTAIN TRAIL
From Sheep Pass to Ryan Mountain is 4 miles round trip with 700-foot elevation gain

This hike tours some Joshua trees, visits Indian Cave and ascends Ryan Mountain for a nice view of the rocky wonderland in this part of Joshua Tree National Park. Ryan Mountain is named for the Ryan brothers, Thomas and Jep, who had a homestead at the base of the mountain.

The view from atop Ryan Mountain is to be savored, and is one of the finest in the National Park.

DIRECTIONS TO TRAILHEAD: From the Joshua Tree National Park Visitor Center at Twentynine Palms, drive 3 miles south on Utah Trail Road (the main park road), keeping right at Pinto Wye junction and continuing another 8 miles to Sheep Pass Campground on your left. Park in the Ryan Mountain

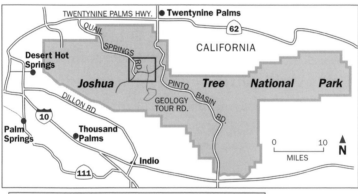

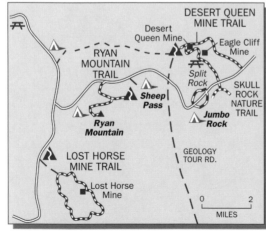

Ryan Mountain Trail

parking area. You may also begin this hike from the Indian Cave Turnout just up the road. Be sure to visit Indian Cave; a number of bedrock mortars found in the cave suggests its use as a work site by its aboriginal inhabitants.

THE HIKE: From Sheep Pass Campground, the trail skirts the base of Ryan Mountain and passes through a lunar landscape of rocks and Joshua trees.

Soon you intersect a well-worn side trail coming up from your right. If you like, follow this brief trail down to Indian Cave, typical of the kind of shelter sought by the nomadic Cahuilla and Serrano clans that traveled this desert land.

Continuing past the junction, Ryan Mountain Trail ascends moderately-to-steeply toward the peak. En route, you'll pass some very old rocks which make up the core this mountain and the nearby Little San Bernardino range. For eons, these rocks have, since their creation, been metamorphosed by heat and pressure into completely new types, primarily gneiss and schist. No one knows their exact age, but geologists believe they're several hundred million years old.

Atop Ryan Mountain (5,470 feet) you can sign the summit register, located in a tin can stuck in a pile of rocks that marks the top of the mountain. From the peak, you're treated to a panoramic view of Lost Horse, Queen, Hidden and Pleasant valleys. There's a lot of geologic history in the rocks shimmering on the ocean of sand below. Not all the rocks you see are as ancient as the ones on Ryan Mountain. Middle-aged rocks, predominately quartz monzonite, are found at Hidden Valley, Jumbo Rocks and White Tank. Younger rocks made of basaltic lava are mere infants at less than a million years old; they are found in Pleasant Valley.

LOST HORSE MINE

LOST HORSE MINE TRAIL
To Lost Horse Mine is 3.5 miles round trip with 400-foot elevation gain

Lost Horse Mine was the most successful gold mining operation in this part of the Mojave. More than 9,000 ounces of gold were processed from ore dug here in the late 1890s. The mine's 10-stamp mill still stands, along with a couple of large cyanide settling tanks and a huge winch used on the main shaft. The trail to the mine offers a close-up look back into a colorful era and some fine views into the heart of the national park.

Many are the legends that swirl like the desert winds around the Lost Horse Mine. As the story goes, Johnny Lang in 1893 was camping in Pleasant Valley when his horse got loose. He tracked it out to the ranch belonging to Jim McHaney, who told Lang his horse was "no longer lost" and threatened Lang's health and future.

Lang wandered over to the camp of fellow prospector Dutch Diebold, who told him that he, too, had been threatened by McHaney and his cowboys. A pity too, because he, Diebold had discovered a promising gold prospect, but had been unable to mark his claim's boundaries. After sneaking in to inspect the claim, Johnny Lang and his father, George, purchased all rights from Diebold for $1,000.

At first it looked like a bad investment, because the Langs were prevented by McHaney's thugs from reaching their claim. Partners came and went, and by 1895, Johnny Lang owned the mine with the Ryan brothers, Thomas and Jep. Peak production years for the mine were 1896 through 1899. Gold ingots were hidden in a freight wagon and transported to Indio. The ruse fooled any would-be highwaymen.

But thievery of another sort plagued the Lost Horse Mine. The theft was of amalgam, lumps of quicksilver from which gold could later be separated. Seems in this matter of amalgam, the mill's day shift, supervised by Jep Ryan, far out-produced the night shift, supervised by Lang. One of Ryan's men espied Lang stealing the amalgam. When Ryan gave Lang a choice—sell his share of the mine for $12,000 or go to the penitentiary—Lang sold out.

Alas, Johnny Lang came to a sad end. Apparently, his stolen and buried amalgams supported him for quite some time, but by the end of 1924, he was old, weak and living in an isolated cabin. And hungry. He had shot and eaten his four burros and was forced to walk into town for food. He never made it. His partially mummified body wrapped in a canvas sleeping bag was found by prospector/rancher Bill Keys alongside present-day Keys View Road. He was buried where he fell.

DIRECTIONS TO TRAILHEAD: From the central part of Joshua Tree National Park, turn south from Caprock Junction on Keys Road and drive 2.5 miles. Turn left on a short dirt road. Here you'll find a Park Service interpretive display about Johnny Lang's checkered career. (You can also visit Lang's grave, located a hundred feet north of the Lost Horse Mine turnoff on Keys Road.) The trail, a continuation of Lost Horse Mine Road, begins at a road barrier.

THE HIKE: The trail, the old mine road, climbs above the left side of a wash.

An alternative route, for the first (or last) mile of this day hike, is to hike from the parking area directly up the wash. Pinyon pine and the nolina (often mistaken for a yucca) dot the wash. Nolina leaves are more flexible than those of yucca, and its flowers smaller. The wash widens in about 0.75 mile and forks; bear left and a short ascent will take you to the mine road. Turn right on the road and follow it to the mine.

A few open shafts remain near the Lost Horse, so be careful when you explore the mine ruins. Note the stone foundations opposite the mill site. A little village for the mine workers was built here in the late 1890s. Scramble up to the top of the hill above the mine for a panoramic view of Queen Valley, Pleasant Valley and the desert ranges beyond.

Lost Horse Mine

WONDERLAND OF ROCKS

BARKER DAM LOOP TRAIL
From Parking Area to Barker Dam is 1.25 miles round trip

One of the many wonders of Joshua Tree National Park is the Wonderland of Rocks, 12 square miles of massive jumbled granite. This curious maze of stone hides groves of Joshua trees, trackless washes and several small pools of water.

Perhaps the easiest, and certainly the safest way to explore the Wonderland is to follow the Barker Dam Loop Trail. The first part of the journey is on a nature trail that interprets the botanical highlights of the area. The last part of the loop trail visits some Indian petroglyphs.

This hike's main destination is the small lake created by Barker Dam. A century ago, cowboys took advantage of the water catchment of this natural basin and brought their cattle to this corner of the Wonderland of Rocks. Barker and Shay Cattle Co. constructed the dam, which was later raised to its present height by Bill Keys and his family in the 1950s. Family members inscribed their names atop the dam's south wall and renamed it Bighorn Dam; however, Barker was the name that stuck.

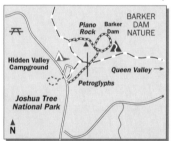

The trail to Barker Dam, while interesting, is not likely to occupy much of a day for the intrepid day hiker. One way to explore a little more of the Wonderland of Rocks is to pick up the Wonderland Wash Ranch Trail to the Astrodomes. Departing from the next spur road and parking area past the Barker Dam trailhead, this path leads to the ruins of a pink house known as the Worth Bagley House. From the back corner of the house, you'll pick up a wash and follow an intermittent trail through boulder clusters. The trail is popular with rock climbers, who use this trail to reach the Astrodomes—steep, 300-foot tall rocks that tower above the wash.

Myriad narrow canyons and washes lead into the Wonderland, but route-finding is extremely complex and recommended only for the very experienced with map and compass skills.

By park service regulation, the area is open only from 8 A.M. to 6 P.M.; this restriction is designed to allow the shy bighorn sheep a chance to reach water without human interference.

DIRECTIONS TO TRAILHEAD: From I-10, a little east past the Highway 111 turnoff to Palm Springs, take Highway 62 northeast to the town of Joshua Tree. Continue 4 miles south to the park entrance, then another 10 miles to Hidden Valley Campground. A dirt road leads 2 miles from Hidden Valley Campground to Barker Dam parking area.

THE HIKE: From the north end of the parking area, join the signed trail that immediately penetrates the Wonderland of Rocks. You'll pass a special kind of oak, the turbinella, which has adjusted to the harsh conditions of desert life. The oaks are habitat for a multitude of birds and ground squirrels.

For the first 0.5 mile, interpretive signs point out the unique botany of this desert land. The path then squeezes through a narrow rock passageway and leads directly to the edge of the lake. Bird-watching is excellent here because many migratory species not normally associated with the desert are attracted to the lake. The morning and late afternoon hours are particularly tranquil times to visit the lake, and to contemplate the ever-changing reflections of the Wonderland of Rocks on the water.

The trail is a bit indistinct near Barker Dam, but resumes again in fine form near a strange-looking circular water trough, a holdover from the area's cattle ranching days. A mechanism resembling a toilet float controlled the flow of water to the thirsty livestock.

The path turns southerly and soon passes a huge boulder known as Piano Rock. When this land was in private ownership, a piano was hauled atop this rock and played for the amusement of visitors and locals.

Beyond Piano Rock the trail enters a rock-rimmed valley. A brief leftward detour at a junction brings you to the Movie Petroglyphs, so named because in less-enlightened times, the native rock art was painted over by a film crew in order to make it more visible to the camera's eye.

Back on the main trail, you'll parallel some cliffs, perhaps get a glimpse of some bedrock mortars, and loop back to the parking area.

Barker Dam

BLACK ROCK CANYON

BLACK ROCK CANYON TRAIL
From Black Rock Campground to Warren Peak is 6 miles round trip with 1,000-foot elevation gain

A hike through Black Rock Canyon has just about everything a desert hike should have: plenty of cactus, pinyon pine-dotted peaks, a sandy wash, dramatic rock formations, a hidden spring, grand vistas. And much more.

Tucked away in the northwest corner of the park, the Black Rock Canyon area also hosts forests of the shaggy Joshuas. *Yucca brevifolia* thrive at the higher elevations of this end of the national park.

More than two hundred species of birds, including speedy roadrunners, have been observed in and around Black Rock Canyon. Hikers frequently spot mule deer and rabbits—desert cottontails and black-tailed jack rabbits. Bighorn sheep are also sighted occasionally. A bit off the tourist track, Black Rock Canyon rarely makes the "must see" list of natural attractions at the national park. Ironically though, while Black Rock is often overlooked, it is one of the easiest places to reach. The canyon is close to Yucca Valley's commercial strip, very close to a residential neighborhood.

Maybe we nature-lovers practice a curious logic: if a beautiful place is near civilization it can't be that beautiful, right? In Black Rock Canyon's case, our logic would be faulty. The canyon matches the allure of much more remote regions of the national park.

Black Rock Canyon Trail follows a classic desert wash, then ascends to the crest of the Little San Bernardino Mountains at Warren Peak. Desert and mountain views from the peak are stunning.

DIRECTIONS TO TRAILHEAD: From Highway 62 (Twentynine Palms Highway) in Yucca Valley, turn south on Joshua Lane and drive five miles through a residential area to Black Rock Ranger Station. Park at the station. The station has some interpretive displays and sells books and maps. Ask rangers for the latest trail information.

Walk uphill through the campground to campsite #30 and the trailhead.

THE HIKE: From the upper end of the campground, the trail leads to a water tank, goes left a very short distance on a park service road, then angles right. After a few hundred yards, the trail splits. The main trail descends directly into Black Rock Canyon wash. (An upper trail crests a hill before it, too, descends into the wash.)

A quarter mile from the trailhead, the path drops into the dry, sandy creekbed of Black Rock Canyon. You'll bear right and head up the wide canyon mouth, passing Joshua trees, desert willow and cholla.

A mile of wash-walking leads you to the remains of some so-called "tanks," or rock basins that were built by early ranchers to hold water for their cattle.

Another quarter mile up the wash is Black Rock Spring, sometimes dry, sometimes a trickle. Beyond the spring, the canyon narrows. You wend your way around beavertail cactus, pinyon pine and juniper.

(Near the head of the canyon, the trail splits. Turning left [east] cross-country will lead along a rough ridge to Peak 5195.)

If you follow the right fork of the rough trail, you'll climb to a dramatic ridge crest of the Little San Bernardino Mountains, then angle right (west) along the crest. A steep, 0.25-mile ascent past contorted wind-blown juniper and pinyon pine brings you to the top of Warren Peak.

Oh what a grand clear-day view! North is the Mojave Desert. To the west is snowy Mt. San Gorgonio, Southern California's highest peak, as well as the San Bernardino Mountains and the deep trough of San Gorgonio Pass. Southwest lies mighty Mt. San Jacinto and to the south (this is often the murky part of the view) Palm Springs and the Coachella Valley. The peaks of the Little San Bernardino Mountains extend southeast, marching toward the Salton Sea.

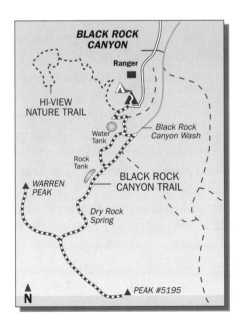

FORTYNINE PALMS

FORTYNINE PALMS TRAIL
To Fortynine Palms Oasis is 3 miles round trip with 400-foot elevation gain

Fortynine Palms Oasis has retained a wonderful air of remoteness. From the parking area, an old Indian trail climbs a steep ridge and offers the hiker expansive views of the Sheephole and Bullion mountain ranges.

On the exposed ridge, barrel cacti, creosote, yucca, and brittlebush brave the heat. As the trail winds up and over a rocky crest, the restful green of the oasis comes into view. At the oasis, nature's personality abruptly changes and the dry, sunbaked ridges give way to dripping springs, pools, and the blessed shade of palms and cottonwoods.

Unlike some oases, which are strung out for miles along a stream, Fortynine Palms is a close-knit palm family centered around a generous supply of surface water. Seeps and springs fill numerous basins set among the rocks at different levels. Other basins are supplied by "rain" drip-drip-dripping from the upper levels. Mesquite and willow thrive alongside the palms. Singing house finches and croaking frogs provide a musical interlude.

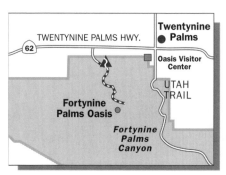

Perched on a steep canyon wall, Fortynine Palms Oasis overlooks the town of Twentynine Palms, but its untouched beauty makes it seem a lot farther removed from civilization.

DIRECTIONS TO TRAILHEAD: From Interstate 10, a few miles east of the Highway 111 turnoff going to Palm Springs, bear north on Highway 62. After passing the town of Yucca Valley, but before reaching the outskirts of Twentynine Palms, turn right on Canyon Road. (Hint: Look for an animal hospital at the corner of Highway 62 and Canyon Road) Follow Canyon Road 1.75 miles to its end at a National Park Service parking area and the trailhead.

THE HIKE: The trail rises through a Spartan rockscape dotted with cacti and jojoba. After a brisk climb, catch your breath atop a ridgetop and enjoy the view of Twentynine Palms and the surrounding desert.

The trail leads down slopes dotted with barrel cactus and mesquite. Soon the oasis comes into view. Lucky hikers may get a fleeting glimpse of bighorn sheep drinking from oasis pools or gamboling over nearby steep slopes.

MASTODON PEAK

MASTODON PEAK TRAIL
3-mile loop trail with 400-foot elevation gain

Mastodon Peak Trail packs a lot of sight-seeing into a three-mile walk: a cotton-wood-shaded oasis, a gold mine and a grand desert view.

Mastodon Peak, named by early prospectors for its behemoth-like profile, was the site of the Mastodon Mine, a gold mine worked intermittently from 1919 to 1932. The ore was of high quality; however, the main ore body was cut off by a fault.

A mile down the trail from the mine is Winona, where some concrete foundations remain to mark the former mill and little town. Winona was home to workers at the Mastodon Mine, as well as workers at the mill, which processed ore from a number of nearby mines.

Views from elephantine-shaped Mastodon Peak include the Cottonwood Springs area and the Eagle Mountains. Clear-day panoramas extend from Mt. San Jacinto above Palm Springs to the Salton Sea.

DIRECTIONS TO TRAILHEAD: Entering the national park from the south (via Interstate 10), travel eight miles north of the park boundary to Cottonwood Spring Campground. Park at the Cottonwood Spring day use area.

THE HIKE: From the parking area, the path proceeds immediately to Cottonwood Spring, a collection of cotton-woods, California fan palms and cattails crowded around a trick-ling spring.

The path continues 0.5 mile, following a wash to a junction. Lost Palms Trail heads right, but you take the left fork to ascend Mastodon Peak. A short spur trail leads to the summit. Enjoy the views from Cottonwood Campground just below to the Coachella Valley beyond.

The main trail descends to the shafts and ruins of Mastodon Mine. Another mile of travel brings you to Winona. Some shady trees—including eucalyptus planted by miners—offer a pleasant rest stop. A last 0.25-mile brings you to a fork in the road. The right fork leads to the campground; the left fork returns to Cottonwood Spring parking lot.

Lost Palms Oasis

LOST PALMS OASIS TRAIL
From Cottonwood Springs Campground to Lost Palms Oasis is 8 miles round trip with 300-foot elevation gain.

Lost Palms Oasis Trail passes through a cactus garden, crosses a number of desert washes, and takes you to the two southern oases in the National Park: Cottonwood and Lost Palms.

Largely manmade, Cottonwood Spring Oasis was once a popular overnight stop for freight-haulers and prospectors during the mining years of 1870 to 1910. Travelers and teamsters journeying from Banning to the Dale Goldfield east of Twentynine Palms, rested at the oasis.

Lost Palms Oasis is a hidden gem. Nearly 100 palms are found in the deep canyon where steep igneous walls sparkle in the desert sun.

DIRECTIONS TO TRAILHEAD: From the south end of Joshua Tree National Park, follow the park road 8 miles to Cottonwood Spring Campground. Park your car at the campground. The trailhead is at the end of the campground.

THE HIKE: Leaving Cottonwood Spring Campground, the trail ambles through a low desert environment of green-trunked palo verde, ironwood and cottonwood trees, spindly ocotillo plants and cholla cactus. Park Service identification plaques describe the area's flora and fauna.

The trail, a bit difficult to follow through the sandy wash, brings you to Cottonwood Spring Oasis in 0.5 mile. Cottonwood Spring is home to a wide variety of birds and a large number of bees.

From Cottonwood Spring, the trail marches over sandy hills, past heaps of huge rocks and along sandy draws and washes. A number of Park Service signs point the way at possibly confusing junctions. Finally, you rise above the washes and climb to a rocky outcropping overlooking the canyon harboring Lost Palms Oasis. From the overlook, descend the steep path around the boulders to the palms.

Little surface water is present at Lost Palms Oasis, but enough is underground for the palms to remain healthy. Lost Palms remained relatively untouched throughout the mining years, though some of its water was pumped to settlements eight miles to the south at Chiriaco Summit. Adjacent to Lost Palms Canyon is a handsome upper canyon called Dike Springs.

Shy and reclusive desert bighorn sheep are often seen around this oasis—particularly in hot weather when they need water more often.

CHAPTER TWENTY-ONE

Anza-Borrego Desert State Park

The state park includes virtually every feature visitors associate with a desert: washes, badland, mesas, palm oases, and much more. This diverse desert park boast more than 20 palm groves and year-around creeks, great stands of cholla and elephant trees, slot canyons and badland formations. Anza-Borrego Desert, California's largest state park at 600,000 acres, extends along almost the whole length of San Diego County's eastern border between Riverside County and Mexico. Travelers are welcomed to Anza-Borrego by what is probably the best visitor center in the state park system. The park offers numerous self-guided nature trails and automobile tours that allow visitors to set their own pace.

BORREGO PALM CANYON

BORREGO PALM CANYON TRAIL
To Falls is 3 miles round trip with 600-foot elevation gain; to South Fork is 6.5 miles round trip with 1,400-foot gain

Borrego Palm Canyon is the third-largest palm oasis in California, and was the first site sought for a desert state park back in the 1920s. It's a beautiful, well-watered oasis, tucked away in a rocky V-shaped gorge.

The trail visits the first palm grove and a waterfall. A longer option takes you exploring farther up-canyon. In winter, the trail to the falls is one of the most popular in the park. In summer, you'll have the oasis all to yourself. Watch for bighorn sheep, which frequently visit the canyon.

DIRECTIONS TO TRAILHEAD: The trail begins at Borrego Palm Canyon Campground, located one mile north of park headquarters. Trailhead parking is available at the west end of the campground near the campfire circle.

THE HIKE: Beginning at the pupfish pond, you walk up-canyon past many plants used by native people for food and shelter. Willow was used for home-building and bow-making; brittle bush and creosote were used for their healing qualities; honey, along with mesquite and beavertail cactus, was a food staple. Notice the shallow grinding holes in the granite.

The broad alluvial fan at the mouth of the canyon narrows and the sheer rock walls of the canyon soon enclose you as the trail continues along the healthy, but seasonal stream. Already surprised to learn how an apparently lifeless canyon could provide all the survival ingredients needed by the native population, you're surprised once more when Borrego Palm Oasis comes into view. Just beyond the first group of palms is a damp grotto, where a waterfall cascades over huge boulders. The grotto is a popular picnic area and rest stop.

From the falls, you may take an alternate trail back to the campground. This trail takes you along the south side of the creek, past some magnificent ocotillos, and give you a different perspective on this unique desert environment. By following the optional route, you can continue hiking up the canyon. Hiking is more difficult up-canyon after the falls, with lots of dense undergrowth and boulders to navigate around.

To South Fork: From the "tourist turnaround" continue up the canyon. The creek is a fairly dependable water supply and is usually running late in the fall. The canyon is wet, so watch your footing on the slippery, fallen palm fronds. The canyon narrows even further and the trail dwindles to nothing. Parallel the streambed and boulder-hop back and forth across the water. The canyon zigs and zags quite a bit. The hike is well~worth the effort though, because most of the 800 or so palms in the canyon are found in its upper reaches. Sometimes you'll spot rock~climbers practicing their holds on the steep red~rock cliffs above you.

The canyon splits 1.75 miles from the falls. Straight ahead, to the southwest, is South Fork. The rocky gorge of South Fork, smothered with bamboo, is in pos~session of all the canyon's water. It's quite difficult to negotiate. South Fork ascends to the upper slopes of San Ysidro Mountain (6,417 feet). The Middle Fork (the way you came) of Borrego Palm Canyon is dry and more passable. It's possible to hike quite a distance first up Middle Fork, then North Fork of Borrego Palm Canyon, but check with park rangers first. It's extremely rugged terrain.

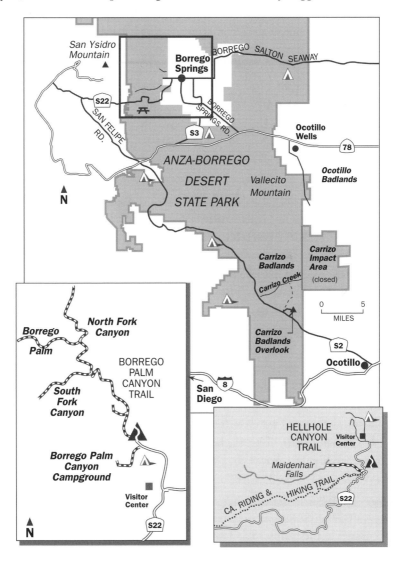

HELLHOLE CANYON

HELLHOLE CANYON TRAIL
From S-22 to Maidenhair Falls is 5 miles round trip with 900-foot elevation gain

Add Hellhole Canyon to the list of great geographical misnomers. Just as Greenland is anything but green, Hellhole Canyon is far from, well . . . hellish. Cottonwood, California fan palms, ferns and mosses thrive in the canyon, which hosts a blissful waterfall.

Certainly this hike's destination—Maidenhair Falls—is no misnomer. Maiden-hair ferns enshroud the thirty-foot high falls. The presence of a lush, fern-filled grotto in the midst of one of the West's most parched landscapes is a small miracle, an example of nature's mysterious ways. Not only is Hellhole Canyon attractive, it's convenient—just a few miles as the cactus wren flies from the park visitor center.

An intermittent trail travels through the long and deep canyon. Caution: While the canyon's riparian growth is easy on the eye, it's difficult to penetrate; expect slow-going through the thick vegetation.

Begin your trek to Hellhole Canyon from the park visitor center or from a trailhead located just off S-22. I recommend the latter trailhead, which shaves a mile from the hike and avoids the sometimes-congested visitor center parking lot.

DIRECTIONS TO TRAILHEAD: From its intersection with Palm Canyon Drive, proceed 0.7 mile southwest on Montezuma Valley Road to the parking area on the right (west) side of the road.

THE HIKE: Follow signed California Riding and Hiking Trail some 200 yards to a junction; the CRHT splits left, while you bear right, heading south-west over the broad alluvial fan. The well-defined, sandy trail crosses a desert gar-den of cholla, creosote bush, desert lavender and ocotillo.

A bit more than a mile out, the path angles toward the mouth of Hellhole Canyon, distinguished by riparian trees and palms (and altogether different-look-ing than that smaller, drier tributary canyon to its right). The trail stays to the left of the fan, as should the hiker until entering the mouth of the canyon.

Once in the canyon, you might find yourself walking next to a wet or dry (depending on the season) watercourse. Try to steer clear of the very bottom of the canyon, an obstacle course of brush, boulders and fallen trees. The thickest of the canyon's scattered palm groves, and the narrowing of the canyon's walls signal that you're nearing Maidenhair Falls.

Ultra-ambitious hikers can continue bushwhacking up Hellhole Canyon, but most travelers will be content to enjoy the soft light and tranquility around the falls and return to the trailhead.

CALCITE CANYON

CALCITE CANYON TRAIL
From County Road S-22 to Calcite Mine is 4 miles round trip with 500-foot elevation gain

Nature's cutting tools, wind and water, have shaped the ageless sandstone in Calcite Canyon into steep, bizarre formations. The cutting and polishing of the uplifted rock mass has exposed calcite crystals. Calcite is a common enough carbonate and found in many rocks, but only in a few places are the crystals so pure.

It was the existence of these crystals, with their unique refractive properties that brought prospectors to this part of the desert. The jeep trail was built in the mid-1930s for miners to gain access to Calcite Canyon, as it came to be called. Because of their excellent double refraction properties, calcite crystals were useful in the making of gun sights. Mining activity increased during World War II.

The calcite was taken from the canyon in long trenches, which look as if they were made yesterday. The desert takes a long time to heal.

This walk takes the jeep road to its dead end at the mine. You'll see the Calcite Mine Area up-close and get a good overlook of the many washes snaking toward the Salton Sea. A return trip through Palm Wash and its tributaries lets you squeeze between perpendicular walls and gives a unique perspective on the forces that shape the desert sands. The awesome effects of flash flooding are easily discerned by the hiker and suggest a narrow wash is the last place in the world you want to be in a rainstorm.

DIRECTIONS TO TRAILHEAD: Follow County Road S-22 west from Highway 86, or 20 miles from the Christmas Circle to Calcite Jeep Road. The jeep road is just west of a microwave tower.

THE HIKE: Follow the jeep road, which first drops into the

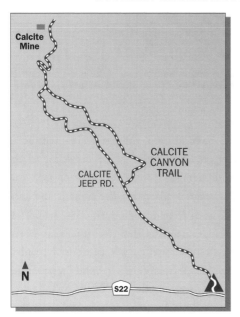

south fork of Palm Wash, then begins to climb northwest. Along the road you'll see long, man-made slots cut into the hillsides for the removal of calcite. Calcite Jeep Road dips a final time, then climbs a last 0.5 mile toward the mine. Two miles from the trailhead, the road ends at the mining area.

Calcite crystal fragments embedded in the canyon walls and scattered on the desert floor glitter in the sun. Behind the mining area, to the northeast, is a gargantuan hunk of white sandstone dubbed "Locomotive Rock." The imaginative can picture a great locomotive chugging up a steep grade. If you look carefully, you'll be able to see Seventeen Palms and some of the palms tucked away in Palm Wash in a bird's-eye view of the east side of the state park.

You can return the same way or descend through tributaries of the middle fork of Palm Wash. Take a last look at the steep ravines and washes to get your bearings. Middle Fork is but a hop, skip and a jump from the mine, but the jump's a killer—a 50-foot plunge to a deep intersecting wash. To get into the wash, you need to descend 0.5-mile down Calcite Road to a small tributary wash. Descend this wash, which is fairly steep at first. The sandstone walls close in on you. One place, "Fat Man's Misery," allows only one fat man (or two skinny day hikers) to squeeze through at a time. When you reach the middle fork, a prominent canyon, follow it 0.25 mile to the brief jeep trail connecting the wash to Calcite Road. Hike back up Calcite Road 0.1 mile to the parking area.

ELEPHANT TREES

ELEPHANT TREES DISCOVERY TRAIL
1.5 miles round trip with 100-foot elevation gain

A rarity in California deserts, the odd elephant tree is much admired by visitors to Anza-Borrego Desert State Park. Its surreal color scheme (was this tree designed by committee?) of green foliage, red-tan twigs, yellow-green peeling parchment-like bark, white flowers and blue berries, is something to behold. The stout trunk and the way the branches taper, vaguely suggests an elephant, but lots of imagination is required.

Enjoy this hike by following the 1.5 mile nature trail and/or by trekking along an alluvial fan to some elephant trees. A herd estimated at five hundred elephant trees grow at this end of the state park. *Birsera microphylla* is more common in Baja California and in the Gila Range of Arizona. The park has three populations of elephant trees, but the one off Split Mountain Road is the most significant one.

Elephant Trees Discovery Trail (brochure available), interprets various desert flora and geological features of this part of the Colorado Desert.

DIRECTIONS TO TRAILHEAD: From Ocotillo Wells (located about 40 miles west of Brawley and 78 miles east of Escondido on Highway 78), turn south on Split Mountain Road and proceed 6 miles to the signed turnoff for the Elephant Trees Area. Follow a dirt road 1 mile to the trailhead.

THE HIKE: Follow the nature trail until signpost #10, where you'll see the first elephant tree on the hike.

(Those experienced hikers who wish to see more elephant trees will leave the trail here and hike west up the broad alluvial fan. You'll encounter bits of trail, but really the route is cross-country. Keep the mountains on the western horizon in your sight. A mile's walk brings you to some elephant trees.)

Return the way you came back to the nature trail, which follows the numbered posts through a dry streambed and loops back to the trailhead.

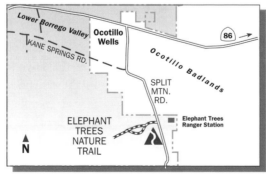

BOW WILLOW CANYON

ROCKHOUSE CANYON TRAIL
Bow Willow Campground to Rockhouse is 7 miles round trip with a 700-foot gain

This enjoyable day hike, for more experienced hikers, explores two intriguing canyons–Bow Willow and Rockhouse.

Early 20th-century miner Nicolas Swartz boasted he took $18,000 worth of gold from his remote desert mine. In the great tradition of Lost Mine Legends, he died without leaving a map. In 1906, Swartz built a rock house in an anonymous canyon that soon picked up the name of his structure.

This looping day hike takes you climbing through a single palm canyon, visits the rock house and its canyon and returns via the wash on the bottom of Bow Willow Canyon. Spring scatters color in the wash. Monkeyflowers, desert stars and a host of wildflowers brighten the sands and gravel bars. Even ocotillo changes its fit-only-for-firewood appearance and displays its new green leaves and flaming red flowers.

DIRECTIONS TO TRAILHEAD: From Interstate 8 in Ocotillo, take County Road S-2 sixteen miles to the turnoff for Bow Willow Canyon and Campground. Follow the good hardpack sand road 1.5 miles to the campground. Park in the campground, but don't take a campsite someone could use.

THE HIKE: Hike up Bow Willow Canyon on the signed jeep trail. Before you get much past the campground, make a 90-degree left turn (south) across a few hundred yards of wash to pick up the foot trail. One-quarter mile up the trail is a beleaguered palm tree. You begin climbing steadily through a desert garden of granite boulders, agave and cholla cactus.

As you near Rockhouse Canyon, the trail descends briefly and intersects Rockhouse Canyon Jeep Trail. Follow the Jeep Trail west for one mile to Swartz's abandoned rock house.

From the rock house, you follow a tentative foot trail that drops down into Bow Willow Canyon. Before long you'll come to a barrier across the wash preventing off-road vehicles from ascending into the upper reaches of the canyon. Past the barrier, the canyon widens and it's an easy 2-mile hike over soft sand back to Bow Willow Campground.

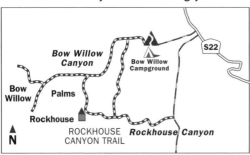

AGUA CALIENTE SPRINGS

SQUAW POND, MOONLIGHT CANYON TRAILS
1.5 to 2.5 miles round trip; Season: October-May

Nothing like a good soak after a good hike. At Agua Caliente Springs in the middle of Anza-Borrego Desert State Park, you can have both an inspiring walk and a soothing mineral bath. A hot spring, along with a good-sized campground, a store and the natural beauty of the Tierra Blanca Mountains, combine to make Agua Caliente County Park a popular weekend retreat.

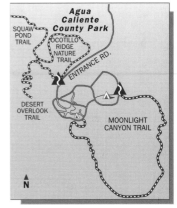

Seismic activity (an offshoot of the Elsinore Fault) that long ago shaped the surrounding mountains also boosted water to the surface to form the mineral springs. The natural springs in the area give life to mesquite, willows and palms and also attract many animals and birds.

Today's visitors can soak away their cares in a large shallow outdoor pool, geothermally heated to 96 degrees and in an indoor pool, boosted to more than one hundred degrees and equipped with Jacuzzi jets.

Two trails explore the county park and visit undeveloped tiny springs (seeps) in the surrounding hills. Squaw Pond Trail visits mesquite-filled Squaw Canyon; Moonlight Canyon Trail fulfills the promise of its name.

Squaw Pond Trail ascends a mesquite-dotted slope above the park's campfire circle and soon comes to a junction. Desert Overlook Trail branches left and climbs a steep 0.25 mile to a panorama of the surrounding mountains. Ocotillo Ridge Trail, an abandoned nature trail, weaves through abundant desert flora and returns to the park entry road. Continue on signed Squaw Pond Trail which descends a teddy-bear cholla-lined draw and soon arrives at Squaw Pond, a boggy, willow-lined area nurturing a single palm tree.

From the campground, Moonlight Canyon Trail ascends briefly, but steeply to a rocky saddle, curves east, then descends into a narrow wash. After passing a willow-lined seep in the midst of the canyon, the trail circles back to the park campground.

DIRECTIONS TO TRAILHEAD: Agua Caliente County Park is located on Highway S-2, some 22 miles southeast of Highway 78. Parking for Squaw Pond Trail is right next to the park entry station (day use fee) in a picnic area. Moonlight Canyon Trail begins at Campsite 140 next to the shuffleboard courts.

THE HIKER'S INDEX

CELEBRATING THE SCENIC, THE SUBLIME, AND THE RIDICULOUS IN SOUTHERN CALIFORNIA

ONLY SPOT ON U.S. MAINLAND ATTACKED BY
THE JAPANESE NAVY DURING WORLD WAR II:
Goleta Beach, February 23, 1942

SPIRITUAL JOURNEYS
Mt. Zion (San Gabriel Mountains), Solstice Canyon (Santa Monica
Mountains), Holy Jim Trail (Santa Ana Mountains), Mt. Rubidoux (Riverside)

FIRST FEDERALLY FUNDED WILDERNESS AREA
SET ASIDE BY THE WILDERNESS ACT OF 1964:
San Rafael Wilderness (Los Padres National Forest)

SOUTHWESTERNMOST POINT IN THE CONTIGUOUS FORTY-EIGHT STATES
International Boundary Marker, Border Field State Park

LARGEST NATIONAL FOREST IN CALIFORNIA
Los Padres National Forest

BEST HISTORICAL HIKE
Mt. Lowe Railway Trail (San Gabriel Mountains)

CALIFORNIA'S MOST EXPENSIVE STATE PARK:
Chino Hills State Park ($47 million spent by the time it opened in 1986)

LEAST-INSPIRATIONAL NAME (Three-way tie)
Inspiration Point (San Gabriel Mountains), Inspiration Point (Santa Ynez
Mountains), and Inspiration Point (Santa Monica Mountains)

SOUTHLAND'S SMALLEST ISLAND
Santa Barbara Island

SOUTHLAND'S LARGEST ISLAND
Santa Cruz Island

MOST INAPPROPRIATE PLACE NAME
Sandstone Peak—it's granite (Santa Monica Mountains)

The Hiker's Index

Second most inappropriate place name
Crystal Cove—nothing is crystalline, and there's neither a cove nor coastal indentation of any kind (Orange County)

Best close-up view of the San Andreas Fault
Devil's Punchbowl County Park

We'll Be Dead Before It's Done Award
To the Santa Monica Mountains' Backbone Trail; after three decades of struggle, the 65-mile long trail is still incomplete

Tallest Lodgepole Pine
World Champion lodgepole in San Bernardino Mountains

Remembering Republican Presidents
Eisenhower Peak (outside Palm Springs), Reagan Ranch (Santa Monica Mountains), (Grover) Cleveland National Forest, Richard M. Nixon's San Clemente Beach Trail

Pardon the obvious
Ocean Beach (Santa Barbara Co.), High Point (Palomar Mountains)

Devil of a time
Devil's Punchbowl County Park, Devil's Backbone Trail (to Mt. Baldy), Devil's Slide Trail (San Jacinto Mountains), Devil's Canyon (San Gabriel Mountains), Devil's Gateway and Devil's Elbow (Los Padres National Forest), Devil's Pit (San Bernardino Mountains)

Honoring Southland naturalists
Edmund Jaeger Trail (The Living Desert), Dick Smith Wilderness (Los Padres National Forest)

But seriously, they're fun places
Rattlesnake Canyon (Santa Ynez Mountains), Suicide Rock (San Jacinto Mountains), Hellhole Canyon (Anza-Borrego Desert State Park), Prisoners Bay (Santa Cruz Island)

Least lyrical place name
Peak 9775 (San Bernardino Mountains); runners-up: Peak 7114 (Los Padres National Forest) Peak 5195 (Joshua Tree National Park)

INDEX

Information Sources

Aliso Wood Canyons Wilderness Park
28373 Alicia Parkway
Laguna Niguel, CA 92677
(949) 923-2200

Cabrillo Marine Aquarium
3720 Stephen White Drive
San Pedro, California USA 90731
(310) 548-7562

Caspers Wilderness Park
33401 Ortega Hwy.
San Juan Capistrano, CA 92675
(949) 923-2210

Catalina Island Conservancy
PO Box 2739
Avalon, CA 90704
Nature Center at Avalon
(310) 510-0594

Charmlee Natural Area
2577 S. Encinal Canyon Road
Malibu, CA 90265
(310) 457-7247

Chino Hills State Park
4721 Sapphire Road
Chino Hills, CA 91709
(951) 780-6222

Cold Creek Canyon Preserve
Stunt Road between Schueren &
    Mulholland
Malibu, CA 90265
(310) 456-5627

Conejo Open Space Conservation
    Authority
Old Meadows Center
1600 Marview Drive
Thousand Oaks, CA 91360
(805) 381-2741

County of Orange RDMD/Harbors
    Beaches & Parks
1 Irvine Park Road
Orange, CA 92869
714-973-6865 or 866-OCPARKS

Eaton Canyon Nature Center
1750 North Altadena Drive
Pasadena, California 91107
(626) 398-5420

Laguna Coast Wilderness Park
20101 Laguna Canyon Road
Laguna Beach, CA 92651
(949) 923-2235

Laguna Niguel Regional Park
28241 La Paz Road
Laguna Niguel, CA 92677
(949) 923-2240 or (949) 923-2243

LAMountains.com
(Santa Monica Mountains
    Conservancy)
(310) 589-3200 or (323) 221-8900

Leo Carrillo State Park
35000 W. Pacific Coast Highway
Malibu, CA 90265
(818) 880-0350

The Living Desert
47900 Portola Avenue
Palm Desert, CA 92260
(760) 346-5694

Malibu Creek State Park
Las Virgenes Road south of
    Mulholland Highway
Calabasas
(818) 880-0367

McGrath State Beach
901 S. San Pedro
Ventura, CA 93001
(805) 654-4611

Mojave Desert State Parks
43779 15th Street West
Lancaster, CA 93545
(661) 942-0662

Mount San Jacinto State Park
PO Box 308
25905 Highway 243
Idyllwild, CA 92549
(951) 659-2607

O'Neill Regional Park
30892 Trabuco Canyon Road
Trabuco Canyon, CA 92678
(949) 923-2260 or (949) 923-2256

Palomar Mountain State Park
Palomar Mountain State Park
P. O. Box 175
Palomar Mountain, CA 92060
(760) 742-3462

Placerita Canyon Park and Nature
    Center
19152 Placerita Canyon Rd.
Newhall,CA91321
(661) 259-7721

Point Mugu State Park
9000 W. Pacific Coast Highway,
Malibu, CA 90265
(818) 880-0350

Rancho Simi Recreation & Parks
    District
1692 Sycamore Drive
Simi Valley, California 93065
(805) 584-4400

Riverside County Regional Parks
& Open Space District
4600 Crestmore Road
Riverside, CA 92509
(951) 955-4310

San Clemente State Beach
225 Avenida Califia
San Clemente, CA 92672
(949) 492-3156

Santa Monica Mountains
    Conservancy
(310) 589-3200, (323) 221-8900

Santa Monica Mountains National
    Recreation Area
401 Hillcrest Drive
Thousand Oaks, CA 91360
(805) 370-2301

Santa Rosa Plateau Ecological Reserve
39400 Clinton Keith Road
Murrieta, CA 92562
(951) 677-6951

Temescal Gateway Park
15601 Sunset Blvd.
Pacific Palisades, CA 90272
(310) 454-1395

Topanga State Park
(310) 455-2465

Torrey Pines State Reserve
16500 North Torrey Pines Road
San Diego CA 92037
(858) 755-2063

Vasquez Rocks County Park
10700 West Escondido Canyon Road
Saugus, CA 91350
(661) 268-0840

Will Rogers State Historic Park
1501 Will Rogers Park Road
Pacific Palisades, CA 90272
(310) 454-8212

NATIONAL FOREST OFFICES
ANGELES NATIONAL FOREST
Supervisor's Office
701 N. Santa Anita Avenue
Arcadia, CA 91006
(626) 574-5200

Los Angeles River Ranger District
12371 N. Little Tujunga Canyon Road
San Fernando, CA 91342
(818) 899-1900

Chilao Visitor Center
Angeles Crest Highway (Hwy 2)
La Canada, CA 91011
(626) 796-5541

Mt. Baldy Visitor Center
Mt. Baldy Road
Mt. Baldy, CA 91759
(909) 982-2829

San Gabriel River Ranger District
110 N. Wabash Avenue
Glendora, CA 91741
(626) 335-1251

Grassy Hollow Visitor Center
Angeles Crest Highway (Hwy 2)
Wrightwood, CA 92397
(626) 821-6737

Clear Creek Information Center
Angeles Crest Highway (Hwy 2)
La Canada, CA 91011
(626) 821-6764

Big Pines Information Center
Angeles Crest Highway (Hwy 2)
Wrightwood, CA 92397
(760) 249-3504

CLEVELAND NATIONAL FOREST
Trabuco Ranger District
1147 East Sixth Street
Corona, CA 92879
(951) 736-1811

LOS PADRES NATIONAL FOREST
6755 Hollister Avenue, Suite 150
Goleta, CA 93117
(805) 968-6640

Santa Barbara Ranger Districtt
3505 Paradise Road
Santa Barbara, CA 93105
(805) 967-3481

Ojai Ranger District
1190 E. Ojai Avenue
Ojai, CA 93023
(805) 646-4348

Mt. Pinos Ranger District
34580 Lockwood Valley Road
Frazier Park, CA 93225
(661) 245-3731

SAN BERNARDINO NATIONAL
    FOREST
602 South Tippecanoe Avenue
San Bernardino, CA 92408
(909) 382-2600

Arrowhead Ranger Station
28104 Highway 18
P.O. Box 350
Skyforest, CA 92385
(909) 382-2782

Big Bear Ranger Station
41397 North Shore Drive, Highway 38
P.O. Box 290
Fawnskin, CA 92333
(909) 382-2790

San Gorgonio Ranger Station
34701 Mill Creek Road
Mentone, CA 92359
(909) 382-2881 (voice)

San Jacinto Ranger District
54270 Pinecrest
P.O. Box 518
Idyllwild, CA 92549
(909) 382-2921

About the Contributors

Cartographer Hélène Webb is an artist and cartographer for maps and illustrated marine charts. A USCG Captain, Hélène shares her expertise and love for the Santa Barbara Channel with charter sail trips and sailing lessons. Contact her at www.aquarelle.com

Editor Cheri Rae is a native Californian who grew up exploring—and appreciating—the mountains, deserts, canyons, and beaches of the Southland. She has a long background in lifestyle sports and served on the editorial staffs of *Runner's World* and *Bicycle Sport* and was the founding editor of *California Scenic Magazine,* which celebrated the history, culure, and natural wonders of the Golden State.

Book designer Jim Cook is a master typography with more 30 years of experience in designing fine books. A native with a deep appreciation for California and the natural world, he decided to evoke the Great Hiking Era in books designed for The Trailmaster.

Cover artist Nadya Penoff is a plein-air painter who has also created stained-glass masterpieces installed in churches in far-flung locations. A member of Southern California Artists Painting for the Environment (SCAPE), Nadya frequently leads and participates in paint-outs in Santa Barbara, California, and Kauai, Hawaii.